Who Cares About Parents?

Carework in a Changing World

Amy Armenia, Mignon Duffy, and Kim Price-Glynn, Series Editors

The rise of scholarly attention to care has accompanied greater public concern about aging, health care, child care, and labor in a global world. Research on care is happening across disciplines—in sociology, economics, political science, philosophy, public health, social work, and others—with numerous research networks and conferences developing to showcase this work. Care scholarship brings into focus some of the most pressing social problems facing families today. To study care is also to study the future of work, as issues of carework are intertwined with the forces of globalization, technological development, and the changing dynamics of the labor force. Care scholarship is also at the cutting edge of intersectional analyses of inequality, as carework is often at the very core of understanding gender, race, migration, age, disability, class, and international inequalities.

Sophie Bourgault, Maggie FitzGerald, and Fiona Robinson, eds., *Decentering Epistemologies and Challenging Privilege: Critical Care Ethics Perspectives*

Cara A. Chiaraluce, *Becoming an Expert Caregiver: How Structural Flaws Shape Autism Carework and Community*

Mignon Duffy, Amy Armenia, and Kim Price-Glynn, eds., *From Crisis to Catastrophe: Care, COVID, and Pathways to Change*

Kim Price-Glynn, *Who Cares About Parents? Temporary Alliances, Exclusionary Practices, and the Strategic Possibilities of Parenting Groups*

Fumilayo Showers, *Migrants Who Care: West Africans Working and Building Lives in U.S. Health Care*

Who Cares About Parents?

Temporary Alliances, Exclusionary
Practices, and the Strategic
Possibilities of Parenting Groups

KIM PRICE-GLYNN

Rutgers University Press
New Brunswick, Camden, and Newark, New Jersey
London and Oxford

Rutgers University Press is a department of Rutgers, The State University of New Jersey, one of the leading public research universities in the nation. By publishing worldwide, it furthers the University's mission of dedication to excellence in teaching, scholarship, research, and clinical care.

Library of Congress Cataloging-in-Publication Data
Names: Price-Glynn, Kim, author.
Title: Who cares about parents?: temporary alliances, exclusionary practices, and the strategic possibilities of parenting groups / Kim Price-Glynn.
Description: New Brunswick, New Jersey: Rutgers University Press, [2025] | Series: Carework in a changing world | Includes bibliographical references and index.
Identifiers: LCCN 2025004723 (print) | LCCN 2025004724 (ebook) | ISBN 9781978824874 (paperback) | ISBN 9781978824881 (hardcover) | ISBN 9781978824898 (epub) | ISBN 9781978824911 (pdf)
Subjects: LCSH: Parents—Social networks.
Classification: LCC HQ799.C65 P75 2025 (print) | LCC HQ799.C65 (ebook) | DDC 306.87406/073—dc23/eng/20250222
LC record available at https://lccn.loc.gov/2025004723
LC ebook record available at https://lccn.loc.gov/2025004724

A British Cataloging-in-Publication record for this book is available from the British Library.

References to internet websites (URLs) were accurate at the time of writing. Neither the author nor Rutgers University Press is responsible for URLs that may have expired or changed since the manuscript was prepared.

∞ The paper used in this publication meets the requirements of the American National Standard for Information Sciences—Permanence of Paper for Printed Library Materials, ANSI Z39.48-1992.

rutgersuniversitypress.org

For Lucas and Lilly

Contents

Who Cares About Parents?

Introduction

My Search for Parenting Groups

There never seemed to be enough care when navigating a dual-earner family with two kids. For the first years of our children's lives, my husband and I relied on ourselves and found friends and at-home care providers.[1] Later, as our children approached kindergarten age, we made connections through a local preschool. No doubt my family operated our care search from a position of relative privilege. Our kids do not have special needs or disabilities; we did not face the simultaneous demands of frequently navigating health care beyond routine physicals, three broken bones, several sprains and concussions, and countless ear infections. We also did not face the scheduling of many therapies that help kids with speech, fine motor, and behavioral issues, for example. We were able to focus our attention primarily on organizing our kids' routine child care. We had a full "constellation of resources" (Garey 1999) to draw upon in this process, including steady and well-paid employment, a flexible work schedule that we could stagger, and homeownership. Though this list may sound full, we still had care gaps, times that we had difficulty finding enough care and resources.

When faced with care gaps, I reached out to parenting groups. For example, when I struggled to nurse my first baby, I phoned a local La Leche League leader to discuss latching techniques. I found the exchange, though technically very useful, perfunctory. It could have been idiosyncratic, but the exchange led me to read La Leche League's books rather than seek out a meeting. Even absent my greater involvement, the group provided me with the invaluable advice I needed. Parent group exclusion has a variety of sources. Though sometimes it may stem from a local personality mismatch, a misinterpretation, or the vulnerability of being a new parent, as in my story, other times, as I document in

1

this book, parents' feelings of exclusion stem from group leaders' and members' exclusionary organization, ideology, and practices.

Our family's ongoing needs kept me looking for support. One afternoon we scheduled afternoon at-home care for our son, and at the last minute the babysitter called to cancel. She was sick with stomach flu. At the same time, I had a meeting that I needed to facilitate; I could not easily reschedule it, nor could I juggle my toddler and the meeting at the same time. My husband was thirty minutes away in his own meeting, so his care was not an option. I needed to find a solution quickly. I called a friend for help. She took my son into her house for a few hours, and when I came to pick him up, she said, "You should join my babysitting co-op for circumstances like this!" As she explained, it was for short-term planned or emergent care needs. She described a group of approximately two dozen other moms whom I could reach out to for help, to fill caregiving gaps and create backups. Finding a ready care network felt like a lifeline, and I eagerly joined the babysitting co-op. Only later did I realize the group would provide both care and community. I met a group of smart, kind, and generous women who were passionate about their kids, parenting, and communities. I am indebted to them for sharing their lives and their stories with me, alongside their carework.

We also participated in parent groups at our children's schools and in our local community, including a local MOMS Club. These groups often provided important resources to our family—fostering friendships, providing emotional support, facilitating playdates, and developing enrichment activities.[2] Parent groups also provided me with access to educational resources, like books on breastfeeding, films about gender and family, and articles on contemporary social issues. Through these groups, I engaged in community outreach—providing meals and care for group members. I learned about broader community resources, considered school board matters, and discussed political issues. Most important, these groups provided care for *me* as a caregiver. Not only did these groups support me in day-to-day practical child care, but they also offered me wider resources. The opportunities for learning, respite from caregiving responsibilities, and broader community engagement enabled me to become a better caregiver. As my children have grown, my search for parenting groups has not stopped. I recently joined a small group of moms who wanted to meet occasionally and talk about parenting teens. In our conversations, for example, we discuss productive ways to reconnect with our kids, like effective ways to foster conversation, validate our teens' feelings, and show affection. As a parent, having another set of parents with whom I can reflect, learn, and share new ideas has helped me better understand new stages and challenges. I continue to learn from these groups, and they help me to be a better parent.

Based on my research and experiences, I often discuss parenting groups with my fellow parent colleagues. Their reactions are polarized. Recently, two sociologists I deeply respect both said that they never joined parenting groups. One explained her reasoning stemmed from a "limited and horrible" experience—she could not relate to the parents and found the experience alienating. Other parents have had more positive reactions joining local neighborhood play and shared caregiving groups. Given these opposing reactions, I think of parenting groups as a sort of Rorschach test. Like the famous inkblot psychology tools, parenting groups lend themselves to many interpretations. Similarly, parents frequently project their own ideas, expectations, and concerns onto them. I have come to expect and relate to these reactions. Through my participation, I saw firsthand groups' strengths and contradictions that left me asking questions, feeling conflicted, and wanting to know more. The beginnings of *Who Cares About Parents?* started with my own parenting group interactions. As a sociologist I was fascinated by the ways that these groups both provide possibilities to address and transform inequalities and reproduce them. These groups have a propensity for problem solving and outreach to parents. Simultaneously, exclusivity emerges from the organizations in daily pedestrian ways and through organizational practices. This book brings a sociological perspective to understanding these groups' complexity.

Parental Care, Infrastructure, and Gendered Social Reproduction

Commonplace understandings about U.S. parental care often reflect individual-level thinking about parents, households, and families. This micro-level focus is driven by social norms and ideology as well as legal, economic, and educational institutions that place the ultimate responsibility for family care squarely on parents. According to the Pew Research Center, "A majority of parents (57%) say they think their children's successes and failures reflect a great deal or a fair amount on the job they're doing as a parent" (Minkin and Horowitz 2023, 10). While some sources of U.S. parenting challenges are idiosyncratic, many parents' struggles have structural causes stemming from existing inequalities and inadequate social supports—the solutions to which lie beyond individual households.

To study structural inequalities, sociologists study people in the aggregate—through their participation in social groups. A central project of sociology is to understand social problems and social change by examining group circumstances through different levels of analysis—micro (interpersonal), meso (community), and macro (societal and global). Using a meso lens, one can see that, contrary to a normative ideology of individualism, American parents engage in wider networks, organizations, and communities. News outlets documented family disruption and parents' tremendous need for broader care resources amid COVID-19 lockdowns and school closures (Cain Miller 2020; Grose 2020;

Kamenetz 2022). During the pandemic, when the Biden administration called for an unprecedented care infrastructure investment, ideas about care as infrastructure became more mainstream in the United States (White House 2021).

Conventionally, the language of infrastructure has focused on water supplies, sewage systems, the electrical grid, roads, and bridges—fundamental systems that enable human life (Carse 2017). The term "infrastructure" is a "collective term . . . that . . . denotes a plurality of integrated parts" (Carse 2017, 27). Thinking of "people as infrastructure" in caregiving recognizes how "complex combinations of objects, spaces, persons, and practices . . . become an infrastructure—a platform providing for and reproducing life" (Simone 2004, 407). The care infrastructure includes a "network of resources, services, and systems that are available to meet the care needs of people" (Duvisac and del Rosario Castro Bernardini 2024, 5). The underlying premise of care as infrastructure is not new to feminist scholars, who have long argued that social reproductive activities such as child care and elder care and sustaining connections and communities are fundamental to the functioning of economic and social life (Fraser 2016; Hall 2020). The language of care infrastructure provides a way to understand the human scaffolding that includes care providers in paid and unpaid positions across a variety of social institutions (Alam and Houston 2020; Li and Laughlin 2023). This work includes paid and unpaid domestic labor; child care, education, and health care; community outreach nonprofits; and—the focus of this study—parent groups' care for caregivers and their families.

This research examines care for parents beyond individual families to consider how parents have come to care for each other through existing parenting groups. I argue that parenting groups are part of our existing meso-level care infrastructure. These groups provide parents with care that has scope and structure that emphasizes people's "collective actions and decisions" and "interdependence" (Tronto 2015, 40). U.S. parenting groups have a long history of providing parent-to-parent care, on not just an individual level but also meso and macro levels. As part of the care infrastructure, parenting groups may provide and work against members' access to a sense of belonging and connection, education and emotional support, resources and respite, and advocacy. Parenting groups exists in a variety of forms, from small to large groups that operate publicly and privately in local communities, across states, or even nationally and internationally. Many are interconnected entities; some have a global reach. Their influence, however, is often blunted by a variety of factors. Chief among them, their organization is often siloed—they are defined by neighborhood, faith communities, income, and gender and tend to be limited by those locations and identities. As they are products of the broader U.S. culture, these outcomes should hardly be surprising. In the broader culture, "warm," home-based, unpaid family care is normatively contrasted with "cold," institutionally based, paid-provider care, when these forms can and do exist in various combinations (Hochschild 1995). Many forms of carework traverse normative care dichotomies, including love/money, family/nonfamily, paid/unpaid, private/public, and home/institution. When carework is siloed, we miss opportunities and "[overlook] similarities and synergies between" forms of care (Folbre 2012, 1). Organizational sociologists have long recognized similar exclusionary ideologies and practices in many social institutions (Acker 2006). However, parenting groups also resist these outcomes in big and small ways. As part of our care infrastructure, parenting groups make inroads into connecting parenting communities, expanding resources, and challenging social problems. In this book, I address the care infrastructure of parent groups and how exclusivity is actively maintained when it could be interrupted, addressed, and dismantled as well as cases in which progressive outcomes are strategically deployed and embraced.

Studying Parenting Groups

Who Cares About Parents? is a qualitative analysis focusing on the care infrastructure of established, well-documented, and popular parenting groups including a babysitting co-op, three dads' groups and their national organization, the National Parent Teacher Association (PTA), La Leche League International (LLL), the UES (Upper East Side) Mommas, and MOMS Club International.[3] I chose these groups for several reasons, chiefly because they represent some of the most recognizable parent groups in the United States today. On behalf of adult family caregivers with children, the groups provide care, participation, education, financial and in-kind resources, and advocacy. These groups also provide crucial access to online and print materials that document their organization, membership, and practice. Websites, podcasts, publications, and news articles provide a wealth of data from which to study.

The title of this book, *Who Cares About Parents*, refers to the actual work of caring for parents, exploring which parents are cared for and by whom, and the very idea that parents need and deserve care. Though researchers have long understood that parents want support, carework-related research does not often conceptualize parental caregivers as warranting care. The literature on the ideology of intensive mothering is one exception (Hays 1996). This research emphasizes the burdens associated with parental caregiving by explaining the demographics, strategies, and extent of hands-on care. Addressing parental care burdens is often a by-product of parenting analyses, rather than the focus in and of itself.

Support for parental caregivers often appears in the form of advice. Sources ranging from the federal government to self-help literature make recommendations about how parents should raise their kids (Beatty, Cahan, and Grant

2006), often proposing individual or micro-level solutions. In the United States, parents retain legal responsibility for their children until they reach the age of adulthood or are emancipated, so, in part, it is logical to begin with parents. However, even when meso-level issues suggest meso-level solutions, micro-level answers are proposed. For example, since a majority of parents are employed, one parenting challenge is navigating paid and unpaid work. Though paid employment occurs at the meso level, suggestions often point to micro-level strategies. Daisy Dowling's (2021) *Workparent: The Complete Guide to Succeeding on the Job, Staying True to Yourself, and Raising Happy Kids* and the *Harvard Business Review*'s Working Parents Series self-help book, *Taking Care of Yourself* (2020) are examples that focus on the tagline "make working parenthood work for you." When support for parents is mentioned in these texts, these sources often suggest turning to one's own family (Cohen 2018). In addition to sidestepping larger scale problems, individualistic family ideologies alongside gender, race, and economic inequalities expand parents' (particularly mothers') caregiving burdens (Calarco 2024).

Research on caring for parents as caregivers often emphasizes those addressing acute, rather than routine, care needs. Examples include parents providing home medical care for family members with a long-term illness or disability (Mong 2020) and parents in the "sandwich generation," who care for children and aging parents simultaneously (Parker and Patten 2013). The U.S. Centers for Disease Control and Prevention's web page for parents caring for children focuses on the content of care for kids and child development and addresses parental needs associated with "stress and coping" and "food insecurity" only related to the COVID-19 pandemic (Centers for Disease Control and Prevention n.d.). Many care researchers argue that caregiving is not simply an emergent, one-directional, or individual phenomenon—no person exists without needing care and parents are no exception (Tronto 2013; Waerness 1984). Not seeing beyond the micro-level toward the meso- and even macro-level issues and existing care infrastructure leaves families with the dubious task of self-rescue. The basis for this book is the need for research to address a wider range of parents' caregiving needs, including both commonplace and emergent, to build a better understanding of the care infrastructure and argue for the possibility of strategic parenting that goes far beyond individual toward collective solutions.

The Challenges of U.S. Parenting

Shaped by ideologies of American individualism and neoliberal economics, U.S. families are normatively seen as self-made and independent. Likewise, family care in the United States is culturally seen as a private concern that families provide directly, outsource to paid caregivers, or both (Glenn 2010; Hays 1996; Mintz and Kellogg 1988; Tronto 2013). In this context, American social institutions have not kept pace with working families' challenges in securing affordable a robust care infrastructure that includes quality child and elder care (AARP and National Alliance for Caregiving 2020; Adams and Rohacek 2010; Clawson and Gerstel 2014; Feinberg et al. 2011; Henly and Lyons 2000; Palley and Shdaimah 2014). Of U.S. households, 40 percent are made up of families with children under the age of eighteen; that is, over 63 million families provide care for kids (U.S. Census Bureau 2020). In the absence of comprehensive care support and given a context of great inequality, this large group of caregivers often struggles to meet ordinary caregiving needs. In effect, parents are expected to provide care for their families regardless of the resources they have for themselves.

Parental caregivers are overwhelmed with caregiving in its many forms—the physical, mental, and emotional components of providing care for others to be sure, but also the planning, overseeing, knowledge-building, resource-gathering, networking, and community-making that accompany these challenges. Parents find it difficult to provide enough care and often struggle to afford it. For many families, job loss and relocation leave them without a stable location and stable access to extended family or community-based networks (Pugh 2015). Additional burdens, especially visible during the emergence of COVID-19, brought families to the brink of crisis and beyond. As care arrangements evaporated during lockdowns, families were left to their own emergent strategies. So overwhelmed by pandemic caregiving, hundreds of mothers called into the *New York Times* primal scream hotline to complain, worry, cry, and yell about their frustrations.[4] However, many parents felt overburdened and isolated well before the pandemic started. Research amplifies parents' concerns. In a recent survey, "almost half (48%) of all parents don't feel they are getting the support they need when they feel stressed" (Zero to Three 2016), and over half of the parents (56 percent) indicate they have only "some support," "almost no support," or "no support at all" (Parker, Horowitz, and Rohal 2015, 82). It is no wonder many parents find child-rearing difficult. As a *New York Times* headline reads, "Parenting was never meant to be this isolating: nuclear families have always relied on a community for practical support" (Grose 2020). Parents still turn to a community for support. Today it may take the form of parenting groups.

Adding to parental burdens are contemporary parenting ideologies such as "intensive mothering" (Collins 2019; Elliott, Powell, and Brenton, 2013; Hays 1996). Emerging in the late eighteenth and early nineteenth centuries, the ideology of intensive mothering presumes that mothers are irreplaceable caregivers responsible for addressing the needs of children (Damaske 2011; Hays 1996; Walzer 1998). The content of "child-centered" care requires expertise gained through deep investments of time and money (Hays 1996, 112). The ideology of intensive mothering assumes that an "individual mother" bears accountability for her child's needs (Hays 1996, 54). Nonparental caregivers are viewed as less trustworthy, loving, invested, and attentive (Hays 1996). There is abundant evidence for the ideology of intensive mothering's vast influence. Some research suggests that the ideology of intensive mothering is a ubiquitous social norm (Elliott, Powell, and Brenton 2013; Hays 1996; Ishizuka 2019; Lockman 2019) informing countless aspects of family life including mothers' self-concept (Johnston and Swanson 2006, 2007), family food practices (Brenton 2017; Chen 2016), and children's vaccine refusal (Reich 2016). Women go to great lengths to mother intensively from work, from prison, and transnationally through developing schedules for increased visibility or through reliance on a variety of surrogate caregivers and telecommunication (Christopher 2012; Edgley 2021; Granja, Cunha, and Machado 2015; Peng and Wong 2013). Other authors suggest that the ideology of intensive mothering is better understood as a hegemonic ideal type legitimizing unachievable expectations and mothers' disproportionate care burdens (Schiffrin et al. 2014). The ideology of intensive mothering has also been critiqued as an idea that applies to a narrower (largely affluent) population and fails to fully capture parenting diversity by race, class, employment, and country (Arendell 2000; Collins 2019; Dow 2019; Taylor 2011; Walls, Helms, and Grzywacz 2016).

My research for this book includes an affluent and largely white women's babysitting co-op that exhibits an ideology of collective-intensive mothering that often increases (rather than alleviates) mothers' caregiving demands. Though the group's gendered organization of care, and its belief in essential gender differences, increases mothers' recognition of their skills, produces camaraderie, creates solidarity among caregivers, and enhances their access to care, it also increases the care these women provide (Price-Glynn 2024).

The central question of this book is this: Can parents in the contemporary United States secure some of the necessary resources to provide care, not only for their children but also for themselves, through parenting groups? This book also asks whether parenting groups can move beyond individualistic models of family care, to organize care for caregivers differently as community-based care infrastructure. The evidence from my research suggests they can.

What Are Parenting Groups?

Parenting group care infrastructure in the United States is vast and diverse. I define parenting groups as voluntary associations designed for adult family caregivers with children. These groups take different organizational forms and may be highly structured, including regular membership and responsibilities, meetings, and online resources. They may also be more informal and temporary. Some groups have long histories, while others have recently formed. They emerge to address a variety of considerations and constituents. The central components of parenting groups' formation are related to participants, locations, and needs. Though these components often overlap, there are also cases that prioritize one component over another.

Parenting group participation is often designed around membership characteristics, like groups arranged for only mothers or fathers. Moms' groups, like MOMS Club International, have organized groups for stay-at-home moms in the United States and other parts of the world. Likewise, City Dads Group is a nationwide organization of local dads' groups designed for fathers.[5] There are also groups organized by demographic characteristics like race, gender, and religion. For example, there are groups that provide outreach among African American parents, like Jack and Jill, and mothers of color, like Mocha Moms; and there are religious parenting groups like those found through Christian churches or Jewish community centers.[6]

Parenting groups are gendered. Participants are most often mothers and less often fathers; this distinction holds for specific parenting groups (there are more moms' groups than dads' groups), and groups open to all parents. Parenting groups may also draw in other family members (e.g., grandparents) and guardians (foster parents). Though groups draw largely on peer or parent-to-parent models, they may also include experts from inside and outside of the organization. Many of these groups address an array of issues; a major organizing principle is bringing together particular groups of parents.

Parenting groups are found in many different places; location serves as another formative component. Parenting group participants may meet in person, exclusively online, or a combination of the two. Some parenting groups are locally focused (e.g., drawing from neighborhoods or cities), while some are national or even international in scope, like La Leche League International. Other groups are geographically dispersed and require lower levels of commitment, particularly in the case of exclusively online groups.

Parenting groups address parents' needs, including emotional support, education, goods, services, and advocacy. Parenting groups may address specific issues and enable parents to connect with peers and experts around their experiences. The internet has exponentially increased the number and types of parenting groups available through various online platforms. They include groups for divorced parents and parents of children with disabilities. The Facebook group "Single Parents: Surviving Single Parenthood" began in 2010 and now has over a hundred thousand members ("Single Parents" n.d.; "Private Facebook Group" 2018). As the name suggests, this online group provides peer-to-peer support and advice for single parents. "Moms of ADHD, Anxiety, ASD, and ODD Kids" is another Facebook group for mothers, offering connection and resources for more than thirty thousand members ("Moms of ADHD" n.d.). There are also court-mandated parenting groups focused on parenting education and skills following divorce, substance abuse, and incarceration.

A major contrast in parenting groups is between those more narrowly formed around specific participants' needs and those formed more broadly. Broad-based groups are those in which participants are identified generally as parents or caregivers and expansive needs are addressed. The PTA is one example with the mission "to make every child's potential a reality by engaging and empowering families and communities to advocate for all children" (National PTA n.d.-h). Advocating for families, communities, and children makes parents' needs more visible and potentially augments parents' resources and alleviates some of their burdens. However, even when groups are ostensibly open to all, they are still most often filled by mothers. A majority of PTA members and leaders across the country continue to be women. The group selected its first male president, Charles Saylors, in 2009, after 113 years.[7]

Parenting Group Challenges and Contributions

Conventionally we often simplify care into discrete tasks (like activities of daily living). However, these tasks are interwoven with a capacity to care based on parental well-being and better care for caregivers. Much like school performance is related to nutrition—you cannot learn if you are not nourished—there is a connection between acts of care and the broader context that surrounds them. I argue that the care offered by some parenting groups goes well beyond emphasizing discrete tasks and providing hands-on tools to address "care as a complex process" entailing a variety of aspects recognized as forms of caregiving in the broader literature on care (Tronto 2015, 8). This more expansive and progressive approach to care includes education and advocacy, for example, for parents as well as the children in their care. With education and advocacy, our approach to care shifts and we are better able to identify, be accountable, attend to, and fulfill care needs (Tronto 2013, 2015).

I focus on four primary forms of care parenting groups provide for parents: (1) emotional support, (2) education, (3) providing goods and services, and (4) advocacy. Table 1 summarizes parenting groups' dimensions of care. Emotional support for caregivers includes fostering community by providing discussion and advice through parent-to-parent meetings and events. Parenting groups provide access to education, bringing in experts, offering informational programming, and creating educational websites. Goods and services provided by parenting groups include providing care for kids and connecting parents with local kids' activities. Though not called respite care, these services constitute a similar form in which parents get outside assistance caring for their children and "short-term relief [as] primary caregivers," including supervision, meals, and financial support (National Institute on Aging 2023). When parenting groups engage in advocacy, we can see their potential for what I call "strategic parenting," or working to address inequalities, expand access, and engage in political

Table 1
Parenting Groups' Organization and Carework

Dimension	Oakwood Babysitting Co-op	Local Dads' Groups / City Dads Group	La Leche League	Parent Teacher Association	MOMS Club International	UES Mommas
Participants, recruitment	Parents (mostly mothers)	Fathers, experts	Parents (mostly mothers), experts	Parents, experts, family, community	Parents (mostly mothers), experts	Mothers
Membership, belonging	Leader/member approval to join, geography	Leader approval to join, geography	Leader/member approval to join, geography	Geography	Leader approval to join, geography	Leader approval to join, geography
Dues	$5 annually	Free	Free for participants, $40 for Leaders	Varies locally, $15–20 annually, $4 to national organization	$25–35 annually	Free
Decision-making	Leadership, member voting	Leadership, member voting	Leadership, member contributions	Leadership, member voting	Leadership, member voting	Leadership, member contributions
Emotional support: online, face-to-face	Facebook, email, and in-person meetings	Facebook and in-person meetings	Telephone, Facebook, and in-person meetings	Facebook, in-person meetings	Facebook, email, and in-person meetings	Facebook, email, and in-person meetings
Activities	Meetings, events, training, moms' nights out	Meetings, events, dads' nights out	Meetings, events, and training	Meetings, events, and training	Meetings, events, training, moms' nights out	Announcements
Education: programs, events	Local	Local, national	Local, national	Local, national	Local, national	Local

(continued)

Table 1
Parenting Groups' Organization and Carework (*continued*)

Dimension	Oakwood Babysitting Co-op	Local Dads' Groups / City Dads Group	La Leche League	Parent Teacher Association	MOMS Club International	UES Mommas
Outreach: web, social media, print	Facebook, email	Facebook, email, websites	Facebook, email, website, phone, books, magazine	Facebook, email, website, phone, books, magazine	Facebook, email, websites	Facebook
Goods and services: in-kind resources	Physical space, food, refreshments, clothing, toys, birth and illness meals	Physical space, food, refreshments	Physical space, food, refreshments	Physical space, food, refreshments	Physical space, food, refreshments, birth and illness meals	Member-initiated ad hoc
Respite care	Kids' activities, playdates, babysitting	Kids' activities, playdates, babysitting	Kids' activities	Kids' activities, playdates, meeting babysitting	Kids' activities, meeting babysitting	Kids' activities
Financial support				Fundraising, redistribution	Mother-to mother, Sunshine Fund	
Advocacy: issues	Individually sponsored	Corporate advertising, changing tables	Breastfeeding, attachment parenting, trans inclusion	Education, vaccines, music, school gun violence, equity	Service projects	Individually sponsored

action. Not all groups provide all forms of care. More often, groups emphasize some forms over others. The unevenness of parenting groups' engagement in these forms of care for parents is the product of specialization around participants, locations, and needs in addition to much cultural ambivalence over whether parents could (or should) provide these resources for themselves.

Since parenting groups are situated in local communities and a broader U.S. context that is segregated by gender, race, and income, resources often circulate narrowly. Exclusivity shapes the origin stories, organization, and recruitment processes of parenting groups. Across parenting groups, I consider how their ideologies reinscribe social inequalities through membership, resulting in a narrow circulation of care resources. Access to parenting groups is shaped by group leadership in ways that make it difficult for members to challenge systemic racism, gender and economic inequalities, and other social problems. Mainstream issues, responses, and voices often prevail within parenting groups' programming, curriculum, and publications, including books and magazines, the web, and social media platforms. Using a conventional lens often favors consensus and a path of least resistance over and above morality and justice. As a result, the groups often silo care around particular populations and reinforce ideologies that underscore essential, intensifying individual and family-based care. Ideologies of essentialism and exclusion are significant barriers to cross, especially when core issues and divisions are ignored or opposed organizationally.

Alongside narrow inclusion, parenting groups also exhibit possibilities for collaborations. Despite deep-rooted problems, some parenting groups provide models of what I call "strategic parenting," or parenting through social change that challenges exclusionary practices and moves toward collective (rather than individual) community-building resources. For example, a PTA in Illinois divides its coffers equitably across schools, district-wide (Brown 2022; PTA Equity Project 2020). LLL, a group dedicated to mothers' breastfeeding, now includes transgender and nonbinary participants and leaders, and educates its members on chestfeeding (La Leche League International n.d.-k). Dads' groups have successfully lobbied corporations (like Huggies) to challenge negative advertising stereotypes around fatherhood (D'Arcy 2012a). Redistributing funds and bringing families together is a far-reaching way to challenge inequalities. Addressing gender diversity expands access to resources and reduces the marginalization of nonbinary persons. Challenging deep-seated stereotypes around gender and care is a step toward new understandings and a more equitable distribution of care. So this book also highlights the possibilities for innovation, collective action, and social change by parenting groups.

I introduce the concept of "strategic parenting" to address how parenting group members advocate for social and organizational change within and beyond parenting organizations with care infrastructure developments that range from constrained to transformative. These actions have much to teach about parent group mobilization and help us understand how exclusivity could be interrupted, addressed, and dismantled, illuminating new care problems and understandings at the collective or meso level. Nonfamilial sources of family and parental support are often sidelined by the U.S. culture's normative focus on nuclear families as the primary source of children's and parents' care. Parenting group organizations connect and divide families in ways that are often undetected by nonparticipants. While too often marred by exclusive ideologies, volunteer-led parenting groups can offer a compelling model for parental care. At their best, when limitations are addressed, parenting groups show the potential to become a care resource providing affordable and nimble care networks to better address parents' care burdens and build an important part of our care infrastructure.

Parenting Group Cases

Given so many parenting groups, I had to make calculated decisions concerning which groups to study. To better enable an in-depth analysis, I prioritized researching parenting groups that are well-established, with vast available data including many online resources, self- or outside authored publications, or media attention. I add to this interviews and observations with Oakwood baby-sitting co-op members and interviews with local dads' group participants. All of the groups have existed for more than a decade, so they have some permanence and history as part of the care infrastructure. The structure and formality of these groups vary, but they maintain a documented organization and set of goals and intersect common attributes including groups' targeted participants, route to belonging, dues, decision-making, geographic location(s), and needs. Table 1 details these dimensions. The groups demonstrate considerable overlap across these dimensions. All target parents through their materials, however most groups' language (including the groups' name), pictures, and recruitment information target mothers. The local dads' group and City Dads Group target fathers, and the PTA has a long history of being run and populated by mothers. They are typical and representative of parenting groups more broadly; they target mothers and parents, include groups that are local and national in scope, and are groups in which participants interact online and in person. Several of the groups also include experts (except the Oakwood baby-sitting co-op and the UES Mommas). Most groups provide participants with a sense of membership that they produce in a variety of ways. Groups may include a process for vetting, sense of belonging, and access to group activities. Four of the groups include annual dues for participants or leaders. Dues may include access to newsletters and manuals (PTA, LLL, and some MOMS Clubs), a pool of monetary resources for the group to allocate (Oakwood babysitting co-op and MOMS Clubs), and a fund to draw on for philanthropic outreach (MOMS Clubs).

All of the groups have a geographic dimension for local groups including members who reside in a particular region, city, or zip code, though several also have an overarching national organization. All organize decision-making with a top-down model of leadership, four groups provide access to member voting, and two provide opportunities for member contributions (though the group is not organized as a voting body). They address a range of needs across the groups' four primary types of care mentioned previously: (1) emotional support, (2) education, (3) providing goods and services, and (4) advocacy. Each of these groups has another commonality that I found in my research—they all engage in exclusionary practices around gender, race, class, and religion. Unless I am using publicly available materials, all people and places are referred to using pseudonyms to protect the confidentiality of parenting group members. In some cases, identifying details have been omitted or obscured.

The cases include local parenting groups. One group is a babysitting co-op, designed for parents' short-term childcare needs. The babysitting co-op began more than two decades ago (in 1999) through a local Christian church in an affluent and largely white community. Although the group was designed (at least on paper) as open to all parents, it is nevertheless populated by a mostly homogenous group of approximately twenty moms. Though church ties have become less central over time, the group's faith-based roots alongside its prevailing family and gender ideology produce a form of collective-intensive mothering that exacerbates the group's care for mothers. I also studied a set of three dads' groups. The groups are affiliated with a national dads' group organization, City Dads Group, that began more than fifteen years ago, but each operates mostly independently on the local level. Designed for homosocial camaraderie, they are a resource to connect fathers and children with other fathers and children. Their central organizing principle is built on both progressive and traditional notions of American masculinity that leave men with connections mired in gendered contradictions.

I examine parenting groups on a larger scale through several prominent broad-based groups, including the PTA, LLL, the UES Mommas, MOMS Club International, and City Dads Group. The PTA provides one of the oldest needs-based groups focusing on children, parents, and families through schools and education locally and nationwide. The PTA began as two groups, the National Congress of Mothers, organized in 1897, and the National Congress of Colored Parents and Teachers, organized in 1911. Without fully addressing tensions over racism, in 1970 these two groups merged to form today's PTA (National Congress of Parents and Teachers 1944; Woyshner 2009). LLL was founded in 1956 by seven white affluent Catholic suburban moms in Franklin Park, Illinois. The group's demographic and faith-based origins have long influenced LLLI's reputation as a well-known needs-based group providing breastfeeding and now chestfeeding support, education, and advocacy both domestically and internationally (Lowman 1978). Though my focus is primarily on the United States, my research on LLL extends to include the Canadian organization. City Dads Group was established by two New York City dads in 2008 and became a nationwide group five years later. Founded to support fathers, City Dads Group has over forty local dads' groups across the United States and Canada, including the three I studied in the United States. They also support two national conferences for dads. The UES Mommas is an online New York City–based moms' group of about forty thousand members that began in 2011 to provide a network for mothers living on the Upper East Side of Manhattan (Lorenz 2020). MOMS Club International was founded in 1983 by California mom Mary James to promote activities and support for mothers of young children (Catania 1995). Both UES Mommas and MOMS Club have been the subject of major news reports about racism, bullying, and exclusion (Coleman 2020; Cummins 2020; Goldberg 2020; Klein 2020; Lorenz 2020; Ludwig 2020). This broad array of parenting groups offers an opportunity for in-depth examination of common parental care infrastructure.

Organization of the Book

Chapter 1, "Parenting Group Beginnings: History and Overview," introduces the groups I studied. In this first chapter, I trace the formation and organization of each group, focusing on how access to parenting groups' peer support is shaped by the group's leadership, recruitment process, and existing membership. Although several groups I researched are part of larger national and international organizations that take a broad and inclusive approach to care, some operate independently on the local level. In these cases, the local leadership's outsized influence and the (often silent) membership majority concentrates power and decision-making. In groups designed around the leadership's direct influence over members, decision-making is consolidated with leadership at the top. The organization of these early and mid-twentieth-century parenting groups provides important insights for understanding how parenting groups operate today.

In chapter 2, "Belonging and Exclusion: Parenting Groups' Objectives," I look at the groups' contemporary practices and how they foster inclusion and exclusion through their missions, membership, and meetings. The groups' practices grow from their formation, organizational structure, and ideology outlined in the previous chapter. Often couched as good intentions, members and leaders participate in gatekeeping access and participation through membership and recruitment, group activities, and their own sense of belonging. I consider how and why parenting groups are built around membership and ideologies that often underscore essential, intensifying individual and family-based care models and exclusionary practices.

Chapter 3, "Educating Parents: Care and Ideology," examines how education shapes parenting groups' care for parents. The groups' programming offers presentations, curriculum, publications, including books and magazines, as well as information and events posted to web and social media platforms. Education is not typically considered a form of care. I argue that parenting groups' education is a form of care designed to teach parents about caregiving resources, reduce parents' feelings of isolation, and boost their self-esteem. Across parenting groups, mainstream issues, responses, and voices often prevail and influence educational offerings. Using a mainstream lens, though less divisive, often favors consensus and a path of least resistance over and above morality and justice.

I address the provision of goods and services by parenting groups in chapter 4, "From Fundraising to Respite Care: Broad Resource Goals and Narrow Allocation." Parenting groups provide access to a range of in-kind resources. Fundraising may be the most familiar kind of support, particularly due to the cultural tradition of PTA bake sales. Collective resources generated by fundraising can be used to provide educational resources, like laptops, saving parents considerable expense. Parenting groups also provide access to respite care, though they do not use the term to capture this service. Providing access to short-term caregivers and playdates enables parents to attend parenting group meetings and have time for themselves, to work or rest. These kinds of goods and services (as well as others) could provide a lifeline to parents in need. However, since parenting groups are situated in local communities and a broader U.S. context segregated by gender, race, and income, resources often circulate narrowly.

Parenting groups are contradictory. Despite their limitations, some parenting groups foster advocacy within and beyond their organizations. In chapter 5, "Parenting Groups as Agents and Opponents of Social Change," I introduce the concept of "strategic parenting," or parenting groups' individual and collective efforts to advocate for resources and social change. Though seemingly counterintuitive, parenting groups are simultaneously sites of social action and public advocacy visible in moments when the groups broaden gender norms, embrace gender and economic equality, and raise awareness about racism to challenge the status quo and foster social inclusion. This chapter addresses the ways that parent groups can help us to understand how exclusivity could be interrupted, addressed, and dismantled.

I conclude by examining how parenting groups illuminate understandings of care at the collective level. In "Building Strategic Parenting Groups," I argue that parent groups provide invisible webs between parents. These are often imperceptible to nonparticipants for a variety of reasons, including nonparticipants' feelings of and experiences with exclusion as well as broader cultural stereotyping and negation and the taken-for-granted character of women's caregiving. While too often marred by exclusive ideologies, volunteer-led parenting groups can offer a compelling model for parental care. At their best, when broader contradictions are addressed, parenting groups show the potential to become a care resource that provides affordable and nimble care networks that better address parents' care burdens.

In the chapters that follow I examine how parenting groups could and sometimes do expand access to broad forms of care for parents. My goal is to provide a fuller view of the history, forms of care, and organization of parenting groups. I hope that parents, as well as those studying and organizing around parental caregiving, will find a deeper understanding of these processes.

1

Parenting Group Beginnings

History and Overview

Take care of one's own, we are told. Blood is thicker than water. Particularly in discussions around care, Americans emphasize family and "kinship" and discount "the importance of care for other social relations," social institutions, and nonfamilial caregivers (Thelen 2015, 497). At least since Alexis de Tocqueville's *Democracy in America*, the United States has been celebrated as a land of individualism, a place that values self-reliance (1899). Families both are products of and reproduce American individualism—they are normatively seen as private, nuclear, independent, and self-sufficient, despite abundant evidence that families live interconnected lives with support from neighbors, friends, teachers, coaches, paid caregivers, and extended kin. This myth of the self-sufficient nuclear family persists in American folklore as part of this elusive American dream of rugged individualism.

In this context, parents' care needs are not being met—far from it. U.S. families face a growing care crisis. The lack of affordable quality child and elder care coupled with an expansive aging baby boomer generation is creating more care needs than most families can meet independently (Adams and Rohacek 2010; Clawson and Gerstel 2014; Feinberg et al. 2011; Henly and Lyons 2000; Palley and Shdaimah 2014). These challenges create real struggles as families strive to close their care gaps often with few resources and a lack of social support programs that lead to "greater exploitation and intensifying inequalities" for careworkers (Misra 2012, 147). Families in the United States do not go it alone in addressing these challenges. American families are part of a web of social institutions that intersect with family life, including those pertaining to government, education, health care, recreation, and faith (Hansen 2004b). In neighborhoods and cities across the country, public schools, parks, athletic facilities, libraries, art and music centers, summer camps, and leisure service departments serve the local collective interests of families. Families may seek out community resources like online and in-person parenting groups, through hospitals, community centers, and libraries, or hospitals and courts may suggest (or mandate) participation related to illness, bereavement, divorce, or domestic violence. Out of economic survival and necessity, parents have long collaborated with other parents in their neighborhoods and communities. Parents may also build their own groups through access to national online platforms like Care.com and Sitting Around that help parents build connections to exchange care with other parents. So, rather than thinking of American families in isolation, it is more accurate to examine the extent to which families are served—or not served—by the care infrastructure, the people and organizations working to provide access to various care resources.

Parenting groups can expand the care infrastructure by promoting a broad-based approach that reaches well beyond individual households. Facilitating interactions between families, groups like the PTA are described as a "forum for fellowship and entertainment" (Cutler 2000, 46). In this chapter I look at the history of parenting group formation, organization, mission, and ideology within popular and successful early to mid-twentieth century and contemporary twenty-first-century parenting groups including the PTA, LLL, the Oakwood babysitting co-op, the UES Mommas, MOMS Club International, and City Dads Group. Though varying in size and scope, these groups' development, leadership, and membership follow similar patterns. By examining the groups' histories, "organizational logic," and system of beliefs reflected in their membership materials, we can better understand how and why they tend to reproduce narrow inclusion (Acker 1990, 147).

Early and Mid-Twentieth-Century Parenting Groups

In the past century, U.S. membership in clubs and organizations flourished. "Americans joined and led voluntary associations not merely to interact with friends and neighbors and solve local problems but also so as to reach out to fellow citizens of a vast republic and build the organizational capacity to shape national culture and politics" (Skocpol 2003, 12). These organizations include "fraternal organizations, veteran's groups, women's clubs, civic associations, study clubs, ethnic groups and even secret societies, such as the Masons" (Woyshner 2021). Organizations like the PTA were enormously popular during this time. Until 1970, the PTA's "organizational infrastructure . . . meetings and . . . communication channels" had "two branches—black and white" (Woyshner 2009, 153). By the 1950s the PTA's white organization had nine million members and the (Black) PTA had nearly two-hundred thousand (Woyshner 2021). LLL was built to "[provide] an infrastructure for reaching and improving the lives of women, babies, and families" (La Leche League International 2010, 444). It also began in the middle of the past century, and nearly a decade later membership included international groups in Canada, Mexico, and New Zealand (McKay 2016). It follows that writings about the PTA and LLL use the term "infrastructure" to capture how they grew into elaborate national and, in the case of LLL, international networks of people and organizations providing care.

The PTA and LLL share many commonalities as large long-standing parenting organizations. Although this book addresses LLL's international influence, including organization-wide social change through their Canadian branch, my analysis focuses on parenting group work in the United States. Founders of the PTA and LLL believed passionately in their causes—education and breastfeeding, respectively. Their identification of care needs stemmed from localized knowledge, lived experience, and nearby communities. While these resources have enabled leadership to understand some parents' needs firsthand, they have also limited the scope of their outreach as founders and leaders have embraced local constructions of family and motherhood. Though their language has often reflected inclusive ideals, early parenting groups reproduced the gender and race segregation visible in the broader society.

Beginnings of the PTA

The PTA began before the turn of the past century during the social movement for women's suffrage. Women's rights were subsumed under their fathers and husbands until 1920, when women secured the right to vote. Within this context, the group's early membership was like many social reform groups at the time. Like the Woman's Christian Temperance Union (WCTU), which fought for women's suffrage and the prohibition of alcohol, the early PTA was dominated by affluent Christian white women (Mintz and Kellogg 1988). The mostly white PTA originated in 1897 and was called the National Congress of Mothers (NCM) (National Congress of Parents and Teachers 1944). The Black PTA launched in 1926 was originally called the National Congress of Colored Parents and Teachers (Woyshner 2009).

The idea for the NCM came from Alice McLellan Birney, who identified parents' needs during a visit to the Chautauqua Institution, a private summer art, faith, and intellectual community in western New York, where the WCTU also traces its beginnings. In the summer of 1895, Chautauquans studied the kindergarten movement (National Woman's Christian Temperance Union

2022). They read about Marguerite Schutz, who began the first Wisconsin kindergarten and whose work inspired Birney (National PTA 1997). Through this study, Birney became convinced that parents, in particular mothers, alongside teachers would benefit from learning the best child-rearing and educational methods. Her plan was to provide mothers with "the opportunity to better educate themselves for intelligent homemaking and child-nurture" (Schoff 1916, 140). In dialogue with others in residence, Birney found tremendous support for her ideas and began conceptualizing her organization (National PTA 1997).

To realize her vision, Birney saw that she needed resources—monetary, political, and human. When she met Phoebe Apperson Hearst, she found a collaborator deeply invested in the growing kindergarten movement at the time (National PTA 1997). Hearst was an educator who became a philanthropist following the death of her husband, wealthy businessman and senator George Hearst, and funded the first free kindergarten and kindergarten teacher training in California. By collaborating with Hearst, Birney had access to both the financial backing and political connections needed to assemble the first NCM convention in Washington, D.C., in 1897. The meeting attracted "more than 2,000 people" including "mostly mothers, but also fathers, teachers, laborers, and legislators" (National PTA 1997, 11).

Statements from the PTA's formative years show the group's aspirations, ideologies, and engagement that shaped which issues gained traction, whom they partnered with, and how successful they were. The PTA leaders' worldview and education shaped how they understood and approached issues. Birney's broad approach would serve all families. "The National Congress of Mothers, irrespective of creed, color, or condition stands for all parenthood, childhood, homehood. Its platform is the universe, its organization, the human race" (National PTA 1997, 12). Though originally a southerner and by all accounts a person who avoided controversy, Birney's inclusivity was likely influenced by her second marriage to Theodore Birney, whose grandfather was a well-known abolitionist. In practice, however, the early PTA was racially segregated "reflective of working relationships, tradition, and Jim Crow laws in communities around the country" (Woyshner 2009, 55).

Setting forth this vision for a national parenting group, the white PTA would enable "the welfare of children and youth in home, school, church, and community" (National Congress of Parents and Teachers 1944, 184). The group aimed to foster a "membership of parents and teachers of all political parties, all religious beliefs, and many different opinions as to the right and wrong of various movements." When Hannah Schoff assumed leadership in 1902, she promoted a PTA that fostered "education . . . [to inform parents on] intelligent homemaking and child nurture, . . . effective cooperation" between schools and homes, and "a sentiment of community responsibility" to address local problems (Schoff 1916, 140). Through her work and that of others, the "PTA . . . stressed the ideal of 'educated motherhood' as the key to the well-being of individual families and the broader society" (Skocpol 2003, 82).

Though fathers were present, they were largely excluded from participation in the early NCM. At the 1899 congress, Birney advocated for men's inclusion: "No true-hearted man will shirk his duty in this crusade for the children, a warfare as glorious, I think, as men ever waged on a field of battle" (Skocpol 2003, 27). Despite Birney's encouragement on behalf of men, change favored teachers' inclusion first; at the second NCM, president Hannah Kent Schoff broadened the scope of the organization through a 1908 name change to the National Congress of Mothers and Parent-Teacher Associations (NCMPTA).[1] It was not until 1924 that the organization removed "mothers" from its title and became the National Congress of Parents and Teachers (National PTA n.d.-q). It would take another eighty-five years for the first man, Charles Say-lors, to become national PTA president (National PTA n.d.-i). Though Birney and Schoff promoted a big tent for the early PTA, in practice it operated like many groups in the United States, segregated by gender as well as race and wealth.

At the national and local levels, parent-group exclusion happens in several ways. The United States has a long history of racially and economically segregated neighborhoods and schools. Geographic segregation reproduces segregation in schools, beginning in prekindergarten (Stockstill 2023). Given the pervasiveness of residential segregation and institutionalized racism, communities of color have long created their own parenting organizations. Selena Sloane Butler was an early advocate of separate support and outreach groups specifically for Black parents and teachers in Black communities (Woyshner 2009). A former kindergarten teacher, Spelman College graduate, and member of the National Association of Colored Women (NACW), Butler was well situated to foster change for Black families within Georgia schools (Woyshner 2009). In 1911, Butler organized and became president of a parent and teacher group at the all-Black Yonge Street School in Atlanta (Woyshner 2009; National PTA n.d.-c). Butler saw the inequalities facing Black children who were limited to "half-time" education "as segregated schools were used for double sessions" (Woyshner 2009, 78). Butler led grassroots efforts with the NACW and the Jeanes Supervising Industrial Teachers to promote school and community improvement through the founding of the National Congress of Colored Parents and Teachers (NCCPT) (Woyshner 2009).

Butler's vision for the NCCPT, with the support of Black organizations, was to prioritize issues facing the Black community. So when Birney approached Butler in 1908 to "organize a black national PTA," Butler declined (Woyshner 2009, 77). Instead, she successfully helped other area Black schools organize their own groups. Her local work culminated in a 1919 statewide meeting, and seven years later she convened a national convention of the NCCPT (Woyshner 2009, 77). To provide a "financial starter," attendees were each asked to provide $6.42 (NCCPT 1961, 10). Among their primary goals was to continue "working in the interest of better trained motherhood . . . and better understanding of the child" (NCCPT 1961, 13). For the group's coral anniversary, the NCCPT commemorative book explained, "Integration is a continuous process; it will not materialize on all fronts at once. There is no doubt that the National Congress is needed now, and it is indeed imperative that it be kept strong. The days ahead look brighter. Through continuous efforts the dreams of the founders are becoming a reality. The members do not predict dissolution of their organization; new and significant chapters will be recorded in the future" (NCCPT 1961, 88). The PTA and NCCPT worked separately for nearly half a century; the Black NCCPT in southern states as well as segregated PTAs in other states operated with limited white PTA engagement (Woyshner 2009).

By contrast to the white mother volunteers who ran the predominately white PTA, the Black PTA groups were led by working moms, like schoolteachers and administrators, who focused on providing resources for parents and schools in addition to their work combatting racism, "making a conscientious and untiring effort for race elevation" (Woyshner 2009, 66). As reflected in the NCCPT publication *Our National Family*, members grounded their work within the family: "The home is the first consideration as it is the foundation of the nation." They emphasized goals that "must be motivated always by the objectives . . . to make better citizens, to make better parents, and to make better schools" (NCCPT 1948, 9). Care provided by both the early PTA and NCCPT extends parents' responsibility to community care, to include care across different families.

PTA integration took place over two decades. Led by the white PTA, "the timeline for desegregation was to be determined by each state unit's leaders. What transpired was the state-by-state annexation of Black PTA units" (Woyshner 2009, 153). The PTA failed to fully reckon with local members' racism and opposition to integration. Even after the U.S. Supreme Court made racial school segregation illegal in *Brown v. the Board of Education of Topeka*, the groups remained separate because of the "violent opposition from the white PTA units in the Deep South" (NCCPT 1961, 151).

In 1970, the PTA and the NCCPT formed one organization by signing "a declaration of unification." After they merged, the new PTA talked little about their struggles. The national PTA's leadership left decisions to local groups, which prevented the organization from providing its broadest support for Black members' full inclusion. The new PTA nearly fell apart over racial tensions. "Many black parents no longer felt welcome in the desegregated units of local schools, and white members in some locations in the South did not want to be a part of an integrated association" (NCCPT 1961, 4). As Cutler argued,

"Parenthood, while a common bond, was not necessarily an antidote to the divisive effects of gender, culture, class, or race. White, middle-class mothers could be insensitive to cultures other than their own and undemocratic in their relations with black, immigrant, and working-class women" (2000, 11). There were also important economic, racial, and experiential differences between the two groups. PTA leaders were less likely to be employed, whereas the NCCPT leaders were often employed as teachers. While NCCPT teachers and parents held a mutually beneficial relationship, they struggled mightily for resources limited by racial segregation and institutional discrimination (Woyshner 2009).

Even fifty years later, PTA coverage of the NCCPT and PTA unification initially failed to address the systematic exclusion of Black PTA members within the new PTA. To celebrate "50 years of unity," the PTA website presents the history of the NCCPT and PTA relations as fact: "As the United States progressed through the Jim Crow era, the Civil Rights Movement and the eventual desegregation of schools and communities, the two associations fought side by side for every child" (National PTA n.d.-e). Addressing the years after *Brown v. Board of Education*, its leadership wrote, "Following the Supreme Court decision that ended segregation, the associations held their conventions in conjunction with one another and worked toward merging in all fifty states" (National PTA n.d.-e). Rather than naming the white racism, widespread disenfranchisement, and fraught struggle leading up to and following the 1970 Declaration of Unification, the PTA presents a revisionist unified front. School leadership in the United States followed a similar pattern of inaction; despite considerable reductions in segregation during the three decades following *Brown v. Board of Education*, researchers argue that the decades since the late 1980s have been periods of "resegregation or stalled progress" particularly for "Black white segregation" (Reardon and Owens 2014, 203).

Two years after the fiftieth anniversary, the PTA further addressed unification through a position statement titled "Say Their Names—Addressing Institutional or Systemic Racism." The PTA wrote, "In the spirit of that unity, let us come together at all levels—national, state and local—to examine our policies, procedures and programs and eliminate any practices that disenfranchise or discourage Black and Brown families. We must look within ourselves and then call upon all other institutions to do the same if we are to end the practices that so adversely affect our children" (National PTA 2022). The statement outlined suggestions for how to "listen," "educate," and "advocate." Position statements are common from the PTA. They have "adopted hundreds of position statements on a wide variety of national education, health, and safety issues since . . . 1897" (National PTA n.d.-l). In these statements the PTA offers perspectives and recommendations; however, they are dependent on the organization and leadership's action to provide more than lip service. While this position differs significantly from the one that precedes it, the organization's approach to leadership is dispersed. The relationship between local and national PTAs is characterized by a common practice of noninterference that, within a broader context of structural racism, means that these kinds of statements will likely have varying levels of influence. Local parent groups can opt out of the PTA in favor of a hyperlocal PTO (parent-teacher organization), based in individual schools. Many schools have shifted to unaffiliated PTOs because they enable parents to make decisions independently to prioritize and benefit their own school, without interaction with the state or nationwide PTA.

PTA challenges surrounding racism are not unique. Parenting groups like LLL reflect the high levels of segregation in the United States throughout the twentieth century. Like the PTA, LLL began with affluent white, Christian women promoting mother-to-mother outreach. LLL's founders expressed a particular set of worldviews, especially early on.

The Beginnings of LLL

LLL's origin story still shapes normative impressions of the group's underlying values. In the decades between 1930 to 1960, breastfeeding rates in the United States were falling. By the 1970s, about one-quarter of infants were breastfeeding at one week old, and that number dropped to 14 percent at two to three months (Fomon 2001). Such was the context for the early years of LLL. It began during the summer of 1956; Mary White and Marian Thompson breastfed their babies at a Christian Family Movement summer picnic (Lowman 1978). At the time they did not think much about their choice until other mothers approached them with questions, sharing stories about their interest and desire to breastfeed as well as their challenges. This experience led them to consider the unmet care needs of mothers and babies. Based on these interactions, they planned to provide free advice and support mother to mother, borrowing the model from their Christian Family Movement affiliation (Bazelon 2008; Blum 1999; Cahill 2001).

The first group to assemble included the seven founders, one of whom was Mary White, who was married to Dr. Gregory White, a physician who played a central role as advisor to LLL. The group also included Mary Ann Kerwin, Mary White's sister-in-law. She and her husband, Thomas, were both lawyers. The other five were Edwina Froehlich, Viola Lennon, Mary Ann Cahill, Betty Wagner, and Marian Thompson. Except for Edwina and John Froehlich, who had three children, all the other founders had larger families. The Whites had eleven children, Viola and William Lennon ten, the Kerwins nine, Mary Ann and Charles Cahill eight, and Betty and Robert Wagner and Marian and Clement Thompson both seven. Their focus on faith and large family caregiving shaped LLL's support for breastfeeding parents.

During their first meeting, hosted by White, Edwina Froehlich recalled that she and most of the others in attendance had never discussed the "depth of . . . [their] feelings about breastfeeding and mothering" (Lowman 1978, 16). Thompson opened the gathering by reading aloud from "Breast Fed Is Best Fed," a *Reader's Digest* article written by Eleanor Lake (Lake 1950; Lowman 1978). Lake's impassioned writing captured the group's core belief bluntly: "Babies have always obstinately preferred their mother to any cow" (Lake 1950, 15). Over the course of the first several meetings, the seven suburban Chicago mothers established their ideas for the group (Ward 2000).

LLL founders did not anticipate the size or scope of their organization. Thompson explained, "In the beginning, we were not thinking of starting an organization. We just thought we were there for the women in our community" (Marinelli 2017, 16).[2] Though LLL's founders understood their contribution to mothers, they were unprepared for how they would "grow to such an extent" that they would need "to explain it to anybody" (La Leche League International 2023). LLL was created in the 1950s, the apex of the U.S. nuclear family ideal with its concomitant increases in marriage rates, declining age at first marriage, emphasis on domesticity, and idealization of women's roles in the household as wife and mother. Like the two establishing organizations that built the PTA, LLL's founders identified care needs through their experiences with other mothers.

Initially the group's focus was not entirely clear, founder Edwina Froehlich explained: "In those days, we were discussing how to present the basic mothering ideas" (Lake 1950, 27). The group was urged to clarify their objectives by Dr. Herbert Ratner, the local director of the public health department in Oak Park, Illinois, and a close friend of the Whites. According to LLL history, Dr. Ratner "kept probing and asking questions almost to the point of irritation. . . . He kept saying, 'what else is it besides the techniques of breastfeeding that you talk about?'" The founders "finally . . . said, 'well-mothering!'" Dr. Ratner was delighted: "That's it. That's what I wanted you to understand. You really are not talking just about the techniques of breastfeeding, because that is not what is so attractive to the mothers and keeping them coming. It's the fact that you're all together supporting each other in your basic belief that this baby needs good mothering." Seeing their group's broader purpose, LLL's founders forged their goal to "help mothers successfully breastfeed their babies, and so successfully mother them." LLL is, as Dr. Ratner saw so clearly, a parenting group (Lowman 1978, 22).

LLL began as a women's group and remains predominately one today. Like the NCM, which also explored including fathers as participants during its formative years, LLL realized that enticement was necessary to get men involved. LLL wanted to include men as supportive, rather than as primary, members in their own separate group meetings. The founders believed that "fathers weren't getting any support" in learning about breastfeeding and how to support their wives (Lowman 1978, 17). LLL hosted "special For Fathers Only meeting[s]," the first of which was directed by Dr. Ratner. Froehlich described having "a lot of trouble getting the husbands to go" to meetings. Husbands of LLL's early leadership offered new members' husbands transportation and beer; members also agreed to spread the word that each other's husbands were going to entice more men to attend (Lowman 1978, 17). Despite these enticements, men's continued resistance to inclusion meant that during the early years the work of parenting groups was disproportionally done by women.

The history of LLL reveals broad consensus in the group's formative years (Lowman 1978). The seven founders' shared vision was shaped by each other, their husbands, their families, and their common community. In a fiftieth anniversary interview, Mary Ann Kerwin and Marian Thompson reflected on the origins of the group's name. Kerwin explained, "We couldn't find a name. . . . We had been struggling with nursing mothers' anonymous . . . you couldn't use breastfeeding, as you know, that was a no-no. . . . And we figured we'd be confused with nurses, with the profession, if we said nursing mothers. We were desperate for a name" (La Leche League International 2023). Mary White's husband, Dr. Gregory White, was integral in the naming of La Leche League, based on a Spanish shrine in Florida with a statue of Mary nursing baby Jesus. The statue bore the Spanish name "Nuestra Senora de la Leche y Buen Parto." The English translation reads "Our Lady of Happy Delivery and Plentiful Milk" (Miller 2008; Shefsky 2013). With little attention to their cultural appropriation, Thompson explained, "In the beginning we called it 'La Lesh'; we thought it was French and then we found out it was really Spanish" (La Leche League International 2023). Taking the name La Leche League provided a way for the group to avoid using the term "breast," a word that newspapers and other sources at the time might have censored (Shefsky 2013). Both women described the name "as a help or, at times, a hinderance" (La Leche League International 2023).

LLL began with a narrow scope; they "started their little neighborhood group for friends" (Lowman 1978, 23). The population of Franklin Park was less than nine thousand in 1950 (U.S. Census Bureau 1950). The group began dispensing free information locally through pamphlets like their first, "For Better Mothers," written in 1957. By their third edition in 1959, "Why Nurse Your Baby," they detailed their perspective that "Mothering is Our Objective" because "the unique relationship between mother and her breast-fed infant affords a natural and sure start in good mothering" (Lowman 1978, 19, 20). They would eventually come to embrace "mothering through complete breastfeeding" (Merrill 1987, 223). LLL has advocated for a particular version of motherhood that centers on the interrelations between "prescriptions of breastfeeding, natural childbirth, and full-time domesticity" (Andrews 1991, 94). Sociologist Linda Blum asserts that LLL is a maternalist organization "exalting women's motherly traits" (Blum 1993; Blum and Vandewater 1993, 285). Discourses of natural mothering entail essential beliefs about gender and parenting, phenomena better understood outside of society and culture, as rooted in women's embodied essence. Using the term "natural" makes the practice seem transhistorical and inevitable, obscuring the gendered assumptions embedded in the ideology and practice, that women are expected to perform greater amounts of care due to the centrality of breastfeeding.

LLL's early local outreach included pamphlets available by word of mouth, correspondence in the form of "fifty or more letters a month," alongside answering women's telephone calls (Lowman 1978, 24). Their first large-scale event occurred when they invited British natural childbirth expert and author of *Childbirth Without Fear* (1942), Dr. Grantly Dick-Read, to speak in Franklin Park. They overfilled a twelve-hundred-seat high school auditorium and in the process raised enough funding to provide printings "for mothers who lived too far away to attend meetings" (Lowman 1978, 21). With their roots in a suburban enclave and Catholic community, they served a growing but largely homogenous group of mothers.

Both LLL and the PTA were often focused on narrow demographic membership in their formative years. Leadership was unable and, to an extent, unwilling to understand or diligently pursue broader access to their groups. Their standpoint reflects their experiences as educated, economically advantaged white Christian women (Harding 1986). These earlier formed parenting groups provided a pattern that many contemporary parenting groups have followed.

Twenty-First-Century Parenting Groups

Contemporary parent groups continue many of the patterns developed by their predecessors. Centrally, both the PTA and LLL underscore that caring for parents includes helping parents care for their dependents, particularly children. Over time, these groups have built extensive organizational structures with access to resources, plans, and support for member groups. Next, I address the contemporary PTA and LLL alongside parenting groups that formed over the past several decades, including the contemporary PTA and LLL, MOMS Club International, the UES Mommas, the Oakwood babysitting co-op, and City Dads Group. These groups, though more recently developed and smaller in scale than the PTA and LLL, provide parents with access to established connections and resources. Related to these objectives are the groups' ideas about gender, child-rearing, and family. It is here that the groups articulate their ideals of community beyond individual households.

Parenting groups' missions, both formal and informal, reflect their central goals, issues, and targeted membership as well as their groups' directives and what they seek to accomplish. They include formal and informal declarations reiterated on their websites, in their membership materials, and in statements from leadership. These are the general components and strategies of the group's "gendered substructure," which includes the organization's broader "rules" and "documents" (Acker 1990, 147). Often framed in idealistic terms, parenting group materials are contradictory and the groups themselves may operate more or sometimes less exclusively than their "rules" and "documents" may indicate. For example, the dads' groups and, until recently, LLL were founded with a gender-exclusive organization. By contrast, the PTA and babysitting co-op both maintain an "organizational logic [that] appears to be gender neutral," even if the groups' practices suggest otherwise (Acker 1990, 145).

The Contemporary PTA and LLL

Advocating for PTAs, the contemporary organization argues that "when a school has a PTA, parents are better informed and more engaged, and the learning environment is more supportive for students—plus, the school has a better reputation in its community." In short, the PTA seeks to be "a relevant resource for families and communities." Care is at the center of these statements. The PTA's position is that parents need engagement and empowerment through education—not just for their children, but for themselves. Since PTAs are often considered organizations that center the needs of children, it is important to highlight how the PTA itself underscores the importance of parents' needs. Similarly, the PTA's mission highlights caring about children broadly, well beyond one's own. Their contemporary mission is "to make every child's potential a reality by engaging and empowering families and communities to advocate for all children" (National PTA n.d.-b). Advocating for a community responsibility to care and promoting children's collective care and education provide parents with much needed support, including respite care, which is addressed in chapter 4, by allocating carework to other adults.

LLL also aligns its mission around collective care, beginning with something normatively seen as private and family bound—lactation and infant nursing—and fostering a broader community around it. LLL captures their work this way: "La Leche League USA helps parents, families, and communities to breastfeed, chestfeed, and human milk feed their babies through parent-to-parent support. LLL USA encourages, informs, educates, supports, and promotes the use of human milk and the intimate relationship and development that comes from nursing a child for as long as mutually desired" (La Leche League USA 2021). Leadership's use of a broad mission expands on the group's beginnings while still centering the infant-nursing relationship within a wider community.

MOMS Club International

Mary James founded MOMS (Moms Offering Moms Support) Club in the early 1980s (MOMS Club of East Lyme n.d.). According to the group's history, James was living in California and could not locate a group of moms to join, so she established one herself (MOMS Club of the White Mountains n.d.). "She posted announcements at supermarkets and playgrounds with a simple message: Stay-at-home moms don't have to be alone. Come join the MOMS Club" (Catania 1995). Over more than three decades, James built a nonprofit organization that helps mothers locate or create their own parenting groups using the MOMS Club umbrella of "support and guidance," including experienced leaders to offer advice, training, "online programs, seminars and workshops...formats for monthly meetings...and service projects" (MOMS Club n.d.-e).

The principles of the group combine central tenets of feminism, that "women must be free to choose their personal path to fulfillment," with traditional motherhood, "for women who choose it, raising children is an important and fulfilling full-time job" and "a family's decision for a mother to stay at home to raise the children often involves considerable financial sacrifice." Group formation is at the core of their principles: "There is no one right way to raise children, but... a major reason for the members to come together is their desire to seek out mothers with a common concern for raising their children in the best possible and most healthful way" (MOMS Club 2013).

James continues to serve as chair of the club's five-member Board of Directors that oversees more than 780 groups in the United States and around the world (MOMS Club n.d.-a). As their online materials explain, "International MOMS Club is a nonmember corporation. Mary James wanted to create something that would continue on beyond one person, so she started MOMS Club as a nonprofit organization that would not be a business but would be a charity supporting at-home mothers.... As a nonprofit, most... coordinators are volunteers. As... [they] grew larger... some jobs became too much to expect someone to volunteer for, so... [they] do have... paid positions" (MOMS Club n.d.-c). According to their 2016 to 2022 tax year filings, James has the only paid position, earning $24,000 each year for her role as chairman, president, and director of MOMS Club.[3]

The MOMS Club board oversees chapters nationwide. Local chapters are organized into conferences by geographic region (MOMS Club n.d.-a). For example, Conference 1, the northern region, stretches up the coast from Central California across the northern states including Idaho, Wyoming, South Dakota, Indiana, and Ohio. There are five conferences in all.[4] Within each conference are chapters overseen by various members of leadership. The chapter's leadership is organized with supervising coordinators, who manage area coordinators, who preside over local chapters with their own officers (president, administrative vice president, membership vice president, secretary) and members (MOMS Club Simi Valley n.d.-b). As one club's website explains, "MOMS Club ... offers opportunities for leadership in a variety of ways, allowing you to contribute to the group and satisfy your need to develop yourself and interact productively with other adults" (MOMS Club Maple Grove n.d.). To join leadership positions at the chapter and conference levels, MOMS Club provides online materials including eLearning courses complete with training tests. Though MOMS Club provides considerable chapter structure, locally "each group chooses the activities that its mothers wish to do and handles its own finances" (MOMS Club n.d.-g).

James designed MOMS Club to connect mothers and children "almost exclusively during school hours" (MOMS Club of Stamford n.d.). Chapter materials emphasize that participation is for "at-home mothers" who "spend the bulk of their time caring for their children" (Catania 1995), echoing the words from the MOMS Club bylaws—MOMS Club is "a support group for mothers who choose to stay home to raise their children" (MOMS Club 2013). Group websites laud the group's merits, as the Simi Valley website elaborates: "We are a group of passionate moms who have a vested interest in supporting each other and creating lifelong friendships for both ourselves and our children. . . . Each and every mother helps us create a village where both moms and children benefit" (MOMS Club Simi Valley n.d.-a). Group websites often contain intense appeals, as the Las Vegas website demonstrates: "We know that motherhood can be tremendously rewarding but sometimes challenging too. That's why we offer a program designed to support the whole *mom* . . . we understand that being *a mother also means being a woman*" (MOMS Club of Las Vegas Summerlin Central 2019, emphasis original). The group's emphasis rests on supporting mothers through their caregiving.

In addition to providing a support group for mothers, the group's "purpose" is "to provide a forum for topics pertinent to children, child-raising, homemaking, personal improvement and the family; to engage in activities to enrich the lives of children in the community; and to undertake and complete at least one charitable, humanitarian or social welfare project related to children each year" (MOMS Club 2013). Within this framework, each "[chapter tailors its activities to meet the needs of members. Some focus on social interaction, while others bring in speakers to talk about health and child rearing. Baby-sitting, [and] moms' night out" are "popular among the clubs" (Catania 1995). They hold events including museum visits, children's play groups, and stroller walking groups. The local chapters "are committed to complete at least one service project per year" (MOMS Club of Copley/Fairlawn n.d.). These projects often include supporting a local charity chosen by group vote. According to MOMS

Club websites, participants pay annual dues of between twenty-five and thirty-five dollars to support the local groups' operations and service (MOMS Club n.d.-f).

UES Mommas

Created in December 2011, UES Mommas is a Facebook group with over forty-one thousand members. The group's tagline reads, "Where NY Mommas come for support, positive and constructive guidance, and community" (Lorenz 2020; "UES Mommas" n.d.). The Upper East Side included in the group's name runs between Central Park and the East River, stretching twenty-seven blocks from Ninety-Sixth to Fifty-Ninth Street. The neighborhood's demographics are majority white (72 percent in 2018–2022), with 65 percent of residents having household incomes at or over $100,000 (NYU Furman Center 2024). The area is well-known for being one of the wealthiest parts of New York City and the broader United States.

The group is private, with considerable structure and organization. According to their Facebook profile, they currently have four administrators who oversee access and posting. The group's rules for decorum are extensive and include the administrators' expectations that members should "be kind and courteous"; not engage in "hate speech or bullying" or discussions leading to "contentious debates or divisive topics"; not engage in "advertising or solicitation" or recommend "fake profiles/names or fake nanny referrals." Any member "real estate" listings or "vaccine posts" carry a "one warning removal policy" by administrators. Participants "screenshotting (anywhere) or sharing posts . . . is not allowed" and results in "immediate removal with no warning" of a member by the administrators. The rules include empowering administrators to "reserve the right to remove and block any member for any reason at all." The group is run by administrators who screen prospective members for access. The group limits membership to moms by explaining that "nannies/caregivers are only allowed in the group if they are also local moms. The nannies in the group must interact in the group as moms rather than as [paid] caregivers." To join, prospective members "must have a public visible matching residence location in [their] profile," must self-identify as a "mom or caregiver," and must identify where they live (city and state) ("UES Mommas" n.d.).

I focus on the UES Mommas primarily because of the group's transparency around members' and leaders' political disagreements, particularly over racism. The group's Facebook page has been the subject of several high-profile social and media investigations, including *ABC News* and the *New York Post*, that document participants' exchanges, including conflict in 2017 over the book *P Is for Palestine* and again in 2020 following George Floyd's murder (Coleman 2020; Klein 2020; Lorenz 2020; Sucharov 2017). I detail the latter story in the next chapter. Since 2020 the group has had several moderators who have considerable control over posts to the forum. As one 2020 moderator explained, "The leadership of the group is what it is and if anyone is unhappy in the group for any reason whatsoever that person is under no obligation to stay in the group" (Klein 2020). Ultimately, the group did add another administrator, "to promote conversations about important topics like racism and not wash over it or have civil discussions with other points of view," and in 2021 the group issued even stricter rules for joining that include documenting a prospective member's pregnancy with sonogram images or legal surrogacy paperwork. Controversy continued in 2023 with news media allegations that one administrator was spying on members' online activities when deciding to ban their access to the UES Mommas page (Kreth 2023). As the media coverage and group rules attest, moderators act as "gatekeeper for a very large group of women" from "one of the wealthiest neighborhoods in Manhattan," situating administrators for "the group [into] a powerful position of influence and privilege." The top-down leadership style exhibited by the UES Mommas provides an organizational context for a group rife with conflict.

The Oakwood Babysitting Co-op

The Oakwood co-op is a relatively recent development, though similar groups have existed for decades. Calling itself a co-op, short for cooperative, is part of a common practice similar to cooperative nursery and preschools in which parents are expected to contribute their labor through participation in direct care and school administration alongside other parents and paid professional preschool staff. Like the groups that predate them, contemporary parenting groups are often formed along educational, economic, gender, race, and religious dimensions that reflect the groups' geographic location and broader organization. The Oakwood babysitting co-op is based in an affluent New England community. Oakwood's population of over sixty thousand is privileged across a variety of measures—more than 70 percent are homeowners with median annual household incomes just under $100,000; residents are highly educated, more than 60 percent have a bachelor's degree or higher; and the majority (80 percent) self-identify as white. For comparison, the nationwide median household income is $61,372, and one-third of adults hold a bachelor's degree or higher (Bureau of Labor Statistics 2017).

Due to its small size and somewhat less formal structure, the babysitting co-op does not use a traditional mission statement, but its membership materials and handbook elucidate its guiding principles. Rotating leadership has revised these materials over the years, however an emphasis on the relationships of parents and children within the broader group remains at the core. The handbook explains that "the co-op was designed to provide high quality, safe and enjoyable child-care by members for other members' children on a *for-time*, not *for-cash*, reciprocal basis. The co-op may also serve to nurture, support, entertain, encourage, inform, and cheer its members" and "offers a forum for discussing parenting, community or school issues. . . . Friendships evolve—some lifelong." Highlighting connections across children and families, the authors write, "Children benefit from visiting a variety of homes and families . . . and toys and become well-acquainted with children among whom some lasting friendships bloom." The welcome letter sent by the chairperson to new members emphasizes the group's many contributions beyond providing child care: "We hope that you'll find the co-op to be a valuable resource not only for babysitting, but also for friendship, parenting advice, and general support." Centering parental as well as children's bonds, the group's formative documents emphasize community building and a less isolated but very hands-on approach to parenting.

A convergence of factors led to the group's organization. The idea for an Oakwood babysitting co-op came from a mom who had participated in a babysitting co-op elsewhere. Hearing about the concept, two members of a local Christian church decided in 1999 to create a babysitting co-op in Oakwood. Both founders were parents of young children who saw firsthand the need parents had for help from a network of other moms. Nearly twenty-five years later, the co-op is still operating, although the group is no longer connected with the church.

Unlike MOMS Club and the UES Mommas, the babysitting co-op's materials demonstrate the group's more complex gendered organization. For example, the babysitting co-op's official documentation, including its name, its jargon, and its handbook, uses language like "parents," "members," "volunteers," "spouses," and "he/she," suggesting group membership is for mothers and fathers.[5] One of their organizing documents reads, "A co-op of parents you trust provides nineteen places you can turn to for a sitter especially on those weekdays when sitters are so hard to come by." Though this language is inclusive, other aspects of the co-op are specifically gendered. The babysitting co-op's scrip, paper coupons used to reimburse members for caring for other members' children, features an image of children on one side and a vintage drawing of a woman on the other.[6] The group also uses the language of "Mom's Nights Out" for activities intended for members only. Membership in the babysitting co-op also belies gender inclusivity. At the time of this research, all babysitting co-op members self-identify as women and almost all are married to men. In two decades, only one stay-at-home dad was briefly a member. Babysitting co-op events and meetings highlight the group's gendered composition—from nail salon visits to fashion-related meeting icebreakers (e.g., share your favorite summer wardrobe accessory). These examples underscore the group's gendered composition, as a babysitting co-op made up of moms.

Membership in the babysitting co-op is limited to approximately twenty participants, and they often have a waiting list. Different from the former groups

Table 2

Babysitting Co-op Demographics ($n = 28$)

Characteristic	Members ($n = 18$)	Spouses ($n = 10$)
Average age[a]	44	43
Married	18	10
Self-identified race		
White	16	10
Asian	2	
Religious affiliation[b]	14	9
Homeownership	17	9
Postsecondary education[c]	15	10
Employment[d]		
Part-time	6	
Full-time	2	10
Volunteer[e]	14	9
Average care exchanges across members[f]	4	

[a] Age range is 34–52 years for members and 35–52 years for spouses/partners.

[b] Religious affiliations are as follows for members: 6 Catholic, 6 Christian, 1 Jewish, 1 Jain, 1 Atheist, 3 N/A; and for spouses: 1 Catholic, 6 Christian, 1 Jewish, 1 nonpracticing Catholic, 1 N/A.

[c] Members' highest degree completed: 1 has 2 associate's degrees, 14 have a BA, 4 also have a master's degree, and 3 are missing. One spouse has a PhD.

[d] Members' part-time work averages 18 hours per week. Ten members are not employed. Spouses full-time work averages 48.5 hours per week.

[e] Volunteering for members averages six hours per week and for spouses between once a year and two and a half hours per month.

[f] Co-op members exchange care with between 1 and 7 different members.

given its smaller scale and horizontal leadership, the babysitting co-op's organization and composition are largely shaped by its members. Members of the babysitting co-op are older moms; their average age is forty-one years, and their first birth was typically in their thirties (see Table 2). They are parents of infants, preschoolers, and elementary-school-aged kids. The majority self-identify as white, and many are active in community faith-based institutions. Babysitting co-op members routinely volunteer, averaging seven hours per week. All but one participant owns their own house. Most have college degrees, several have master's degrees, and one has a doctorate. About one-third of the group is employed outside the home, though many move in and out of the paid labor force.

The co-op's membership reflects the broader demographics of Oakwood, but even within a predominately white and affluent city, members argue that the group draws disproportionally from its most affluent neighborhoods. Pia, a thirty-eight-year-old white mother of two who works full-time for a local non-profit, described how geography and connection operate in the co-op: "Our side of the town tends to be more white, people in a certain socioeconomic status, because of the school districts and everything that we have around it. Also, the recruiting mechanism is people you know. . . . It's not an open group. It's an invitation kind of group, so you're going to invite people who are like you." Similarly, Ava, a forty-four-year-old white mother of one who works part-time in leisure services, associated geography with her discussion of diversity. "I think [co-op members] have this vision that it is kind of a very liberal group . . . I guess we're diverse in terms of our life experiences, but in terms of . . . like racially, we're not that diverse . . . in terms of sexual orientation, marriage, we are pretty traditional, so to speak. . . . If you take a look at [Oakwood] . . . if we were to really break [it] down, do we have a lot of families who go to [schools in less affluent and more diverse areas]? We probably don't." Ava's comment illustrates how members use their privilege and confidence to claim diversity and simultaneously use their own vetting to exclude and foster racial segregation within the group. Similarly, though Oakwood is widely considered to be a racially diverse community, studies of its schools have documented ongoing racial imbalance, leading some to be majority white and others to be majority Latino, Asian, and Black.

The babysitting co-op's organizational rules, both formal and informal, structure members' expectations for intensive caregiving. The mothering ideology of the co-op reflects the group's historical roots, as research on path dependence would suggest (Ghezzi and Mingione 2007). The group's members embrace an ideology of collective-intensive mothering that reflects historical links to a Christian church that places women squarely at home and releases men from parenting responsibilities. Reproduced over many years, the group's documents alongside members' stories highlight the intensified labor expected from current and prospective members. In keeping with an ideology of intensive mothering, it is the "individual mother" who bears accountability for her child's needs (Hays 1996, 54). However, with collective-intensive mothering, mothers assume this responsibility in tandem through shared reproduction and reinforcement in members' practices. As Margaret, a forty-four-year-old white mother of two who works part-time in education, describes, "My husband will be like, 'oh just use the co-op, use the co-op,' but I tell him those coupons don't come for nothing, that's also my time!" These practices encumber babysitting co-op mothers with carework, despite and due to their extensive resources.

The babysitting co-op's organization shapes members' expectations for intensive caregiving. Joining the babysitting co-op involves a multistep process, first done by members who propose new recruits, and second by broader co-op members who socialize with recruits on at least two occasions. According to membership materials, before joining potential new members must attend two events, including one meeting. Once they have joined, new members are asked to host a "new member tea" at their home. The tea provides a chance for members and their kids to learn where the new member lives, see their home, and meet their family. This detailed review process is labor-intensive for those who join and enables the babysitting co-op to control who has access to the group. In effect, the group relies on their privilege and confidence to sufficiently vet new members, without resorting to a more formal review process including background checks.

Local care infrastructures, including the MOMS Club, UES Mommas, and Oakwood babysitting co-op, often geared toward moms and building parent-to-parent caregiving connections, follow a script far more common among mothers. Co-op members never mentioned dads' groups or dads joining their group until I brought it up. In part, this contrast in awareness and relevance is due to the size and scope of parenting groups more generally as well as broader gendered parenting norms. The central purpose of the dads' groups is to facilitate connection and camaraderie between men, and those who form and join dads' groups often embrace similar views on masculinity and fatherhood. Dads' group members often make comparisons to moms' groups and highlight the importance of creating dads-only space, especially in a parenting group context that is so often built by and for mothers.

City Dads and Local Dads' Groups

New York City schoolteachers Lance Somerfeld and Matt Schneider longed for "parental camaraderie" with other dads, online and on "playdates and outings with their children," but they could not find a fathers' group until they formed City Dads Group in 2008. Over the first five years, the group grew to more than nine hundred members. Somerfeld and Schneider expanded nationwide five years later. Today, City Dads Group has more than 13,500 members and more than thirty-seven groups across forty-one states in the United States and Canada (Meetup n.d.). City Dads Group developed around major urban areas with larger populations from which to draw membership, access to museums and activities for parents and kids, and more liberal politics.[7] Politics are important since dads' groups reflect a sort of selection bias and are more likely to recruit men who embrace progressive ideas about masculinity and fatherhood. As political distinctions between urban, rural, and suburban politics "have become more pronounced over the past two decades," "rural areas have moved in a Republican direction and urban counties have become even more Democratic" (Parker et al. 2018, 29). In addition to providing digital content and acting as an umbrella organization for many local dads' groups, City Dads Group has supported national conferences, like one I call Dads Collaborate, that bring dads together to network, share ideas, and advocate for reframing fatherhood with slogans like "Dads Don't Babysit (It's Called Parenting)."

On a local level, through individual dads' groups, and on a national scale, through the overarching organization and national conferences, City Dads

Group seeks to bring fathers together and redefine fatherhood positively, as central to contemporary parenting. Dads' groups are different from the other three cases in two major ways. First, they are the only group populated exclusively by men. Second, they do not claim inclusivity; they are overtly gendered in their membership rules, ideology, and practices that exclude moms. Partly, dads' groups' exclusivity is in response to a broader context dominated by moms' groups that often feel inaccessible to the men. Dads' groups also promote an ideology of comradery and similarity at the local and national levels.

For example, consider City Dads Group's promotion of Father's Eve, a time for men to go out together the night before Father's Day. The promotion reads, "Fatherhood is a team sport. . . . Connect and have fun with other dads going through the same things you do . . . celebrate the Brotherhood of Fatherhood" (Fathers Eve 2025). Essentialist arguments are used as evidence for the divergence of mothers and fathers into separate parenting groups. These beliefs, in turn, shape the groups' broader philosophy and actions. Like the Oakwood babysitting co-op, the national City Dads Group and its local affiliates do not have formal mission statements. However, the national organization does provide some approximations. For example, they highlight four priorities in their guidelines for starting a City Dads Group: "1) Dads can be caring and capable parents; 2) Dads want to be involved in the decisions, drudgery, pains and joys of parenthood; 3) Dads benefit from opportunities to socialize and support each other; and 4) Dads come in all stripes: stay-at-home and breadwinning, single and married, gay and straight, and from different races, nations and religious beliefs" (City Dads Group n.d.-c). Like other parenting groups that emphasize their inclusivity, these ideas suggest a perspective that runs counter to the essentialist thinking I saw within the group. These priorities reflect the ideals City Dads Group outlines for fatherhood—skill, involvement, connection, and diversity—that together provide a clear sense of the group's mission. They address, at least in part, the ways in which fatherhood is normatively defined as something men do independently. Men's collective activities often highlight sports-related participation and viewing (McKenzie et al. 2018; Messner 1992). Men's group activities are not assumed to include care, particularly for young children, and City Dads Group seeks to address that.

This research focuses on their U.S.-based parent organization and three regional groups in the eastern, midwestern, and western United States. All of the three dads' group leaders have ties to the broader City Dads Group organization online and in some cases attend national conferences and participate in the broader group's leadership. They describe these connections as invaluable for networking with other dads, telling stories, and answering questions. For many of the dads' group members, their only contact with national organizations is through their initial online searches. Most of the dads I interviewed found their local dads' group through a general online search or a search on Facebook, Instagram, or Twitter. On the local level, the East Coast, midwestern, and western U.S. dads' groups operate independently.

Like the PTA, since the dads' group governance is not shared, their composition and practices are shaped mostly by the group leaders' outreach and members' influence. Each group provides independent web-based information, including a discussion forum and notifications of kids' outings, monthly dads' nights out, and potlucks at members' homes. All the dads' groups limit membership to fathers. The eastern and central dads' groups also limit online participation to dads. Even men who try to join with shared online accounts (for example, with emails or profiles that include their wives' names) are scrutinized and turned away. The western group limits membership to dads but currently allows wives to participate online. Despite the moms' inclusion, at the time of my interviews women had minimal online involvement.

Like the co-op members, most members of the dads' groups are married white fathers of young children—infants, preschoolers, and elementary-school-aged kids. Dads' group demographics are listed in Table 3. They are older parents; members' average age is 38 years. According to the CDC, the mean age at first birth in the United States was about 25.5 years for men in 2018 (Martin et al. 2019). Most of the dads' group participants self-identify as white, educated, and affluent. Most of the fathers and their spouses have college degrees, and all but one of the dads own their own homes. More than two-thirds of the fathers are employed, 80 percent working part-time, averaging seventeen hours per week. All the spouses work more than full-time, averaging approximately fifty hours per week. Similar to the co-op members, men cite their flexible employment as playing a major role in facilitating the time for their dads' group participation.

Understanding Inclusion and Exclusion

From the PTA's beginnings in the early twentieth century to the Oakwood babysitting co-op in the twenty-first, some parenting groups have used inclusive language that invites all parents to join. Other groups, like LLL, MOMS Club, and the UES Mommas, use gendered language to target mothers. Similarly, City Dads and the local dads' groups use gendered language to target fathers. For the parents they serve, parenting groups provide a source for parent-to-parent support. Their fellowship and caregiving provide some parents with a place to take their questions, resources to augment what they have, and access to other parents for solace. However, these groups often serve a narrower population than they claim. All of the groups I studied engage in exclusionary practices. These practices take a variety of forms including recruiting members from existing networks and local neighborhoods. There are few checks on the groups' choices to not prioritize diversity and inclusion. While the parent groups at times highlight inclusion, these attempts lead to little organizational

Table 3
Dads' Group Demographics ($n = 24$)

Characteristic	Members[a] ($n = 15$) Leaders ($n = 3$)	Spouses ($n = 6$)
Average age[b]	38 years	35 years
Married	15	8
Self-identified race		
White	13	5
Alaskan Native	1	
Asian	1	1
Religious affiliation[c]	13	5
Homeownership	13	5
Postsecondary education[d]	12	6
Employment[e]		
Part-time	8	
Full-time	1	6
Volunteer[f]	12	3
U.S. region		
East	7	1
Central	6	3
West	3	2

[a] Eighteen interviews were conducted with 15 men. Three of the men were interviewed twice, once as members and once as group leaders.
[b] Age range is between 27 and 50 years for members and 33 and 36 years for spouses/partners.
[c] Members' religious affiliations include 6 Catholic, 7 Christian, 3 N/A; and spouses'/partners' religious affiliations include 2 Catholic and 3 Christian.
[d] Highest degree completed for members include 8 BAs, 4 MAs, 3 high school diplomas; and for spouses/partners, 3 MDs, 1 PhD, and 1 BA.
[e] Five fathers are not currently employed and one is a student. Members' part-time work averages 18 hours per week and spouses'/partners' full-time work averages 50.1 hours per week.
[f] Members volunteer on average 4 hours per month, and spouses/partners volunteer 1 hour per month.

or demographic change. Local PTAs, LLL, and dads' groups are often disconnected from their umbrella organizations. Decisions at the national and local levels lead to groups that often exclude parents based on their economic status, race, gender, and religion. Conversely, groups like MOMS Clubs and UES Mommas demonstrate that strong leadership can also exclude. Other groups like the Oakwood babysitting co-op have a rotating leadership drawn from members and a horizontal organization that creates little authority to challenge the group decisions.

Conclusion

By examining the specific historical processes, we can understand parent groups' formation, organization, leadership, and which populations they serve (and do not serve). This background makes visible how and why particular ideologies take shape. The parenting groups studied for this book are popular and privileged by many measures. Their founders and members have demographics that are disproportionally middle- and upper-middle-class (measured through education, income, and homeownership), white, heterosexual, and cisgender. Parenting group participation requires resources that are reflected in participants' affluent backgrounds, privileges translated into having the time and mental space to participate in these communities. Privilege also shapes members' expectations for parent communities and empowers them to decide which connections they forge with other parents within their neighborhoods, broader communities, school districts, and nationwide. The groups' racial homogeneity reflects the residential segregation of the communities from which they are drawn, a common feature across the United States: "Residential segregation by race remains a defining feature of most metropolitan areas and continues to exert strong and multifaceted impacts on the life chances of segregated populations" (Crowder and Downey 2010, 1118). Geography matters, but so do the intentions and actions of the groups.

The groups often favor essentialist understandings of gender and family that center care within heterosexual partnerships with women and mothers guiding that care. The exception is the dads' groups that challenge that centering and argue for greater visibility and attention to fathers' participation and needs. Some of these groups, like the PTA and babysitting co-op, to some extent begin with gender inclusivity on paper but have a history of women-only membership. Other groups, like LLL, MOMS Club, UES Mommas, and the dads' groups, are narrower in scope and sought out a gender-based membership. For LLL, "representations of mothering and breastfeeding in the six editions of *The Womanly Art of Breastfeeding* promote a traditional version of heterosexual mothering at the same time that they promote mothers' individual authority as experts" (Hausman 2003, 158). Not until 2014 did LLL formally include transgender and nonbinary members as full participants and possible leaders within their organization and expand their understanding of nursing to include breast and chestfeeding (*Milk Junkies* 2012c). MOMS Club continues to limit membership to mothers and particularly mothers who are not employed. Their call for at-home moms is reflected in their overarching organization as well as their local club websites. Similarly, UES Mommas' rules emphasize their inclusion of mothers as the central caregivers. The babysitting co-op also centers mothers' participation and knowledge. Like the other groups that sideline men, the co-op intensifies women's labor while simultaneously making men's contributions less likely. In effect, the babysitting co-op outsources to other women labor that might also be shared (or at least negotiated) with their husbands. Essentialist thinking also fosters obstacles to broader communities of care and collaboration across parents and parenting groups.

Racial and economic segregation within these organizations stems from a variety of factors—historical, geographical, and ideological to be sure—but chief among them is the lack of effective leadership and resistance from membership. There has been much attention to the whiteness of LLL membership and the group's exclusion of employed women through a model of mothering that promotes breastfeeding on demand (Blum 1999; Bobel 2002; Hausman 2003). Likewise, the babysitting co-op coalesces around mothers' participation during the workday that makes it difficult for employed mothers to be involved. The PTA has been critiqued for both its segregationist history as well as its contemporary struggles with racism. In diverse school settings, the PTA often serves affluent white parents to the exclusion of Black and Latinx families (Calarco 2018; Cutler 2000; Koerber 2013; Posey-Maddox 2014).

As products of their culture and organization, parenting groups reproduce normative social patterns "shaped in particular by those who have acquired the power to define the situation" (Hallett 2003). Situated in a U.S. context, these groups are influenced by the race, class, and gender politics of their leadership, constituents, as well as the broader culture. Heteronormative and cisgender patterns are represented by the privilege afforded to two-parent nuclear families. The PTA, LLL, MOMS Club, UES Mommas, and babysitting co-op have privileged white middle-class mothers' needs and values, often promoting an ideology that centers those mothers' beliefs while it relies on many mothers' labor. In part, these decisions are linked to how each group understands and envisions their constituents and goals. In the next chapter I turn to the effects of exclusionary formation, organization, and ideology on parenting group practices.

2

Belonging and Exclusion

Parenting Groups' Objectives

As part of the broader care infrastructure to which they belong, parent groups supply parents with many resources. Parent groups can nurture members, providing a source of social support, leading parents to feel less alone. These groups also give members access to parenting advice to build parents' skills. Alongside many participants' sense of belonging, parenting groups can also alienate current or potential members, limiting or eliminating their access to these resources. Parenting groups may exclude parents through overt mechanisms like limiting access to particular people, although they often do so through less visible practices. Given the parent group histories outlined in the previous chapter, it is perhaps not surprising that members of these groups struggle to challenge exclusionary practices. These practices grow from the groups' formation, organizational structure, and ideology.

One way groups accomplish exclusion is by simultaneously facilitating and stifling members' communication, particularly around issues like racism, gender exclusion, and economic inequality. For example, we can see how these groups' "everyday racism" incorporates "daily attitudes" and actions that culminate in "the reproduction of systemic racism in terms of the experience of everyday life" (Essed 1991, 2). It is through recognizing these larger processes that we can see possibilities for change. To illustrate, I open this chapter with an example from UES Mommas. The context for the group's actions is the aftermath of May 25, 2020, after two highly publicized acts of U.S. racism cemented these stories together.

In New York City, Christian Cooper, a Black man and avid bird watcher, asked Amy Cooper, a white woman, to comply with Central Park's dog leash requirements for her unleashed dog. In response, Amy Cooper called the police and falsely claimed that she was being threatened by a Black man. On the same day in Minneapolis, Minnesota, George Floyd, a Black man, was being arrested under suspicion of using a counterfeit bill. Derek Chauvin, a white Minneapolis police officer, restrained and suffocated Floyd to death while he pleaded for his life. Both cases generated considerable outrage. The story that follows reflects one parenting group's reactions.

In the summer of 2020, UES Mommas took to their Facebook page to discuss the actions of Amy Cooper and Derek Chauvin. Several news reports on the group's private Facebook exchanges explained that some "members defended Cooper, saying that people should wait before judging her. When discussions around police brutality came up, some people in the group implied that the outrage was outsized" (Goldberg 2020). During these exchanges, Black members protested that their posts were being removed. Member Pearl Brady said, "I commented on a few different posts, 'the silencing of black women is not OK, the admin needs to apologize and stop'" (Lorenz 2020). Other members called for UES Mommas to appoint a Black moderator to better review and address matters related to racism in the group. In response, the white administrator wrote, "I have no intention to adding admins right now. I have worked my ass off to attempt to lead this group in a way that accounts for what its members want." Other members chimed in: "People who were unhappy should leave the group and start their own" (Klein 2020). Despite these objections, the group did eventually add a Black and an Asian moderator. The ensuing struggle led some members to leave the organization in protest (Lorenz 2020).

These conflicts are, at least in part, a product of their historical moment. Following Cooper's false allegations and Floyd's killing, Facebook posts were often oppositional (Dixon and Dundes 2020). More broadly, however, these divisions within parent groups reflect a more commonplace nationwide polarization over how to address systemic racism, white privilege, and police violence. They are also the direct result of the groups' organization. Both groups operate in ways that are difficult for members to challenge. The UES Mommas' leadership-centered organization and exclusionary ideology prevented Black women's attempts to post or moderate within the group, blocking any open discussion about racism. Organizations generally are vulnerable to a consolidation of power in place of broad participation (Michels 1962). Access to power is predicated on leadership's ability to simply not negotiate and unilaterally make decisions. Members' disenfranchisement can also happen through attrition and the tendency for day-to-day objectives to supersede change-based or political ones. Perhaps paradoxically, at the same time the smaller-scale grassroots dynamics that make these groups vulnerable to suppression and exclusion also make them nimble and enable them to act quickly and mobilize on behalf of parents.

As this chapter makes clear, parenting groups are rife with challenges partly because they have a long history of simultaneously fostering both belonging and exclusion. To be sure, not all parents join parenting groups, and these examples of exclusion underscore a reason why. For those who do join, like those in this study, many describe being compelled by what the groups aim to offer. Parenting group organizers look to their communities and see parents in need, sometimes by study and sometimes by chance. How to be better parents, how to foster connections between home and school, how to provide nutrition for infants—these are pressing issues for parenting groups. This chapter examines the effects of the groups' leadership and organizational structure—in particular their current missions, meetings, and membership—on inclusionary and exclusionary ideology and practices. As UES Mommas so vividly illustrates, parent-to-parent outreach from these groups includes discriminatory practices around race as well as economic status, gender, disability, and religion.

There are organizational similarities across these groups. As the last chapter demonstrated, although each group delineates a distinct perspective and orientation, these parenting groups' organization and formative statements reflect a desire to center parenting within their discussion about communities, households, families, and children. All have undertaken to recruit parents into their groups. They also all seek to mobilize caregiving beyond individual children or families, recognizing that both children *and* parents need connections and support. In so doing these groups make visible and seek to address parents' need for a broader parenting community. A primary task of parenting groups is to bring their members together. This is a unique and important resource that parent groups provide. While there are many ways for parents to meet—some parents find each other organically through common activities and locations and having children of similar ages or interests—meeting other parents is not always easy. Given geographic mobility, challenging schedules, and the intense combination of paid work, housework, and child-rearing, many parents reach out to parent groups to make parental connections. What parents find depends on their social location. For some parents, these groups enable them to find fellowship—sharing time, stories, and reassurance through parenthood. For others, like those who challenged and left UES Mommas, they find mixed messages and exclusion.

Developing Parents' (Dis)Connections

Meetings, in-person activities, and online dialogues are the foundation of parenting groups' formation. The success of parent group initiatives is critical to community building. Although some initiatives are designed specifically around children's needs, all (including those targeting kids) are designed to care for parents—to give them tools to address important issues, access to resources they can provide for kids, and parenting information. By collecting, curating, and distributing these tools, parent groups save parents the time and effort necessary to procure these things by themselves. With well-honed resources, parent groups can become known and trusted. To provide these resources, parent groups need to cultivate their membership. In so doing, these groups foster both inclusion and separation. Looking at different examples from group meetings enables us to see how these practices operate.

Talks, Collaborations, and Community in the PTA

PTA meetings have long forged relationships between parents by gathering them together in a common space and facilitating connections with the PTA and each other. PTA meetings take a variety of forms on the local and national levels. Some meetings are tailored to immediate concerns and business within particular schools or the wider national organization. Within these meetings parents who get a seat at the table may understand and deliberate how to address their needs and those of their children, the broader school, and the group. Beyond these more business-driven meetings are topical meetings on an array of issues.

Sample meeting agendas and materials available through the PTA website include multicultural reference guides and meeting suggestions. Under the heading "How We PTA," they outline several categories for group outreach that include advocacy, building a community, social and emotional well-being, distance teaching and learning, bridging the digital divide, and addressing food insecurity. Several of the meeting examples focus on "digital life" (National PTA n.d.-b). One program from New York addresses how families can better understand online communication—through social media and gaming platforms. The school invited two experts, a university professor and school psychologist, to "[help] parents and students see online interactions from different perspectives" (National PTA n.d.-b).

To be useful, parent groups need to adequately address important issues and provide access to that information's development and discussion. For Heather Osterman-Davis, a long-term illness kept her from participating in her local PTA (2021). Most of the PTA meetings and events were in-person, and her illness made in-person attendance difficult. When the pandemic brought PTA meetings and events online, she described being able to participate in "conversations about everything . . . improving the feedback loop between frustrated parents and overwhelmed teachers. Brainstorming solutions lit me up." After participating in the spring, in the fall of 2021 the PTA leadership offered her a position, explaining that "they wanted a major push toward improving communications and building community" (Osterman-Davis 2021). The pandemic brought both tremendous risk and devastation to disabled persons, but it also brought possibilities for change. Organizations like the PTA could suddenly see the value and necessity of broadening their access through online meetings and events. Osterman-Davis describes access to participation in the PTA as a "silver lining of the pandemic" (2021). The PTA is, of course, not alone in their pre-pandemic inaccessibility and ableism.

In some cases, PTAs collaborate with other groups to hold meetings that address broader community issues. Beginning in 2019, the Austin Council PTA collaborated with several groups affiliated with the Austin Independent School District (ISD) in Texas to create a dialogue around race. Working in conjunction with the Austin ISD Race Equity Council, Cultural Proficiency & Inclusiveness, Equity Department, and Parent & Community Engagement Support Office, the Austin PTA hosted a series of ninety-minute Zoom meetings titled "RaceTalks." A July 27, 2020, promotional post to the Austin Council PTA's public Facebook page features a photograph of two hands, one darker skinned and one lighter skinned, simultaneously opening a set of doors that are slightly ajar, letting some bright light emerge from the center. The event's flyer highlights that "RaceTalks opens the door for Austin ISD parents and caregivers to have on-going conversations about race in our community" to "start a conversation about race in our community" including a "monthly conversation with a different focus on race and why it matters" ("Austin Council PTA" n.d.). The National PTA profiled this work on their national web page under "PTAs Leading the Way in Diversity, Equity and Inclusion."

To facilitate participation, Austin PTA organizers and collaborators set up a separate "breakout room for white allies and one for people of color." Ultimately the participants included more people who self-identified as white, and the organizers attributed lower participation by people of color to being "exhausted with the conversation . . . and . . . those spaces . . . [being potentially] harmful." Though the PTA did not provide a tally, they explain that the "first few sessions drew in a large group of participants . . . [as] people were curious to see what RaceTalks would be about" (National PTA n.d. a). The topics included discussing "[participants'] racial autobiography," "white supremacy," "experiences around race and racism," and "action"; in the words of one leader, they provided "a refuge to really let go and be honest and feel and lean in on this type of conversation and work."[1]

In its summary, the National PTA described the Austin "RaceTalks" as receiving both support and some "minor pushback by some who felt they weren't included in the decision-making." Local PTA organizers did conclude the meetings were a success because of both the teamwork that went into building them and their ability to respond to the historical moment unfolding as the talks were held. They described how greater awareness with George Floyd's murder and the participation of "white leaders in positions of power in [the school district] . . . mattered." In her evaluation, PTA leader Laurie Solis explained that by collaborating with other organizations "who are really experts in this work to help lead it and be a part of it" they avoided "another PTA thing where we think we're the expert and we're really not." One of the PTA leaders involved, Nina Wilson, explained that "there's a lot of harm that can be done with this kind of thing, and it's not something that you jump into lightly. It needs to be someone who's steeped in doing their own work first, who leads and connects with humility, and is connected to a community" (National PTA n.d.-s).

The Austin "RaceTalks," through their collaboration and careful framework, illustrate what PTA groups can accomplish for parents with an organizational commitment to addressing issues. Promoting structured dialogue and an ongoing place to bring parents together around challenging issues provides a unique community resource. The "RaceTalks" framework is not without potential shortcomings. Though the organizers did include the words "white supremacy"—a term that suggests a focus on structural underpinnings—in their flyers, they first highlight a focus on and race as an individual attribute though autobiography and experience. This juxtaposition of personal narratives and racism as a systemic social problem does not necessarily lead to a conversation about the important differences between these perspectives. This seems especially likely when their flyers say "race and why it matters," suggesting that some might need convincing that race does matter by using the racially accommodating and obfuscating term "race" and not "racism," a term that highlights a system of oppression (Cazenave 2015). However, fostering parent-to-parent conversations, building allies, and discussing related actions can all contribute toward acknowledging racism's presence within parent organizations and their broader communities.

Meetings, Mothering, and Breastfeeding in LLL

In 1964, LLL held its first international conference in Chicago, with over four hundred people in attendance (Marinelli 2017). Seven years later in another high-profile event, LLL held its fourth conference in Chicago to tremendous fanfare as Princess Grace of Monaco served as a keynote speaker (La Leche League International 2016). Princess Grace used language that underscored her commitment to and admiration for the group's educational work: "I had never considered anything else but breastfeeding when I should have children. I would have liked to have nursed my babies for a longer period of time, but in the beginning, when they needed me and I them, there were no compromises. State had to wait on mother. You who have done and are doing such magnificent work, without fear or failure, in aid of the health and happiness of mother and child." Throughout her speech, the room echoed with the sounds of fussing babies. By the organization's twenty-fifth anniversary, its conference grew to several thousand adults and children in attendance. While national high-profile meetings drew early attention to LLL, their small-scale, local meetings are at the center of their organization and outreach.

Drawing prospective members to parent group meetings is a challenge all groups face. To encourage local meeting attendance, La Leche League's website lists the following questions: "Why attend LLL gatherings?" "What do you find that you can't find elsewhere?" Their answer provides a context for the education and camaraderie the groups can provide. The website explains, "Breastfeeding and mothering are often learned by example. A mother or parent who has no role model, no one with whom to compare their experiences and feelings about breastfeeding, may find it much more difficult to breastfeed. If they know one or two people who have breastfed, they will already have better information. But this information will inevitably be limited to the personal experience of the women in question. Whereas a group, especially if it's part of an international organization that's been in existence for decades, can offer information and support based on the experience of thousands and thousands of people" (La Leche League International 2024c). This explanation promises better information and support for parents, beyond or to augment what their personal networks can provide.

LLL members often describe meetings as a lifeline—a place to share experiences, to learn, and most of all to gain support, friendship, and camaraderie alongside other nursing mothers. As one state LLL website explains, at meetings "parents are encouraged to share their . . . experience, offer suggestions, and provide encouragement to one another. La Leche League meetings are a wonderful place to create friendships as you travel along your parenting journey" (La Leche League of Connecticut n.d.). Psychologist, researcher, and advocate Niles Newton described her first LLL experience: "There were nine breast fed babies at that meeting and many of them got discretely nursed. For the first time in my many years of breast feeding four children I didn't feel odd—I felt I was in a group where breast feeding was natural, the customary thing to do" (Martucci 2015, 55). Newton, like many LLL members, found both a group and a sense of belonging that is part of LLL's central commitment.

LLL meetings have a suggested structure, outlined in the *Leader's Handbook*. The group's suggested format begins with introductions, including participants' names and their children, followed by an introductory question. As the handbook explains, the goal is to get everyone participating before moving on to more topical and personal issues related to breastfeeding. The handbook encourages leaders to include "the LLL philosophy before asking" for participants' responses to a topic or question. For example, "La Leche League believes that for the healthy, full-term baby, breast milk is the only food necessary until the baby shows signs of needing solids, about the middle of the first year after birth" (La Leche League International 2022a, 67). The handbook explains that "clarifying LLL's philosophy in advance allows newcomers to choose whether to talk about personal experiences or opinions that differ from LLL." The book's argument is that advanced notice promotes the group's transparency and enables participants' choices; however, these words could just as likely alienate and silence those participants whose practices do not align with LLL (La Leche League International 2003, 38).

LLL also shapes understandings behind their meetings through its influence on local leadership. The LLL Leader Applicant's Resource Kit's "statement of commitment" requires group leaders to affirm, "I am personally committed to good mothering through breastfeeding" (La Leche League International 2019, 48). What is "good mothering though breastfeeding"? According to LLL, "Breastfeeding is a connection as well as a food source, a baby's first relationship. . . . It's a way of *mothering* your baby—a relationship that develops feeding by feeding, building trust, closeness, knowledge of each other, and a deeply connected attachment that lasts long after weaning" (xxi). LLL foregrounds the contributions of mothers: "It's remarkable how much wisdom there is in the stories of mothers from many years ago; although the world has changed, much about breastfeeding is timeless" (xxiii). Connecting lactation with parenting, LLL advocates not just for a particular form of feeding through breast and now chestfeeding, but also for the care and family organization that work entails, built on the idea that "breastfeeding helps a mother by enhancing her natural mothering instincts" (La Leche League International n.d.-g).

LLL's expectations for nursing present parents with an all-or-nothing framework. As historian Lynn Weiner explains, "To meet league standards of on-demand breastfeeding, mother and infant must remain together" (1994, 1359). This imperative includes always being available, day and night. To promoting cosleeping, *The Womanly Art of Breastfeeding* plays on a host of maternal concerns, including infant safety and health (even the specter of death) and maternal sleep deprivation. The *Womanly Art of Breastfeeding* reports, "Babies under about six months of age who are near enough to hear their mothers breathing and moving are less prone to sudden infant death syndrome because the sounds stimulate them to breathe. But he has to provide his own warmth, and he doesn't feel as safe without your body curled around him. And in order to nurse he has to rouse both himself and you much more than he'd have to if he were right next to you. Co-sleeping works best when you and your baby are touching" (Wiessinger, West, and Pitman 2010, 224). The *Leader's Handbook* emphasizes consistent proximity as the basis for success: "Mother and baby need to be together early and often to establish a satisfying breastfeeding relationship and reliable milk production." Later, on the same page, they attribute this time together to the baby's very existence: "In the early years, the baby has an intense need to be with his mother which is as basic as his need for food" (La Leche League International 2022a, 9). Through these kinds of messages, the group presents a "maternalist ideology" that promotes the "ideal role for women [as] . . . full-time motherhood focused on the natural needs of the baby" (Weiner 1994, 1359, 1374). LLL's perspective on mothering has done more than advance breastfeeding knowledge and skills; the group has advocated for what Sharon Hays called an ideology of intensive mothering (1996).

For the past several decades, the middle-class model of intensive mothering has been idealized as the favored model of American parenting (Hays 1996). Intensive mothering is a deeply gendered parenting ideology that idealizes mothers as the primary caregivers for kids (Damaske 2011; Hays 1996; Walzer 1998). When caregiving is organized through an intensive mothering ideology, tasks are wide-ranging, requiring resources that are not available to all, including expertise, time, and money (Hays 1996). Rachel, an LLL member, served as the opening participant described in Sharon Hays's influential book *The Cultural Contradictions of Motherhood.* Hays portrayed Rachel as "active in La Leche League and for twelve months" while she "breast-fed on demand (against the advice of her pediatrician and friends)" (6). In both her breastfeeding and caregiving, Rachel was emblematic of embracing an intensive mothering ideology: "Appropriate child rearing, for Rachel, [included] lavishing copious amounts of time, energy, and material resources on [her] child" (8). The babysitting co-op embraced a similar ideology, but in its collective form, a concept I call collective-intensive mothering (Price-Glynn 2024). I documented this ideology in my interviews and fieldnotes and with the Oakwood co-op.

A Typical Oakwood Babysitting Co-op Meeting

Babysitting co-op meetings are for adults only, though babies are welcome, and hosts' small children sometimes make an appearance. Meetings, held at members' homes, provide a time for parents to chat, organize co-op business, and make babysitting plans. My fieldnotes document conversations that are familiar and friendly, focusing on kids, schools, and activities. From birth stories, the moms migrate to lighthearted complaints about their kids. Nora, a forty-five-year-old white mother of two who is not employed, groans, "My second is such a terror; that child will truly be the end of me. I turn around and the kid's up on the counter! I keep telling my husband that he's spent too much time at the playground honing his skills!" Margaret, whose oldest child recently began attending preschool, talks about the tremendous amount of stuff associated with her kids' transition from home to preschool: "Now I need two of everything—extra clothes, extra shoes, an extra lunch box—the duplication helps me have what I need in both places, but ugh, there's so much to pack and remember!" Other moms nod and lament the proliferation of stuff and how they strive but often fail to stay organized. Lily, a fifty-year-old Asian American mother of two who works part-time in education and is a longtime member, arrives in new yoga pants and describes a gym she recently joined: "I've spent the last dozen years focusing on my kids—how they look, what they're wearing, what they're doing—I think it's about time I focused on me!" She receives strong vocal agreement from the other moms and compliments on her new fitness focus. Though some of the conversations clearly signify frustrations, they all preserve the centrality of the mothers' hard work on their children's behalf. They also foreground the mothers' resources, in particular their access to time and money to support playground visits, supplemental preschool supplies, clothes, and gym memberships.

Once everyone has arrived and gotten refreshments, co-op members assemble and take turns introducing themselves, including their kids' names and ages and their answer to that night's icebreaker question. Icebreakers range from questions about food ("What is your favorite go-to weeknight dish or takeout restaurant?") to book recommendations ("What is your favorite children's or parenting book?"), seasonal activities ("What are your favorite day trips with kids?" "What's your favorite winter tradition?" "Finish this sentence: I knew it was summer/vacation when [fill in the blank]"), parenting tips ("What's the best advice for preschool to make life easier?" "The smartest parenting advice I've ever received is [fill in the blank]"), and fashion ("What's your favorite summer wardrobe accessory?"). Though the group's mission and materials are inclusive, the meetings are geared toward mothers.

The meeting's business includes scheduling activities, like a mom's night out or other events. The kids' playdate is scheduled, and members discuss a happy hour sit that includes up to five kids per host (minus their own). Each meeting ends with babysitting needs. Members pull out phones and print calendars. Unlike the parents in sociologist Tamara R. Mose's research, all of the co-op members recognize that "sits" are both playdates and child care (2016). They go around the room, gathering members' requests for care to cover doctor's appointments, date nights, school conferences, and babysitter cancellations. Members dutifully respond with their availability and take turns offering their time. Chiefly, care decisions are made based on synchronicity, proximity, fit, and friendship. Many sits are organized pragmatically; the members' schedules mesh well, or they live in the same neighborhood, or errands are closer to one member's house than another. Other times sits are based on having kids of the same age or with the same interests. Care exchanges often happen more narrowly among smaller groups of co-op members. Members often try to recruit neighbors in addition to friends into the group; these previously established relationships facilitate easier and less time-consuming sits. The kids are already familiar with each other, the parent(s), and the house; and transitions also take less time, in terms of commuting, introductions, and instructions. Those who are unavailable to babysit often explain their conflicts before waiting for the next request. Those who cannot fulfill their babysitting needs from those in attendance submit their requests again online to the entire group. Meetings adjourn at nine o'clock, however members often stay late to discuss co-op business, make plans for activities, and socialize. The gendered, child-centered, and labor-intensive aspects of these monthly meetings capture members' affinity toward a collective-intensive mothering ideology, the common ground upon which the co-op is built.

National Conferences and Local Outings in Dads' Groups

Men are far less often the providers of unpaid care, even within their own families (Gerstel and Gallagher 2001). City Dads Group flips this script, centering their outreach toward those who self-identify as engaged fathers. The dads' group members connect through national and local networks online as well as a variety of in-person activities. Locally, the dads' groups hold regular kids' outings, dads' nights out, and potlucks at members' homes; they do not have regular structured meetings like the PTA, LLL, and the Oakwood co-op. Nationally, however, the group participates in an annual conference that I call Dads Collaborate.[2] After nearly a decade in existence, the Dads Collaborate annual conference draws men from across the United States.[3] A recent meeting included nearly four hundred dads.

Dads Collaborate is a well-organized event with generous advertising. Partnering with corporations offsets attendee costs and promotes attendance by providing free goods and activities to conference goers. A recent Dads Collaborate offered free men's skin and hair products with a pop-up barbershop. A separate ballroom featured a cooking contest sponsored by a major food company. The room had an *Iron Chef* format, with several kitchen stations. In another part of the hotel, a large conference room featured a stunt designer who trained participants in sword fighting. Near the lobby, a whisky company served free drink samples. A barbershop shave, competitive cooking, mock sword fighting, and liquor drinking are all activities with a conventionally masculine spin. The dual signifiers of manliness alongside men's caregiving are common themes within Dads Collaborate.

A recent three-day conference featured several large and small sessions.[4] In one of the smaller sessions on how to build a dads' group, Bryson, a married middle-aged white father of two working part-time, who founded and leads a midwestern dads' group, implores his audience to "have the passion . . . to connect with guys. And just be honest with them . . . about why this is important. We need comradery." For fathers, isolation is compounded by gendered expectations around masculinity, caregiving, and employment that make dads' group participation challenging. Additionally, local infrastructures are often geared toward caregiving moms. Bryson's earnest plea is counterbalanced by an audience member who calls out, "Like beer and hatchet throwing!" In response, most of the men laughed.

All dads' group leaders share recruitment challenges. Bryson found recruiting dads complicated by men's indifference, pride, and even distrust. He thought a brewery location would encourage men's attendance, but as he sat down in the industrial-style taproom and ordered his beer, his phone started pinging with regrets: "Hey man, sorry, things are getting crazy at home"; "My kid just popped a fever"; and "I'm not going to make it." He described the event as "a complete disaster. All of these guys [said], 'yeah this is going to be great, yeah, I'm going to be there.' I'm like, 'sweet, I'm going to have five or six guys. It's going to be awesome!' Nobody showed up. It was me sitting at a brewery, waiting on guys who said they were going to show up, to not show up. . . . Lo and behold, the owner of the brewery came up [to me and] was like, 'hey, what are you doing?' and I got talking to him and he got on board. He's like, 'what can I do?' 'I'm a dad too; I want to help in whatever kind of way.'" Bryson's story reflects a typical challenge in community building—people fail to show up. It also reflects a common grassroots organizing tactic—groups begin by contacting individuals.

When I asked men why they joined dads' groups, many of those I interviewed led with descriptions of their isolation. Respondents reach for dads' groups after moving, when their family circumstances make it geographically challenging to have connections and help from extended family, leaving them providing care for their kids alone and without support. John, a thirty-eight-year-old white midwestern dads' group member, father of one, and full-time musician, explained, "We landed . . . far enough away that I can't go ask my mom to come over and just take care of our daughter for a couple of hours while I go out and do something else. But yeah, I mean, that moving to a new place with such a young baby definitely could very easily lead to a sense of isolation. And I mean, that it did to some extent, but having . . . the . . . dads' group really helped." Likewise, Paul, a forty-year-old white father of two and midwestern at-home dad, lamented, "And then when you have little kids you're not, you know, going out to social events. I mean you are somewhat, but it's not the same. . . . So, we just didn't have any friend group. We didn't know anyone . . . [we were] isolated from friends and family." Both fathers have extended families who care deeply about their kids but who for geographic reasons cannot care for them (Hansen 2004b).

There are many recruitment avenues, but for dads' group members they often straddle what Raewyn Connell calls hegemonic and marginalized masculinities that capture normatively exalted and derided performances of masculinity (Connell 1995, 2000; Connell and Pearse 2015). The oscillation between sharing earnest feelings and injecting the meeting with humor to disrupt the intimacy (rather than expanding it) reflects the public masculinity visible at Dads Collaborate. Within a community of dads, this is reflected when Bryson encourages other men to seek connections while another man cracks a stereotypical joke. The joke embraces conventional tenets of masculinity to preserve "within the male homosocial group, emotional detachment" that "is viewed not only as desirable but as imperative" (Bird 1996, 125). A story from Jeremy, a middle-aged white dads' group leader in attendance, further illustrates the challenges men faced when fostering connections.

Jeremy cautioned other fathers about how dads' group media attention could be spun in unintended directions. During an interview about his dads' group, a sympathetic journalist homed in on his use of the word "support" to describe the fathers' interactions. Jeremy warns the audience, "Don't call it a support group 'cause we're not supportive, we're a social group. Our support comes from our family, that's where our . . . support is. Our support comes from other dads [too, but] this is us going out, and having fun with our kids, and socializing with them." Jeremy's outrage is palpable. He seemed most concerned with the stigma he and other dads might experience as members of a "support group," terms that evoke groups who need to share feelings with others. He laments, "I wouldn't say backlash, but there were a few [negative online] comments. I wish [the journalist] never would have done that."

Following Jeremy's story, Bryson attempts to address the contradiction by saying that dads' groups are part of the solution, "a place for . . . camaraderie, for support . . . give the guy a chance to actually be vulnerable, sit down and talk." Many men I spoke with echoed Bryson's perspective, highlighting the importance of support. Thomas, a thirty-five-year-old white father of one and West Coast Dads Group member, explains, "The Dads Group and the City Dads Group definitely helps with [parenting], you know, you can send the message out and get help. . . . Some dads end up getting depressed right in the beginning because it's not easy to take care of a baby. . . . That's the hardest. Your whole life changes." This contrast—Jeremy distancing himself from dads' homosocial support in favor of his heterosexual family and Bryson and other dads, like Thomas, reaffirming dads' groups as a place for connection, camaraderie, *and* support   shows how presentations of masculinity and fatherhood may entail considerable variation and impression management to navigate participation in the dads' group.

Across these groups, members cultivate relationships through various kinds of in-person and virtual meetings—some are more regular and structured like those for the PTA, LLL, and the babysitting co-op, and some are less structured, like the dads' groups. All incorporate activities and socializing, even when they address the groups' business. The parenting groups share a perspective that care for parents is a worthy group endeavor. Each group situates caregiving around group norms that reflect gendered, raced, and affluence-based expectations. Though the groups evoke gender differently, they all embrace, to some extent, essential underpinnings. These essential ideas center women as caregivers and situate men as outsiders in providing care (in evidence even as the dads' groups seeks to reclaim fatherhood's importance). Race-based exclusion is visible in the babysitting co-op and dads' groups demographics and predominately white membership (Tables 2 and 3). Affluence is reflected in the sizeable resources needed for participation, including securing housing to reside within or near the group's community, making time for meeting attendance and travel for conferences, and paying for child care (if not included) and refreshments (if not provided). The groups also foster a sense of exclusivity through their locations and the content of their meetings—like the home and conference hotel-based meetings of the co-op and dads' group meetings, respectively. Though these costs could be minimized or subsidized to promote inclusion, the groups do little to reach beyond their demographics and neighborhoods.

Parenting Group (Dis)Association

For all parenting groups, mobilizing people into the same space is the hallmark of group organizing and one of the biggest obstacles. To exist, parenting groups must continually recruit and build their membership. Beyond basic functioning, these groups require members to achieve their goals, provide member resources, and achieve growth and sustainability. However, these groups not only build membership but also curate it. Despite variation in size, these parenting groups over time arrange caring through leadership and membership that engage in a variety of inclusionary and exclusionary practices.

PTA Membership: Numbers, Racism, and Getting a Dad to the Front of the Room

By one estimate, there were one thousand PTA members at the turn of the century and twenty thousand members ten years later. In the two decades that followed, PTA membership increased exponentially to nearly two hundred thousand by 1920 (Woyshner 2009, 39). For decades through the middle of the twentieth century, the PTA's success was emblematic, and the group experienced tremendous growth, eventually having "more members than any other secular organization" with a "membership encompassing eventually nearly half the families in America" (Putnam 2000, 55). Yet by 1960, PTA membership numbers were dropping drastically. In his famous *Bowling Alone*, political scientist Robert Putnam argued that decreasing membership in the past century was significant beyond PTA ranks, to indicate a loss of community: "[PTA] membership declined from a high in the early 1960s of almost fifty members per 100 families with children under eighteen to fewer than twenty members per 100 families with children under 18 in the early 1980s" (Putnam 2000, 56). This translated into a loss of 25 percent by 1960 and 50 percent by 1980 (Woyshner 2009, 4). Putnam recognized, but eventually discounted, the southern PTA members who fought "bitter battles over school desegregation in the 1960s [that] caused wholesale disaffiliation from the National PTA in several southern states." Putnam ultimately attributed the PTA's declining membership to "disagreements about school politics, as well as about national dues" that led "some local parent-teacher organizations" to become "disaffiliated from the national PTA either to join competing organizations or to remain wholly independent" as PTOs (Putnam 2000, 57). The result was that the PTA lost members who defaulted to an even more local solution of creating their own independent parenting organizations.

Today, 43 percent of parents "attended a meeting of the parent-teacher organization or association," according to the U.S. Department of Education's 2019 National Household Education Surveys Program (National Center for Education Statistics 2019). According to the PTA's own 2019–2020 Annual Report, it has more than 3.5 million members, with charters in all states, across 22,000 local groups, making the PTA arguably the largest parenting organization in the country (National PTA n.d.-m). The initials PTA are often used interchangeably with PTO and sometimes with HSA (home school association), but groups with these acronyms operate differently. PTOs are individual school and community groups without a broader national affiliation. HSA can be analogous to a PTO or related to homeschooling parents; HSA is a less-used acronym for a PTO-like group that operates individually in local schools. Although students are central to all groups, those PTAs and PTOs that add an "S" for student (PTSA and PTSO) are groups that include positions and opportunities for students to participate in their leadership.[5]

However, as chapter 1 demonstrated, not everyone has been included in PTA organizing. The PTA did not consistently embrace Black participants or men, though they were sometimes the targets of outreach. While the separation of the PTA and NCCPT provided NCCPT members with space to discuss racism and education with other Black parents, the racial segregation of the PTA and NCCPT divided members who served different communities. Integrating the PTA further alienated "African American parents, teachers, and other community members [who] no longer found a home for their issues and concerns in the integrated National Congress. The ultimate move toward inclusion, [and] desegregation ended up excluding [Black] members, parents, and citizens" (Woyshner 2009, 194). At least in terms of contemporary membership, the numbers may be changing.

An examination of the data alongside participants' reports show conflicting results. According to the 2020 PTA member schools' profile, students of color represent 57 percent of the total students whose schools are PTA affiliated (National Congress of Parents and Teachers 2020). National PTA presidents now include the first Black woman, Lois Jean White (1997–1999); the first Black man, Orth Thornton (2013–2015); and the second Black woman, Anna

King (2021–2023). Despite these changes, King reflected back on her first national PTA meeting by saying she was "by herself in a place she'd never been, surrounded by people she didn't know who all seemed to be each other's best friends." At that meeting Orth Thornton approached her: "He said, 'You look lost.' I told him I didn't know what I was supposed to do, and he showed me around.' King continued, 'He asked me if anyone had spoken to me, and I said no. Then he looked right at me and said something I have never forgotten: 'If they don't speak to you, you speak to them. We are all in this together'" (Goodrich 2014). These practices, like not welcoming or, conversely, approaching newcomers, provide vivid examples of exclusionary and inclusionary practices. King's reflections clearly speak to both the continued need for change and the role meetings and leadership play in obfuscating and providing some pathways within the PTA.

The PTA has been more successful at drawing in moms than dads. For example, when interviewed by *Education Word*, Charles Saylors, the first man to hold the office of national PTA president, addressed a common stereotype by talking about how men tend to view PTA participation and meetings: "Too many dads believe that they don't have the time [to be active in the PTA]. They believe PTA meetings are boring. They believe that PTA has nothing to offer them. Well, as a fellow dad I believe that I can help change that mindset. Moms have done and are doing a great job—but we need dads too! When I interviewed for the nomination as president-elect, I told our committee that if you want to get dads' attention, you need one in the front of the room" (Delisio 2007). Sayers described his work as "a tremendous opportunity" to lead an organization "made up of about 5.5 million people that do wonderful work all across the United States . . . roughly 10 percent of that number represent men" (Raz 2009). Nearly ten years later, when James Accomando became president, men's share of membership had more than doubled to 22 percent (Lambeck 2017). Getting a dad to "the front of the room" is one step in making a group look more representative. However, drawing more men into the PTA will likely take longer-term social change and outreach since the group is beginning from such a low participation level.

LLL's Grapples with Diverse Gendered Lives

LLL's membership was fueled by the interest, lack of support, and isolation that characterized women's breastfeeding in the early to mid-twentieth century. LLL's size grew very quickly in the organization's early years, and their growth is well illustrated through their publications. In 1958, the first edition of *The Womanly Art of Breastfeeding* was released by La Leche League, with 17,000 copies (La Leche League International 1963). In 1963, when the second edition of *The Womanly Art of Breastfeeding* was released, Karen Pryor published "They Teach the Joys of Breastfeeding," highlighting the group's work in *Reader's*

Digest (1963). Mainstream attention drew many new mothers to the group. The 1972 publication of the 1963 edition of *The Womanly Art of Breastfeeding* listed cumulative printings. From 1963 to 1965 there were 20,000 printings each year. In the next five years, that number grew cumulatively to 165,025 printings. In 1971, Princess Grace of Monaco spoke at that year's LLL Convention (La Leche League International 2016). This high-profile attention increased mothers' interest in LLL. Measured in books, between 1971 and 1972 cumulative printings of *The Womanly Art of Breastfeeding* increased to 100,000, or 50,000 per year (La Leche League International 1963). More than two decades later, Blum and Vandewater reported that LLL's membership in the 1990s was second only to Alcoholics Anonymous (AA) (1993).

Currently, LLL has groups in places around the world, including the United States, Canada, the European Union, Great Britain, Latin America, Africa, the Middle East, Asia, and Australia and New Zealand (La Leche League International n.d.-j). They report having "5,256 accredited leaders, with almost half being outside of North America" (La Leche League International 2020b). In the United States, the organization has 1,020 leaders who "volunteer . . . hosting monthly meetings and providing support via phone and email." Membership is more difficult to measure since the group does not require dues to participate. However, U.S. membership can be estimated by readers of LLL's *New Beginnings*, a free quarterly publication sent via email to over 8,000 subscribers, and the group's 384,000 Facebook followers. LLL Canada claims "over 75,000 weekly visitors" to their website, "4500 Instagram" and "12,750 Facebook" followers and "900 registered users" of their virtual library (La Leche League International n.d.-j). In 2020 LLLI reported having a total of "5.1 million website users, 3.8 were first time visitors" around the world (La Leche League International 2020b).

LLL's publications provide some evidence about the members the group seeks to serve. Despite the changes in women's and in particular mothers' employment, the 2003 edition of LLL's *Leader's Handbook*, a book of almost 270 pages, provides only five and a half pages to employed mothers' breastfeeding (La Leche League International 2003). This section's language reflects specific considerations that employed moms face. Some of the information is intuitive—like details on breast pumps and navigating work schedules. Other text warrants further consideration. It suddenly referred to working mothers as "people," instead of as parents or mothers. Consider the following passage: "People are often tired by the end of a busy workday. Much as they might want to come to a scheduled meeting, when the day actually arrives, they may be tempted to stay home. Preregistration and payment can strengthen commitment to a meeting" (La Leche League International 2003, 185). La Leche League fees are optional and at the discretion of the group's leader. However, to suggest that working mothers, who already likely face different transportation and childcare expenses than mothers who are not employed, should be urged to pay for the meetings they attend shows LLL's continued indifference (and likely disdain) toward working moms. In addition, LLL's recommendations for "planning your baby's care" explains that "babies' stress levels are lower when they're cared for by someone who loves them—a parent, grandparent, or other person very close to the family. That's quality of care that a day care center simply can't provide" (Wiessinger, West, and Pitman 2010, 266–267). The subsequent 2022 version of the handbook includes meeting planning considerations related to participants, "employed outside the home or not, and so on," a half page on "working and breastfeeding," and related web links (La Leche League International 2022a, 61, 205).

It is through this lens of LLL's reluctant inclusion of women's work that we see how a lack of diversity, by employment, race, and class, is implicated in the organization's broader politics. Contradictions in the group's attempt to address employed mothers persist even while the majority of mothers with children under the age of eighteen are employed (Bureau of Labor Statistics 2020). Blum's incisive analysis of motherhood and breastfeeding explored how "La Leche League's maternalism . . . represents a racialized class-enhancing project for white middle-class women" (1999, 63). In her analysis, "The whiteness of La Leche League . . . is more than the lack of non-white members but also the absence of the standpoint and identities of women of color who are mothers." Black women in Blum's research opposed universalizing prescriptions of motherhood as oppressive and problematic, among them the necessity to breastfeed (Blum 1999, 103).

Gendered lives are far more diverse than the founders understood. In part, LLL's ambivalence toward mothers' employment has had a disproportionate effect on lower-wage workers, the poor, and Black and Hispanic women because of their employment patterns. LLL "demonstrates a surprising lack of action for low-income mothers and the enhanced social provisions they need to nurture their children" (Blum 1999, 104). Lower-wage workers are more likely to have insufficient health care, time, and economic resources to nurse on demand, at home or at work. Black women with children are the mothers most likely to be employed, 72.2 percent compared with 71.1 percent of white, 65 percent of Asian, and 63.9 percent of Hispanic mothers. Black families are also nearly twice as likely to be female-headed than Hispanic families (42 vs. 25 percent) and nearly three times as likely to be female-headed than white and Asian families (15 and 12 percent, respectively). Black women's employment also shapes their experiences as they are disproportionally employed in jobs like "nursing, psychiatric, and home health aides (36 percent); security guards and gaming surveillance officers (31 percent); and licensed practical and licensed vocational nurses (30 percent)" (Bureau of Labor Statistics 2019). Particularly for women performing direct care and security, these are jobs often associated with low pay, mobile work, and few benefits (Bureau of Labor Statistics 2024a, 2024b). Economic precarity and challenging work circumstances make the possibility of breastfeeding on demand far less likely for lower-wage earners than for more affluent women with employment circumstances that provide greater pay and benefits alongside stationary locations or the possibility for remote work from home. LLL further demonstrates its exclusivity through its inability or unwillingness to see how poverty and race have impacted women's circumstances.

Because LLL was organized around white, Christian, affluent mothers (and assumed each was part of a heterosexual marriage), leadership provided advice that anticipated men's potential resistance to their wife's participation. *The Leader Handbook* explains in its section on father-inclusive meetings, "Some fathers are wary of LLL and don't quite understand why people would want to get together to talk about breastfeeding. Other fathers may disagree with information or ideas their partner heard at meetings. For these reasons it is important to make a good first impression. Your professional and levelheaded demeanor, as well as an introduction describing Leader accreditation, can help. Talking about LLLI and its global influence, LLL publications, the Professional Liaison resource network, and opportunities for continuing education all demonstrate our credibility. Speak with confidence and avoid nervous or apologetic laughter" (La Leche League International 2003, 182). Though the group operates some couples' meetings and may opt to allow men or have special inclusive meetings, the central "Series Meetings" have historically excluded men. As the LLL *Leader's Handbook* explains, "Traditionally, Series Meetings have been open only to women. In some situations, women might be uncomfortable breastfeeding their babies or reluctant to ask certain questions in a mixed group. A single mother or a mother whose spouse is not interested in attending might feel out of place if others at the meeting were all couples" (La Leche League International 2003, 52). This tension between the inclusion and exclusion of men is in evidence across LLL materials.

Just as the historical moment of the mid- to late twentieth century, characterized by low breastfeeding rates and a lack of support for nursing moms, mobilized members of LLL, historical circumstances likely fueled parents' interests in the babysitting co-op and dads' groups. Both began just after the financial crisis of 2007–2008. The Great Recession, as it has been dubbed, had a tremendous negative impact on families' incomes and stress levels (McCorkell and Hinkley 2018). Though neither group publicly cites financial concerns as formative, the economic upheaval of the years preceding the groups' development likely influenced their arrival. In particular, changes to men's employment (or their unemployment) may have created both the time and the circumstances for dads' group participation. An examination of the reemergence of babysitting cooperatives provides further evidence for this claim.

Collective-Intensive Mothering in the Oakwood Babysitting Co-op

Babysitting cooperatives are not easy to measure—they are not businesses or nonprofits that are registered and tracked.[6] Well-known examples include the Capitol Hill Babysitting Co-op, which has existed since the 1970s and is used (and debated) as an economic allegory by members and economists (Sweeney and Sweeney 1977). A LexisNexis newspaper search for "babysitting cooperative and co-op" produced over 600 articles.[7] Beginning in 1977, there were relatively few news articles, and the count remains low through the 1980s (37). In the 1990s, the number of articles nearly doubles (68). However, this increase is nothing compared to the early aughts. Between 2000 and 2009 the number of articles grows exponentially (376) and spikes between 2007 and 2009 (208), with coverage reducing again in the 2010s (105).[8] The surge in newspaper attention overlaps with the Great Recession, beginning in 2007, and the content of many articles addressing babysitting co-ops as a money-saving idea reflects this relationship. The articles range in scope from a brief mention to interview-based columns. From these news articles, a partial picture emerges of babysitting co-ops as a nationwide phenomenon including cities, suburbs, and small towns from California to New York and in places in between like St. Louis, Atlanta, and St. Petersburg, Florida.

Like other affluent wives, the women in the Oakwood babysitting co-op shoulder a lot of labor between their paid and unpaid work. Their structural and interpersonal circumstances foster unequal caregiving burdens with their husbands (Bianchi 2000; Ostrander 1984). These complex relationships are indicative of "different patterns of combining employment and motherhood . . . [that illustrate] the complexity of the interactions and contradictions between classed and gendered processes, showing how these processes are lived" (Armstrong 2006, 103–104). Members join the co-op due to their care needs that stem, at least in part, from their unequal gendered division of labor at home. As Noelle, a thirty-eight-year-old white mother of one who works full-time in education, describes, "Because [men] normally don't participate in their families . . . like even on the individual level, when it comes to scheduling, they don't do any of those pieces. Like when they are at work, they're at work. They switch off from home life. We [moms] don't. . . . So, it continues [in the babysitting co-op] . . . that the primary weight of children still stays with the mom." Similarly, Kaitlyn, a thirty-eight-year-old white mother of three who volunteers at her children's preschool, explains, "I guess the fathers that I know, they always kind of push [child care] off on their wives. . . . Even when you go to family cookouts and stuff, it's always the moms that go, and take care, and they fix the plates for the kids." Noelle and Kaitlyn's reactions are emblematic of the way most in the babysitting co-op view carework for kids— as the primary responsibility of mothers, not fathers.

Babysitting co-op members do not question the group's gendered composition and were surprised when I asked about men's involvement. Kaitlyn sees fathers' participation as unlikely: "Sometimes the dads do help out, but it seems like it's all done by the moms [laughs]." Most members, like Kaitlyn, had not considered why fathers, including their husbands, do not participate. Margaret expresses her ambivalence: "Do you mean father's involvement in terms of being actual sitters instead of the moms? . . . I'm just not sure how people would feel about it. And, in fact, I'm not sure how I would feel. . . . I realize that my comfort [with the moms] comes from probably knowing the women so well now." As Kaitlyn and Margaret describe, the group's gendered expectations for babysitting co-op membership shaped participants' assumptions about who would provide care (mothers), regardless of the more inclusive membership materials. Carework is culturally defined as women's work. The co-op members' husbands I interviewed were surprised when I asked about their co-op participation; they agree that the co-op operates as a moms' group. As Patrick, a forty-five-year-old white father of two employed in a healthcare industry, replies, "When you say *participated*, what do you mean?" Jake, a forty-four-year-old white executive and father of two, responds with an incredulous gasp: "Am I allowed to [be] a member? No! To me, this is a moms' group. I never knew [laughs]! If you're telling me right now that fathers are welcome to be part of the babysitting co-op, I guess I never knew that. I always thought this was a mom's thing." Fathers' involvement includes attending adult-only co-op events like dinners and wine tastings. Most of the men interviewed (eight of ten) engage in these social activities. By contrast, three of the fathers interviewed cohost babysitting with their wives. A similar number help with babysitting transportation, and most care for their own kids while their spouses host or attend co-op meetings.

Babysitting co-op members use gender as an organizational resource by excluding fathers (Acker 1990, 1992). They frequently joke about fathers' caregiving credibility and underscore mothers' skills. Several members laughed when I asked about fathers' involvement in happy hour sits, saying the "moms are really in charge." Happy hour sits occur in the early evening and are organized around two parents who can watch up to ten children together, minus their own. Carol, a forty-two-year-old white mother of two and local community volunteer, discusses how dads acknowledge this: "It's funny. So even couples that we're friendly with, guys who I think are great dads with their kids, great husbands, like supportive, will joke about the little that they do." Though her comments can be read as indicative of a mom's frustrations, discounting men's caregiving also reinforces mothers' particular activities and skills.

The group's composition is based on well-established recruitment practices shaped by employment, location, familiarity, and parenting practices. Since current members must sponsor new members, it is not surprising that this is a homogenous group. Drawing members from existing neighborhoods is partly for convenience and proximity for shared care. Inadvertently or not, the practice reproduces the babysitting co-op's exclusivity by sharing resources more narrowly among those with both time and money to offer forms of care for other parents' kids. Access to flexible paid and unpaid work makes exchange-based participation possible. One-third of the sample is employed part-time (averaging eighteen hours per week), and a little over 10 percent work full-time (see Table 2).

The babysitting co-op's recruitment is based on the interpersonal connections and parenting practices of prospective members. Julia, a fifty-one-year-old white mother of two and school volunteer, explains she joined the co-op because of its recruitment process that screens for "trustworthy" new members: "The most important question I'll ever ask another human being, as a mother, is can I trust you with my child? And I need to know that I can trust you. . . . I think [the co-op has] a little bit of a vetting process, you can't just join. You have to know somebody to get in." Nell, a fifty-year-old white mother of three who is a church and school volunteer, specifies the importance of parenting approaches in members' recruitment practices: "Because everyone is kind of prescreened, if you will, . . . it takes out some of the legwork when you have to meet people for the first time, and assess them, and decide whether or not you're comfortable with their parenting style and . . . the care that they would give your child." The "vetting" and "prescreening" is a multistep process first done by members who propose new recruits. These practices enable the group to actively narrow inclusion based on in-group recruitment. The obligatory meeting and the new member tea in the recruit's home are part of the process. These in-person events, like monthly meetings and activities, are important for group formation. During COVID-19, when in-person meetings were not possible, the group moved to Zoom meetings and story hours online.

Members recognize parents who would not be a good fit for the babysitting co-op, as Julia elaborates: "My friend, who I wouldn't sponsor [to join the babysitting co-op], . . . she asked me to bring my [kids] over at her house and let her watch them. . . . I did it, reluctantly, because . . . I knew what was behind it was she wanted her daughter to play with my children, and that's fine. . . . So, I did that, and I ran out and did whatever. I came back and they were unattended in her backyard. Now, fortunately, her backyard was almost completely fenced in. . . . So, they were there, unattended, she was in the house, and I was upset . . . it was because of that, that I would not invite her [to join the babysitting co-op]. Because, you know, it's sort of your own reputation too, if I were to bring somebody in and they would do that, that would look quite badly on me too." Among babysitting co-op members, there is broad agreement that it is unreasonable to leave kids completely unsupervised, particularly preschool-aged children as in Julia's story. This need for direct supervision is central to developing a collective-intensive mothering ideology. It sets the stage for parents' caregiving expectations. Further, Julia's reputation would be at risk if she referred someone who strayed so far from the group's accepted practices. Across interviews, members told similar stories about friends or neighbors who would not fit with the group's caregiving expectations and would not be invited to join.

The group's solidarity comes from sharing common ground, particularly about caregiving. Lily explains the importance of having similar experiences: "Obviously most people aren't in a co-op, but I think it's important to stay connected to people . . . who are going through exactly what you're going through [gestures to the toys around her living room]." Tess, a forty-four-year-old white mother of two employed part-time in media, emphasizes the group's cohesion in terms of shared objectives: "I think since the goal is to help . . . I mean, we're doing each other favors. . . . I think it's easier to get along since we have a common goal." Co-op members value a similar ethic of care, as Noelle explains: "Everybody [is] trying to work together. You know, I think that there's lots of mom guilt, for whatever reason, and lots of women who are trying to do it all. And it's a group of relatively like-minded women who are just helping each other out when they can. . . . I think that community is really important. . . . I think we're all fairly like-minded, but yet with enough . . . diversity of opinions and ideas that makes it interesting."

The group's collective identity comes from sharing a common goal, particularly regarding caregiving, and validating as well as absorbing some of the insecurity members shared over being good enough moms. As Tess explained above, the group's shared objectives and mutual respect stem from their common co-op goals of working together to provide parenting support and short-term childcare assistance. Babysitting co-op moms navigated their circumstances together and valued a similar ethic of care, as Noelle describes: "Everybody [is] trying to work together. You know, I think that there's lots of mom guilt, for whatever reason, and lots of women who are trying to do it all. And it's a group of relatively like-minded women who are just helping each other out when they can. . . . I think that community is really important." The mom guilt Noelle describes stems from self-doubt, as Mia, a forty-four-year-old white mother of three who volunteers at her children's school, explains: "I feel like I'm constantly trying to . . . improve upon my way of doing things, constantly looking at each situation. Did I handle it in the right way? Did I not like the way I handled it? I'm probably pretty hard on myself, so I rely on the support of others in the co-op . . . I think I probably talk too much about . . . parenting situations because I felt need to bounce things back off . . . other people." Solidarity and group membership help ease some of the mental burdens of mothering work by sharing these burdens with others through collective-intensive mothering.

The co-op provides a sense of belonging and enhances members' self-esteem, as Grace, a forty-three-year-old white mother of two who is employed part-time in social services, describes: "I just love all the other moms in [the co-op] and I'm . . . proud to be a part of that community. . . . It makes me feel like, hey I'm part of this community of really awesome moms. Some are working, some aren't working, but they're all brilliant. . . . I feel like they're all so smart, and successful, and thoughtful, and caring. So, . . . it just makes me feel like maybe I'm some of those things too." Like Grace, Lucy, a forty-six-year-old white mother of one who is not employed, highlights mutual "respect" within the group: "[The co-op is] a good support network for whatever choices [members make], . . . it also provides . . . for me . . . some of that social support that I don't get . . . and a lot of respect and appreciation for what we're all doing for our kids that I think is hard to find in other sources." Alice, a white mother of one in her mid-forties who is not employed, echoes members' shared admiration: "I think [co-op members] tend to bring their best . . . parenting to the table . . . and I think it sort of elevates everyone else's idea. Well, that one's doing that, I should be like that too, in a good way in this group. . . . Like this group seems to . . . fold in and become better together." The group's camaraderie stems from their mutual respect and common purpose. Part of the group's work is creating a collective set of ideas about parenting. Cooley, writing about primary community groups, asked, "What, in our life, is the family and the fellowship; what do we know of the we-feeling?" (1998, 184). The co-op provides that "we-feeling," the "village" of caregivers it takes to raise kids.

Dads Seek and Struggle to Create Separate Groups

Within the dads' groups, participation is limited to dads. The primary difference for the dads' group members is their engagement not with conventional men's activities but with carework that is centered within members' interactions with each other. Bryson explains that he "would definitely regulate who gets in" to the group. From his perspective, "there are a lot of moms' groups" and "a lot of moms' groups are exclusive." He argues that men should "switch that up" and let prospective dads' group members know, "If you're a mom, you're going to get dumped out of the group. This is a dads' group." By contrast to the other three parenting groups, local dads' groups center social activities around which fathers connect, rather than formal meetings, whereas national City Dads Group representatives gather at annual conferences.

Dads' group members by and large assume that men's and women's parenting groups are naturally separate due to men's and women's diverging communication and parenting styles and, in effect, adopt a *Men Are from Mars, Women Are from Venus* understanding (Gray 1992). In the dads' groups, fostering a space for men enables men to use gender as an organizational resource to distinguish their parenting from that of moms (Acker 1990, 1992). In effect, "homosociality promotes gendered segregation and clear distinctions between men and women in social groups" (Arxer 2011; Lipman-Blumen 1976). Randall, a thirty-seven-year-old white father of one working part-time in food services and serving as an East Coast dads' group leader, points to men's "likemindedness" when "talking about different stuff" as a primary reason behind dads' group exclusivity. Zach, a fifty-year-old Asian American father of three who is enrolled in graduate school, says that he "joined to get to know other dads . . . and . . . to get an idea . . . [of] what are their challenges day-to-day"; from there he hoped to "get an idea of how to handle these kinds of situations, do we have things in common . . . what are the things that other dads also face which is really perhaps unique from moms." Although many of the men foreground camaraderie, they frequently mention the differences they expected to see between mothers' and fathers' parenting and reasons why, collectively, they exist in separate parenting spheres.

When asked, dads' group members struggle with the idea of cross-gender parenting groups. John emphasizes that the dads' group enabled him to connect with other dads in unique ways. "I figured it would lead to this—and it definitely has—the getting together with other dads and our kids, taking them to museums, and playgrounds and such. And having that relationship with other guys who are similarly dedicated to taking care of our kids and . . . in a way that might be a little different from the way moms do it." Randall explains why he thinks dads' and moms' groups should be separate. In a dads' group "you have . . . people to talk to and . . . express concerns about . . . certain issues in parenting . . . I feel like sometimes you don't want to go to woman because you might be judged and . . . it's nice to have like another dad to go to." Bryson provides specific examples of topics that might generate discomfort in cross gender groups: "Women . . . talk about . . . the birthing process, breastfeeding . . . they just don't feel comfortable talking about it to a guy . . . guys, if they want to talk about . . . vasectomy and masturbation and . . . difficulties in . . . marriage . . . they might not want to talk about that around other women." For men, both the content of conversations as well as the specter of mothers' judgment shaped their preference for fathers-only groups.

Throughout their interviews men often highlighted gendered reasons for maintaining separate groups from moms. Dads emphasized how fathers' interactions reflect likeness and differ from those of moms. Benjamin, a forty-five-year-old white father of two working part-time in entertainment, highlights different gendered childhoods: "We might just want to talk about bands we loved in high school. So, it is just a little bit different, there is just a little bit more common ground just based on that, on shared interests and being socialized as a guy instead of a woman. . . . It's a question of solidarity." Nathaniel, a thirty-five-year-old father of two working part-time in various jobs, explains, "Women . . . maybe tend to dictate the conversation in a good way . . . and [in the dads' group] . . . you can even sometimes vent a little bit . . . you think it might sound stupid coming out of your mouth, but someone else is probably, you know, struggling with the same thing. It's very easy to talk to other guys in this situation or scenario." Even when men like Paul seek to distance themselves from stereotypes, they often reaffirm them: "I guess I'm . . . reticent to say anything that comes off as . . . guys are a certain way, and women are certain way. But, you know, I think that's just true . . . we are the way that we are and we're different. And I think that guys' kind of . . . we don't hold the same types of grudges, and we don't care as much. . . . We really just wanna hang out with another dude, and have a beer, and not worry about that stuff." Men's notions of their like-mindedness relate to essential difference, a refrain that runs across the interviews.

Dads' group members are often the primary caregivers for their kids during some weekday hours. New parents, in particular mothers, know that providing care for very young children can be isolating (Miller 2007). Douglas, a thirty-four-year-old musician and father of one, describes how loneliness framed his experience: "It is definitely because of the isolation. You know, everybody that I've talked to, everybody that I've invited to the group and told about it, they are just amazed that there is a group of other dads out there and they're not the only one. . . . If you don't know it's out there, it can feel very lonely. I mean all of the ads on TV and radio, and magazines, parenthood is for mothers, you know." Stay-at-home dads in sociologist Catherine Richards Solomon's research responded to similar "isolation and exclusion" from parenting networks and community parenting spaces by withdrawing or seeking "online communities" (2017). By contrast, dads in this study sought out local dads' groups, both online and in person. Solomon's research did not address whether dads in her study knew about or participated in local in-person dads' groups. Therefore, it is impossible to pinpoint a reason for this difference apart from the relatively easier access men would have to online communities that do not require as many resources like time for travel and energy for in-person interactions.

As Jackson, a forty-one-year-old father of one employed in real estate and West Coast dads' group leader, explains, viewing fatherhood positively can provide a source of solidarity: "We get the dads who are interested in producing healthy high-quality human beings. And, you know, that builds the network because if you're trying to do something good and positive in a vacuum, you know, the vacuum of will eventually get to you. And then you're gonna go least resistance . . . but if you have a community that supports you like you . . . oh, you'll only want your kid to eat organic? Oh, perfect. You know, that's fine, you know, because I don't . . . yeah, GMOs? Yeah, I'm with you there. Oh, yeah, you know, something like that, you know? Oh, you're teaching your kids Spanish at age three? Awesome. You know, hey, get . . . let's . . . you know, bring my kid in and get some more kids, you know, things like that." He underscores how dads' groups have shaped how he approaches other members: "I'm gonna do everything I can to keep it nonpolitical, you know, like . . . because I have me and this other guy, we're super great friends until politics comes up. And then we had a bitter texting feud about eight months ago, and then we didn't communicate for two months. And then we had to like reset our relationship." Despite efforts to depoliticize dads' groups, men's recruitment into parenting groups remains difficult.

Conclusion

Narrow recruitment, rigid binary understandings of gender and family, and a lack of support for diversity are common challenges for parenting groups. Rather than seeing care expansively, parenting groups limit their scope by siloing their care around particular populations. For example, their missions often underscore gender-neutral components; however, like many carework organizations, parenting groups are highly gendered in their membership, ideology, and practice. As we saw in chapter 1, group leadership and membership's demographics often skew white, affluent, and Christian, and this shapes prospective members' sense of inclusion and belonging, as workplace diversity, equity, and inclusion initiatives have shown (Minkin 2023). Contrary to their mission statements that promote broad inclusion, in practice these groups operate independently and frequently fail to uphold their stated goals.

An emphasis on stereotypical underpinnings to gender, parenting, and group cohesion has informed the organizing approach for all the groups, preventing—or at least limiting—a truly inclusive vision. Shaped by local leadership's beliefs and the (often silent) membership majority, parenting groups can exclude and alienate prospective members. As a result, these groups often fall short of where broader inclusivity could take them. Groups like LLL, MOMS Club, UES Mommas, the Oakwood babysitting co-op, and the dads' groups simply narrowed their scope from the start, recruiting largely white married women and, in the case of the dads' groups, white married men. These groups are also primarily affluent, are educated, and have flexible work schedules. Parent groups often overlook potential members to target those with resources to give as well as take. This may make organizational sense for the smooth running of the groups. Parents with flexible employment can more easily allocate time from their schedules for activities and accommodate the added meetings parenting group membership entails. However, those who are likely most in need of these resources and least equipped to provide them are often left wanting.

Parenting groups could bring parents together across geographic and demographic characteristics far beyond what happenstance can provide, but they often fail to do so. Their narrow circulation of care resources tends to reinscribe social inequalities. These groups often handle diversity poorly. For example, when conflict arose over racism in the UES Mommas and the PTA, leadership defaulted to their own priorities, stifling dialogue and leading to greater exclusion. Of course, talk of diversity is not tantamount to full inclusion. That would necessitate input and participation from members. In part these groups act with what Joan Tronto has called "privileged irresponsibility," in which "care exposes the mechanism by which ignorance serves to prevent the relatively privileged from noticing the needs of others" (1993, 121). As products of their culture and organization, parenting groups reproduce normative social patterns "shaped in particular by those who have acquired the power to define the situation" (Hallett 2003). Situated in a U.S. context, these groups are shaped by the politics of their leadership, their constituents, as well as the broader culture. Group organization and membership shapes how they arrange caring and who "takes on the burden of meeting those needs" (Tronto 2013, 34). This research suggests that even when groups see other groups' needs, they may choose to ignore them. In these groups one can see shortcomings, but also opportunities (both realized and missed) for organizational change. The groups demonstrate ways that parenting groups can provide collective care by networking parents with each other. In the next chapter I address how parenting groups use education to promote issue-based outreach and often individual-level solutions.

3

Educating Parents

Care and Ideology

According to the Pew Research Center, most parents surveyed (88 percent) consider parenting "at least somewhat harder" to "a lot harder" than they anticipated (Minkin and Horowitz 2023). Not surprisingly, "advice for new parents" is a Google search that produces billions of results addressing new parents' questions, normalizing their concerns, and providing suggestions. While researching this chapter, I conducted this search to see whether "join a parent's group" might be a popular answer. It is not. While by no means comprehensive, this exercise yields some telling results. The search yielded individualistic ad hoc answers to seeking support through personal inquiry. Many websites advocate that new parents accept help from friends and experts, seek out other new parents, and build their own "tribe" of similarly situated parents (with kids of the same age, from families who live nearby and enroll in the same activities and preschools). One website did suggest parent groups (behind "expect stress") and while promoting its own group encouraged parents to join and share their successes and their challenges, quoting a variation of "a sorrow shared is a sorrow halved" (William James College n.d.). Sharing parenting successes and challenges is part of the logic of parenting groups, but parent groups reach far beyond reassurance. As part of the care infrastructure, parent groups set up their parent education by routinely curating and distributing information and empathy across many parents within their organization. Members and leadership decide what information and support are provided, addressing a range of issues including those that may be distinctive and internal to their own groups, widespread parenting issues, and current events.

By sharing information collectively, parent groups can educate parents on a range of issues and foster parent-to-parent support. During the pandemic, a Philadelphia PTA member explained how her group provided education and care for parents. She describes a meeting in which "parents expressed concerns about virtual learning and students returning to the school building. In that meeting, [PTA leaders] were a sounding board for frustration, but we also provided direction to those parents, so they have a clear path to getting their questions and concerns addressed" (School District of Philadelphia 2021). The PTA has provided support and education to immigrant parents, as Reina Medrano, a Greenwich, Connecticut, PTA copresident explains: "When her oldest started kindergarten, [she] knew nothing about American public schools, and the PTA taught her how to read a report card and ask teachers questions" (Kroeker 2018). On a larger scale, Carol Kocivar, a former California PTA president, describes how her organization created a program to educate parents: "One of the things the state PTA has been involved in is creating parent academies, where parents are invited into the school and are given skills and resources to understand how the school system works. Because, as we know, we have a lot of parents who are new to the United States, or didn't finish high school or go to college and give those parents the skills and resources to be advocates for their kids" (Stupi 2014). This range of skills and collective care provide invaluable parent resources that are emblematic of parent groups' contributions to care infrastructure that is not readily available elsewhere and is unnecessarily cumbersome to collect ad hoc. Alongside this provision of resources, however, parent groups also limit education through the ways they shape content that often favors individual solutions, tokenism rather than full participation, and consensus with the status quo over dissent and social change, as this chapter demonstrates.

Education as Integral Care for Parents

Parent education has a long history across various academic, community, faith, and popular sources (Croake and Glover 1977). Early records date back more than two centuries to an "1815 . . . mother's meeting . . . held in Portland, Maine" (Bridgman 1930, 35). Educating parents has long been central to the mission of parenting groups. The PTA, for example, has been described as a "clearing house of information for parents" (Woyshner 2009, 2). Historian William W. Cutler argued that organizations like the PTA long "justified their existence" by advocating for "parent education" (2000, 47). Likewise, education and care are central reasons why parents join parent groups—to address the questions they have, seek guidance, and receive support to make them feel less alone. By recognizing this need, parent groups offer a collective path forward.

However, the relationship between education and care is not always obvious. Though related, they are often considered separately even when their missions deeply overlap. For parent groups, providing education involves a range of resources and information sharing as well as things like reassurance and normalization. In other words, for parent groups education is not just about imparting information to parents but also about supplying them with care. There are other reasons to consider how these two concepts intertwine. Some research suggests that forms of parent education can fuel intensive caregiving practices that increase parents' (particularly mothers') workload, rather than enabling parents to better accommodate or reduce it (Hays 1996; Villalobos 2014).

Parent group education often follows a self-help model like that found in self-help books that endorse individual solutions to many parenting problems starting before birth through young adulthood. These resources weave together education and care. A best-selling book like *What to Expect When You're Expecting*, now in its fifth edition, has had enormous success, selling "more than 42 million copies . . . published in 38 countries and in 44 languages" and is now a franchise including a series of websites, spin-off books, and a nonprofit outreach organization (Murkoff 2016; What to Expect 2024). The book has been controversial for its focus on mother-to-mother medical advice from Murkoff, who lacks medical credentials, and for its content and tone that often reflect fearmongering and mother shaming (Kantor 2005). In this context, it is not surprising that research finds women "who have the least to do with expert parenting literature and with medical experts" may face lighter parental burdens (Villalobos 2014, 220). Still, what likely draws mothers to Murkoff is the promise of education alongside care and camaraderie. Murkoff's brand mission is "I'm here for you. What to Expect is here for you—and we're all in this together."[1]

The relationship between education and care in parent groups is complex and multifaceted. Cultivating parents' education promotes parents' understanding alongside their broader access to group information and skills. Parent groups often draw from the core issues of their organizations—schooling, nutrition, mothering, and fathering. Parent group education in caregiving includes insights into how parents can provide better care for kids, for themselves as a parent, and for other parents in their parent group, broader community, and beyond. Parent education also includes teaching parents about issues that challenge their abilities to care for their children, themselves, and others, like how to help their children navigate schools. The content of parent groups education is also designed to boost self-esteem and ease isolation. In combination, expanding parents' care resources helps parents provide better care for themselves and their kids. Parent groups education adopts a growth mindset orientation—that struggles can be overcome, skills can be learned, and parenting can improve. By not assuming a fixed mindset—or what you see is what you get—parents are never doomed to failure; they can always try again or use a different approach. Most importantly, parents learn that they do not have to go it alone. There are groups, resources, information, and support available. Through this process, education for parents also becomes a form of care performed by parenting groups.

Organizational Challenges to Knowledge Production

Access to shared information can make parenting feel less like reinventing the wheel, providing them with access to collective care, the knowledge to contribute toward providing it, and a broader sense that they are not alone in their experiences. Parent groups learn from and lean on other parents and experts for guidance. Parent groups have mobilized various modes of outreach through different kinds of media for groups and individuals, online and in person. Parent groups decide which issues are important, how knowledge gets dispersed, and who provides it. As such, they exert considerable influence over what and how knowledge gets communicated.

Parent groups cultivate their own knowledge base parent to parent and also gather information from experts and authorities. Who speaks, who listens, and which issues gain traction (and which do not) are organizational questions shaped by those with access to influence. Among the groups I studied, educational issues may represent leadership's interests or the membership's concerns. For example, MOMS Club provides member groups with "educational services, classes, online programs, seminars and workshops for support groups for at-home mothers, including developing formats for monthly meetings" (MOMS Club n.d.-e). The form parent group education takes—online, email, Facebook, website, and Zoom-based education; in-person forums; and electronic or print newsletters, magazines, and books—all provide different modes of outreach and different levels of access. Some of these modes may democratize access, like email and Facebook, which allow participants to introduce ideas. Zoom meetings and in-person forums may allow participants an opportunity to respond. However, as we saw from the UES Mommas Facebook page and the Austin PTA "RaceTalks" examples in chapter 2, leadership may also play an outsized role in structuring how conversations get organized, what topics are addressed, and who gets to participate as well as who does not.

Some groups are predisposed to a more limited scope due to their histories and organization. Leaders may more narrowly define issues and defer to their own worldview or that of their most powerful members, rather than broadening their scope to consider other constituents' or prospective members' concerns. Many have adopted a top-down approach that favors expert and leadership-driven information that leaves little room for dialogue or dissent.

In those cases, the groups may provide education also as a disciplinary practice, designed to manage and steer parents' ideology and behaviors. Sometimes their limitations are more issue-based—as when the groups have zeroed in primarily on one aspect of care to the exclusion of others (as in LLL). Groups are more often reactive rather than proactive in the information they provide. Each group has faced challenges favoring solutions within existing pathways, particularly individual ones, rather than thinking more systemically about possibilities for change. This chapter examines how education within parenting groups is complex, is contradictory, and often centers mainstream issues, responses, and voices. Briefly tracing the history of early parenting groups' education enables us to see how these groups have long shaped knowledge production in similar ways that situate some issues and perspectives to gain traction while others do not.

Early PTA Parent Education

The National Congress of Mothers (NCM), the precursor to the PTA, was a leader in early support for parent education (Ladd-Taylor 1994). The primary goal of their first meeting was "the establishment of parent education study groups" as their first "fundamental initiative" (National PTA 1997, 23). The NCM recruited participants for newly formed groups and acted as an umbrella organization for the previously formed mothers' study groups. Early groups "functioned outside of the schools, even while cooperating with the school staff to help educate adults" (National PTA 1997, 12). Within this framework, care included the education of parents collectively through "home-school cooperation as represented by the partnership of parents and teachers; and full utilization of the services of all agencies concerned with child welfare." PTA meetings enabled women to learn from experts and each other "to apply new educational theories" (National PTA 1997, 15). Early PTA mothers' advocacy included educational and health-based outreach through pregnancy and following childbirth (National PTA n.d.-p). Underscoring both the private and public responsibilities of motherhood, early NCM leader Hanna Kent Schoff argued, "Parents can never do their full duty for their own children . . . until they make it their business to see that all children have their proper treatment and proper protection" (Ladd-Taylor 1994, 45). Women in the PTA embraced the idea of mobilizing beyond their own families to volunteer within their local schools all the way to the national organization "to serve the greater good" (Woyshner 2009, 6).

Steeped in maternalism—emphasizing the special skills and responsibilities of mothers while defining the limits of appropriate behavior for women—these early groups advocated for a community approach to caregiving across and beyond individual families (Ladd-Taylor 1994). They addressed both "progressive and conservative causes" (Grant 1998, 55) and a range of perspectives, including "mothers and experts, grassroots activists and political reformers, and . . . traditional and modern concepts of childcare" (Ladd-Taylor 1994, 43). In effect, this early education was often intended as a correction alongside care for parents. The goals of these early parent education groups were to both "teach mothers how to care properly of their own children and to awaken their maternal responsibility to improve social conditions affecting all children" (Ladd-Taylor 1994, 35). Historian William W. Cutler argued, "In the 1920s, it was widely believed that Americans did not know how to bring up their children. This problem was not confined to black, immigrant, and working-class homes" (2000, 46). The PTA believed that what parents did not know could be taught.

Though Hanna Kent Schoff, the second NCM president, promoted broad-based parent access to the NCMPTA, in practice it operated like many groups in the United States, segregated by gender, race, and class. The racial segregation of the PTA and National Congress of Colored Parents and Teachers (NCCPT) divided the groups into serving different communities. The NCCPT built on the work of "parent-teacher associations in segregated schools [that] supported homemaking and other practical curricular activities to give black youth essential skills of their health and survival during the lean years of the early twentieth century" (Woyshner 2009, 67). Both Black and white PTA groups developed their own member publications. In 1906, under the leadership of Schoff, the PTA developed a new vehicle for educational outreach, *Our Children*, a magazine that is still published twice a year (Woyshner 2009, 26). The NCCPT's official publication produced quarterly was titled *Our National Family*. Both publications begin with a message from leadership that provides an opportunity to outline and address issues. The same model appears in the unified *Our Children* publication today.

LLL's Maternalism and Consensus

Though narrower in its focus than the PTA, LLL has broadened breastfeeding education to encompass all parts of family life, from birth to forms of infant and toddler care, including natural mothering, cosleeping with infants and toddlers, and attachment parenting (Bobel 2002). For the LLL founders, educating mothers about breastfeeding was more than a practice; it was inseparable from their worldview (Lowman 1978). Early in their history, LLL founders addressed women's questions, espoused breastfeeding's benefits, and detailed their methods through face-to-face meetings. In their first manual from 1958, they described how the group's meetings educate mothers: "Their purpose is to explain, discuss, and advise on breastfeeding to a living room full of interested mothers . . . grandmothers, et al. A series of five meetings has been worked out which points out the advantages of breastfeeding to mother and baby; explains the necessary how-to of nursing; discusses weaning and the baby in relation to the rest of the family; suggests good procedure during pregnancy and at the time of delivery; takes a stab at promoting really good nutrition for the nursing mother (and the rest of the family too, of course)" (Lowman 1978, 16–17).

To reach additional mothers, LLL's founders wrote letters to address individual women's breastfeeding questions. These letters became the foundation for the first volume of *The Womanly Art of Breastfeeding* in 1958. Their promotion of breastfeeding was evident in their first pamphlet, titled "For Better Mothers," which they later retitled "Why Breastfeed Your Baby," to highlight the group's position (Lowman 1978). They presented breastfeeding as inseparable from quality mothering in many of these publications (Wiessinger, West, and Pitman 2010).

Like the early PTA, LLL came to embrace a maternalistic orientation. Many women were drawn to LLL's teachings. As Chris Bobel explains, "*The Womanly Art of Breastfeeding* . . . had a . . . life-transforming effect" for some of her research participants" (2002, 88). One mother explained "how the authors articulated precisely what she felt but had not been able to express," a feeling that "pervaded natural mothering discourse" (89). In its formative years, LLL grappled with a simultaneous embrace and rejection of medical and men's knowledge in breastfeeding education. The contributions of Dr. White and Dr. Ratner to early LLL notwithstanding, the medical establishment's promotion of infant formula and nine-month baby weaning was an existential challenge to LLL's mission. As founder Edwina Froehlich explained, "It gradually dawned on us . . . that we were asking the wrong people. Doctors were men, and why should they know more about it than mothers? Since [weaning] wasn't a medical question, their medical education was no help. That was why no good answer could be found in the medical books. We decided that it would be much more likely to be a woman, a mother, who would know" (Lowman 1978, 23). This struggle over questioning and ultimately jettisoning some medical knowledge regarding infant formula and weaning helped center the group's embrace of mothers' unique understanding, voice, and experience as a key attribute of LLL's mother-to-mother education and support.

LLL's promotion of breastfeeding ran counter to mid-twentieth-century wisdom that favored bottled formula. Though infant formula had existed for more than a half century, since the late 1800s, it took time before it was widely adopted. Infant formula production expanded, and "by 1883, 27 brands of patented infant foods were available. . . . However, relatively few infants were fed commercially prepared formulas" (Fomon 2001, 409S). Better knowledge and implementation of safe and clean water, milk production, storage, and nutritional guidelines led doctors and the broader culture to believe that "formula feeding was about as safe and satisfactory as breast-feeding" (Fomon 2001, 412S). By the late 1950s, doctors and manufacturers enthusiastically advocated for trusted bottled formulas (Fomon 2001). Early manufacturers with familiar names, like Nestle, produced "commercial products and formulas" made of "powdered . . . carbohydrates such as sugars, starches, and dextrins that were to be added to milk" (Stevens, Patrick, and Pickler 2009, 36).

For decades the formula industry and the American Medical Association (AMA) worked hand in hand. In "1929, the [AMA] formed the Committee on Foods to approve the safety and quality of formula composition, forcing many infant food companies to seek AMA approval or the organization's 'Seal of Acceptance.'" This relationship was symbiotic with formula companies invested "through the funding of scientific meetings and the open support of published infant nutritional research" (Greer and Apple 1991, 285). Connections between infant formula manufacturers and medicine included corporate advertising in medical journals like the *Journal of the American Medical Association* and attendance at medical meetings (Greer and Apple 1991). The AMA remained supportive and instrumental in infant formula promotion until the late 1980s and early 1990s, when infant formula producers decided to market their products directly to consumers (Greer and Apple 1991; Stevens, Patrick, and Pickler 2009). At that point, the AMA pivoted from their earlier support because "physicians were concerned about the advertising claims of these products and generally felt that indications and directions for their use should be the province of the physician" (Greer and Apple 1991, 282).

LLL advocates promoted stark contrasts between breast- and bottle-feeding. For example, Sears and Sears, a doctor and nurse couple widely cited by LLL, argued that "for years, doctors told formula feeding parents that by holding and interacting with their babies during feedings they could imitate breastfeeding, and their babies could then receive any intellectual and social benefits associated with breastfeeding. This was true to a point (it is better to hold the bottle and talk to your baby than to prop the bottle and walk away), but research is now showing that the smart stuff is in the milk, and it's not just the mothering that matters" (Sears and Sears 2018, 4). The science underpinning the "small and unverified claims" of health-related benefits associated with breastfeeding makes such strongly held statements seem dubious at best (Blum 1999). Though LLL challenged prevailing medical and popular understandings of feeding and care, their promotion of maternalism and intensive breastfeeding practices made their education by design most accessible to affluent stay-at-home mothers with the time and resources to follow their teachings.

Contemporary Education and Consensus

Parenting groups dispense education through in-person and virtual meetings and their development of informational materials and curricula, including toolkits, handbooks, websites, and podcasts. In smaller groups, like MOMS Clubs, UES Mommas, the local dads' groups, and the Oakwood babysitting co-op, educational resources are often distributed by referral to books, sites, and community organizations. Larger groups, like the PTA and LLL, for example, also produce magazines and books. Though groups target members, their education is often widely circulated to reach the public and recruit new members. We turn next to contemporary education and outreach from smaller parent groups.

Local Education: Parent to Parent and Through Invited Guests

On a more intimate scale, groups like UES Mommas, the Oakwood babysitting co-op, and the local MOMS Clubs and dads' groups exchange information primarily through various in-person activities and online forums. These relatively smaller organizations, or smaller groups within a broader national membership (like the dads' groups as well as local MOMS Club, PTA, and LLL groups), plan their own educational events for parents. The MOMS Club website explains, "Each chapter has a monthly meeting with an interesting speaker or topic for discussion. Speakers can be anyone from a children's librarian speaking about early reading, to a gardener talking about what grows well in your area, to a psychologist talking about child development, to the Superintendent of Schools talking about school choices in your community—whatever the moms are interested in, they can arrange a speaker for" (MOMS Club n.d.-f). The Birmingham–East Alabama MOMS Club holds "a monthly enrichment meeting with a speaker or fun activity. We might . . . learn creative ways to save money from a financial advisor" (MOMS Club of Birmingham-East, AL n.d.).

Groups also provide local resources and parent-to-parent education, including direct referrals to family resources (information about group outings and activities, for instance). Babysitting co-op members emphasize the group's important role in helping members get to know their neighborhood and learn about broader community opportunities. As Julia explains, "I'm just learning a lot about the environment . . . services or schools or recreations, it's just a well of public information that comes from the co-op that's helpful." Similarly, Noelle says, "They know—they are very resourceful with a lot of things that they know about the town. Given that I am relatively newer than most of the people in the town, they know a lot of camps and just classes and activities and events going on." Connecting parents with resources reduces parents' workload for research and reviews. It also provides a sense of community for parents to join and do what other families are doing. Sharing extends to more personal exchanges as well, including parenting stories, resources like helpful books, and feelings of camaraderie.

Within the Oakwood babysitting co-op, education provides a way to transmit caregiving beliefs. In particular, the idea of education as a vehicle for continual improvement, of always being able to be better and do better, as a mom, intensifies mothering practices. As Julia details, "I enjoy hearing other people's stories . . . you just bounce ideas off of each other. . . . You know, my parenting technique is not working because my child is not listening and she's acting out, and she's doing this and this person is doing that, so I'm going to try this. . . . I find that I'm a better mother because of it. I've learned a lot—great references like try this book if you're dealing with temper-tantrums, or acting out, or things like that." Carol highlights the role of regular discussion within the group: "It's nice that when we have our meetings, we go around and share a thought or idea about all these issues about you know, things going on in the society or these activities to do and strengthening the relationships in the family. To . . . help each other with raising kids." Access to information also helps quell co-op members' fears, as Nell describes: "I go to the dark side all the time, and I know it. And it's difficult. I have to have other people help me sometimes to allow my children to stretch the cord a bit. And it's purely a safety issue. It's not a 'they can't handle it,' or 'this is too difficult for them.' It's not that. I know it's my issue. But that's the other part of the village. I don't fill my village with people who are as crazy as I am, just people who understand it and respect it, and can provide a light, if you will. This path is okay because I've tested it, and so it's okay to do this. And then I can say, okay, good. Because I can spend all of my time testing all the water. So, you have to have other people you can trust."

Nell's comments reflect the ways in which the babysitting co-op acts as a deep resource for mothers. The babysitting co-op enhances intensive care, screening for like-minded moms who can support both mother and child, and wards off collective fears in an increasingly economically precarious, media-saturated, and panic-provoking social landscape (Nelson 2010; Villalobos 2014). So, while filling a need for support and encouragement, the babysitting co-op also extends caregiving with an emphasis on not just doing better but also doing more—more deliberation, more searching for answers, and more participation as a group in intensive mothering practices, a process that I call collective-intensive mothering. By contrast, though dads' group members also use their groups to share parenting education, they approach their groups with less intensive expectations and outcomes.

Like the babysitting co-op members, dads' group members use local online Facebook and X (Twitter) forums for a range of information and support, including suggestions about how to approach parenting challenges. As Kyle, a thirty-nine-year-old father of five who is not employed, explains, "It is nice to hear sometimes . . . the way [children] behave and seeing that it is actually normal, that other people are going through it as well, that is a good sign . . . if you have a problem and you may not have the right answer, you know, but along the line someone has good advice." He continues, "So whenever there are questions, . . . like my four-year-old . . . totally . . . has temper tantrums where she is like totally zoned out. So, I posted asking for advice and a lot of it was like, . . . that age . . . they basically lose their concentration, and they can't hear what you are saying. So, they give you advice on questions like that and stuff like that." The camaraderie evident in Kyle's description is indicative of the online information exchanges among dads' group members. Benjamin tells a story about an exchange online, between the group and a dad who reached out for support with a problem he was having: "That was a cool moment [online] because this guy sounded like he was really struggling and everybody else sent a lot of positivity his way, which also I don't think is the most common thing that groups of men do with each other, so that was kind of neat."

Dads' groups' resources include the national online network. As Thomas explains, "A lot of questions end up going usually through City Dads Group" that includes the group's Meetup, Facebook, Instagram, and X (Twitter) platforms. "I mean, you can almost . . . you can think of the question to search for, and someone's probably already asked it, but a lot of dads on there have a lot of good information too . . . like I usually ask ones about sleep stuff because we had some issues with [our child] sleeping a few months back. . . . people point you in maybe a different direction or [provide a] link to different websites." Bryson, a group leader, explains how information gets circulated from the National City Dads to local groups: "I'll share from City Dads Groups because they have . . . a blog too. . . . I'll share . . . some of their stories. Like it's parenting stories mostly, but it's . . . the dad point of view . . . or . . . dad-related parenting issue or what posts or articles or studies that are done that, you know, research and stuff like that." He also takes material from articles or books on parenting and "[poses] a question from out of that." His outreach, as a leader, is designed to share useful information, spark interest, and keep conversation and participation active.

Some dads participate vicariously by reading threads from past discussions. As Jacob, a thirty-three-year-old father of one who is not employed and belongs to the Western dads' group, clarifies, "I do [follow] the nationwide City Dads Group on Facebook. I wouldn't necessarily say that I'm participating, but I have definitely looked at . . . articles and what other dads are saying on it." Providing access to online discussions and information that connects but does not require parents' active participation enables both local and national resource sharing. Unlike the stay-at-home dads in sociologist Catherine Richards Solomon's research, who sought only "online communities," men in this study sought out local dads' groups for online and in-person activities (2017). Given their flexible work schedules, with the majority working part-time, both the employed and stay-at-home dads I interviewed had the time and flexibility to take advantage of what the dads' groups have to offer.

Unlike the moms' groups, dads are not following a typical script. They are foregrounding their fatherhood and discussing direct care for their kids, sometimes as primary care givers, alongside other men. In adapting to the changing social landscape, the dads' groups act as a safe space for men to express and perform a range of masculine performances including normatively marginalized forms of masculinity in the company of other men. For both the Oakwood babysitting co-op and dads' groups on the local level, access to information and resources is done directly, parent to parent, within the groups. For national organizations, information within their local groups is transmitted in similar ways. However, these larger groups also create more widely distributed resources through their group's article and book publications.

Education Through Publications: The PTA and LLL

The PTA and LLL promote education by developing their own curriculum and publications, including books and magazines, on the web and through social media platforms. These publications are emblematic of the group's priorities and serve as recruitment tools. Collectively they make clear the group's targets in their educational missions and the cultural messages they seek to support. Publications also reflect the groups' diversity discourse, or the rhetoric the groups reproduce to signal their inclusivity of various racial/ethnic and gendered groups. While this discourse is set up to demonstrate the groups' plurality and embrace of diversity, research shows that a "diversity discourse can be valorized, deployed, and leveraged in ways that insulate racial hierarchy" (Rajasekar, Aguilar-Champeau, and Hartman 2022).

The contemporary PTA's educational outreach contains competing voices, as it did in members' resistance to racial integration. Usually, however, the organization tends to speak with one voice, following rather than leading on contemporary issues. In effect, they adopt strategies to avoid the appearance of contention, promote consensus, and support the status quo. For example, gun control, an issue I examine later in this chapter, is limited and redefined by PTA education as more or less a nonpolitical safety issue. The group's biannual magazine, *Our Children*, offers a major pathway to PTA voice.[2] The magazine contains short articles, member profiles, advice columns, as well as creative features like poetry, recipes, and activities for parents and kids. Designed for information and recruitment, the magazine draws on the scope of the organization, including articles from across the country. Several presidents have used the magazine to reflect on historical inequalities and exclusion in the PTA for their "President's Message." Former PTA president James Accomando invoked a common belief in American meritocratic education when he wrote, "At PTA, we believe public education is our nation's great equalizer—in our schools, our children have access to opportunities, experiences, and knowledge they would never encounter otherwise" (2018, 5). PTA president Leslie Boggs echoed Accomando in "A Call to Courage," an essay that encouraged members to "speak out and make sure every child in America attends schools that are safe, equitably funded, and structurally sound" (2019, 5). These messages often set the stage for the articles that follow to unpack some of their ideas. They also provide an opportunity to restate the organization's core beliefs for parents.

Our Children educates members on group recruitment through members' connectedness with other parents. As PTA member Sarah Marjoram explained in her *Our Children* article, "This may sound strange, but I think it's an important point to make. Our children provide us with a valuable way to meet people. As they learn, grow and make new friends, we are naturally presented with opportunities to interact and engage with other adults. Through volunteering, we often make new friends and connections ourselves" (2019, 19). The desirability of the kinds of connections that Marjoram described is woven through *Our Children*'s articles. These connections can work in both directions—drawing parents to make connections through PTA and drawing parents with connections into PTA—as Collin Robinson, a featured leader, explained. He was encouraged by other Oregon parents to "use [his] influence and experience as a youth soccer coach to connect with other parents in [his] community" by pursuing a PTA leadership position (2019, 25). Articles reflecting these parent-to-parent experiences show how both recruitment and community building take place on the local level and how to reproduce them.

Over the past five years, across three PTA presidents, *Our Children* has covered a range of substantive matters. Four of the eight issues are thematic and focused on the environment, reading, STEM (science, technology, engineering, and math), and technology. The other half is eclectic, covering child advocacy, family schedules, children's social-emotional health, technology use, food preparation ideas, volunteering, and crafts. Half of the issues contain at least one article (some contain a few) about diversity—by ethnicity, race, gender, and nationality—including strategies to integrate Spanish-speaking children in schools (join the PTA), improve school experiences for African American students, build girls' confidence through running, cultivate dads' participation in their kids' education, and help immigrant families. These articles reveal some of the PTA's diversity discourse, a rhetoric that signals diversity's importance but does not broadly substantiate words with corresponding actions.

Many of the articles reflecting the PTA's diversity discourse in membership, issues, and outreach produce contradictory results and fall short of truly addressing the issues they raise. As products of their culture, local and national PTA organizations reproduced normative social patterns "shaped in particular by those who have acquired the power to define the situation" (Hallett 2003). Members' voices are amplified or silenced through publications that document the organization's interactive processes, ideology, and substructures (Acker 1990, 1992). Situated in a U.S. context, the PTA has been formed by exclusionary ideologies and practices around gender, racism, ableism, and economic inequalities. PTA texts emerge from these circumstances and often capture conventional perspectives, like promoting awareness and outreach. They stop short of calling for significant social change or fully addressing barriers to inclusion. Instead, they work within existing structures to promote more diversity and involvement from various groups.

For example, articles educating members on community inequalities in education and ideas for participation are reflected across *Our Children*'s articles, which often feature one representative and school. Charlene Shanahan, a volunteer representing her Washington State school's PTA, authored one such article that shares how her school developed an Equity Team in response to the "huge disparities in educational achievement, largely based on race" in her community. Her response is emphatic, "I had to join and work to make a difference in our school." Her children's school's first gathering was designed to promote cultural awareness and enable parents to "share their cultural heritage in a low-pressure way." It was a "Family Heritage Potluck," with families sharing native dishes and dress. Shanahan explains, "The [PTA Equity] team wondered if there would be a big turnout and worried it wouldn't be well received or attended, but the potluck was a success and is now an annual tradition." Her response highlights broader family participation in the event: "Most memorable for me is that we see families at this event that don't always participate in other school events" (Shanahan 2018, 35). What is not elaborated in the article is how (or whether) the PTA Equity Team reached out to families in advance (instead of "wondering" and "worrying") regarding the potluck and the extent to which those "who don't always participate" are brought into dialogue and encouraged to become part of the planning. Though we do not know the inner workings of this group, the descriptions hint at similarities with PTAs from previous decades that rely more on narrow responsibility than on direct communication and outreach. Regardless, by profiling these articles within their national publication, the PTA elevates this group's experience to educate others. Similarly, LLL has long used publications to distribute information, educate, and provide care for members.

At the core of LLL's education is its book, *The Womanly Art of Breastfeeding*. In 1958, the first edition of *The Womanly Art of Breastfeeding* was released by LLL with 17,000 copies (La Leche League International 1963). In 1963, at the same time as the first hard copy edition was released, Karen Pryor published "They Teach the Joys of Breastfeeding," highlighting the group's work in *Reader's Digest* (1963). This mainstream attention drew many new mothers to the group. In addition to books and conferences, LLL began a twice-monthly member publication in 1958, first called *La Leche League News*; they changed the name to *New Beginnings* in 1985. In 2014 *New Beginnings* transformed into the online magazine called *LLL Today* (La Leche League USA n.d.). Webpage readers are instructed, "When you can't attend a meeting, you can find encouragement and support in *LLL Today*" (La Leche League International n.d.-e). *LLL Today* is now called *Breastfeeding Today*, and the newest edition of *The*

Womanly Art of Breastfeeding has been retitled *The Art of Breastfeeding*, to reflect the group's gender inclusivity of trans and nonbinary persons, though the term "breastfeeding" and not "chestfeeding" remains in this context (La Leche League International 2024b).

Over twelve years and forty-two online issues, *Breastfeeding Today* provides mother-to-mother stories and letters, health- and illness-related articles, global news reporting, book reviews, nutrition information and recipes, and lots of LLL promotion (La Leche League International 2022b). The core of the issues are first-person stories that appear in every issue. These short pieces cover breast-feeding challenges, insights, and personal understandings on postpartum depression, having second children, military service, and breast cancer, to name a few. The underlying message from these pieces is that breastfeeding can be challenging, but the personal and child fulfilment far outweighs the demands. In a piece titled "Softening into Motherhood," Naomi Stadlen explains "soft-ening" as an LLL concept for prioritizing a nursing infants' schedule: "When a mother keeps fulfilling her baby's needs, he gazes at her with a look of adora-tion for the wonderful person she is. She may not expect to be seen like that. She may be critical of how she looks, of her abilities, and much else. Yet mothers who allow themselves to receive their babies' loving gaze, report that self-criticisms seem to melt away. It's an extraordinary experience of softness and peace" (2020). "Mothers who allow themselves" to experience this process, of course, do not include those who are required to work outside the home. In this context, the reality that a system might prevent some mothers from pri-oritizing breastfeeding is not even considered. In keeping with individual-level solutions, breastfeeding is framed as something mothers can solve themselves, through their relationship with their child. The implication is that if a mother fails, they must not be "allowing themselves" to succeed.

Breastfeeding Today also attends to fathers. Titles include "101 Tips for the New Father," "The Fatherly Art of Parenthood," as well as "Father Stories" like "Bonding," "A Breastfeeding Toddler's Dad," and "Promoting Dad's Role in Breastfeeding." Most recent articles expand the focus to include "The Role of the Partner in Breastfeeding: How the Support of Dads, Co-Moms and Other People Makes a Difference." A 2020 issue makes clear in a boxed insert, "A baby's father is not the only kind of partner who can support breastfeeding. A partner may also identify as a co-mother or co-parent, or may be a grandparent or other relative, a close friend, a doula, or anyone else that the nursing parents identify as their partner in breastfeeding." The article then proceeds through several suggestions for how partners can help by educating themselves with LLL resources, recognizing the effort breastfeeding entails; "[being] a gatekeeper" for phone calls and visitors to protect the nursing mother's energy; and pro-tecting her time for self-care by pitching in with "practical help" (Schnell 2020). Since the magazine is written for members, these pieces are partly propaganda and partly a guide for securing their partner's help and support. In other words, these articles educate mothers that they are not alone in their need for help. LLL comforts parents about their care gap and further educates them in how to address it.

Across issues, the magazine maintains LLL's diversity discourse through a scattershot international focus. Covers feature racially diverse women nursing, kissing, and cuddling their babies and children. Inside, over the decade, the issues incorporate bilingual articles, including stories and recipes in Spanish and Greek. They cover global issues like "Breastfeeding Around the World," reference work by the World Health Organization, include photos and laws from South Africa, and provide recipes from Bulgaria and Ireland. In terms of marginalized groups, the magazine addresses HIV-positive mothers in one article. In another article from 2019 on "Black Breastfeeding Week Celebrations," they mark an annual celebration that began in 2012. The week is held to "[raise] awareness of disparities in black mothers' breastfeeding rates compared to other groups, and possible remedies for these disparities" (Attanasio 2019). Far more prevalent are articles promoting LLL that relate to milestones (like LLL's fifty-fifth and sixty-fifth anniversaries), those highlighting new editions of *The Womanly Art of Breastfeeding*, and pieces calling attention to meetings, groups, children's attendance, and leadership recruitment. Like the PTA, LLL's diversity discourse seems designed more to amplify their appearance than to document substantive change.

As opposed to the other groups, LLL's group education includes training through which members can becoming accredited leaders through a structured process that involves several steps (La Leche League International n.d.-i). To apply, prospective leaders must divulge their breastfeeding and mothering biography. The website reads, "*Our* goal is to accredit Leaders whose knowledge and skills reflect a balance of the practical, physical, and interpersonal aspects of helping others experience 'mothering through breastfeeding.'" LLL emphasizes the importance of "leadership skills and attitudes." Candidates are trained in how to support others in breastfeeding, including techniques and challenges, and are urged to read the core texts, *The Womanly Art of Breastfeeding* and the *Leader's Handbook*. They are also tasked with reading a "comprehensive book on giving birth." Though alternatives are accepted, *The Womanly Art of Breastfeeding* and the *Leader's Handbook* are encouraged. Training also includes webinars, meeting with leaders, and relevant birth experience, if applicable. *LLL* provides insight into what becoming a leader entails, through its "preview" that incorporates "practice emails, texts, or phone calls; role-play; discussion; [and] mock meetings."

Among the resources available for leaders are several books and an online Center for Breastfeeding Information research database compiling additional resources. LLL has published its *Leader's Handbook*, outlining the responsibilities for group leaders, *Leader Today*, a publication for leaders, and *The Breastfeeding Answer Book*, as a reference for leaders to address common to uncommon issues. The commitment to lead an LLL group is considerable and includes staying "up to date on all important breastfeeding information, taking advantage of LLL's opportunities for continuing education, and publications, meetings, correspondence, and the network of resource Leaders" (La Leche League International 2003, 226). The handbook contains an entire chapter on LLL's Education and Member Services Department. Leaders and members are encouraged to purchase these books for their library: "If you let a mother know that information or a suggestion was found in *The Womanly Art of Breastfeeding*, it's an easy transition to suggesting she might want to own a copy" (La Leche League International 2003, 160).

Over its sixty-five-year history, LLL has become an international parenting education source. Born out of opposition to mainstream medicine's embrace of infant formula feeding, the group has been slow to embrace groups that make breastfeeding more challenging or decenter motherhood, like employed and trans chestfeeding parents, as we'll see in chapter 5. The language used in the handbook makes many references to mothers who are active in their kids' schools and providing transportation by car. For example, in the introduction the authors write, "In evaluating their commitment to [LLL], some Leaders have commented that there are many who can act as volunteers in their children's schools or other activities, but only a limited number of women are able to help mothers breastfeed." Their advice for time management includes multitasking: "Find and use hidden time. For example, keep reading material in the car for times that you are waiting to pick up children. Make telephone calls . . . while cleaning the kitchen" (La Leche League International 2003, xv). Though designed to recruit and retain, these descriptions clearly target mothers who do considerable household and child-related labor.

LLL has promoted a kind of intensive embodied mothering in which "the ideal role for women was full-time motherhood focused on the natural needs of the baby" (La Leche League International 2003, 1374). The *Leader's Handbook* explains, "Mother and baby need to be together early and often to establish a satisfying breastfeeding relationship and reliable milk production" and "in the early years, the baby has an intense need to be with his mother which is as basic as his need for food" (La Leche League International 2022a, 9). The embrace of intensive mothering has continued, even as the group has begun to address employed moms, who today make up most mothers with children under the age of eighteen (Bureau of Labor Statistics 2017). LLL's expectations for nursing have presented mothers with an all-or-nothing framework. As historian Lynn Weiner explained, "To meet league standards of on-demand breastfeeding, mother and infant must remain together" (1994, 1359). This imperative has comprised being available day and night, including cosleeping. LLL's centers its expectations for women around what sociologist Dorothy Smith called a "mothering discourse," which makes mothers "responsible for practically everything that might conceivably happen to their children in the future, and particularly that everything that could go wrong [for their children] in school was due to their imperfections as mothers" (Smith 2004, 2).

Feminists have often regarded LLL with caution. As scholar Bernice Hausman suggests, feminists "approach League as an ideologically suspect organization with rigorous social controls over the women who become involved with it—much like a cult" (2003, 161). Feminists have also viewed with suspicion the discourse around breastfeeding that LLL has championed. Over the past two decades, titles like *Unlatched: The Evolution of Breastfeeding and the Making of a Controversy* (Grayson 2016), *Breastfeeding and Media: Exploring Conflicting Discourses That Threaten Public Health* (Foss 2017), *Breast or Bottle? Contemporary Controversies in Infant Feeding Policy and Practice* (Koerber 2013), *Mother's Milk: Breastfeeding Controversies in American Culture* (Hausman 2003), and "The Case Against Breastfeeding" (Rosen 2009) have all signaled continued debates surrounding this practice. Is breastfeeding, as Rosen calls it, "this generation's vacuum cleaner—an instrument of misery that mostly just keeps women down" siphoning time, energy, as well as milk away from overworked mothers (2009, 64)? When parenting groups confront these criticisms, new possibilities for debate and expansion emerge. However, these groups are often predisposed to the influence of their leaders, more powerful members, their histories, organization, and politics, that often limit their scope.

Stress, Safety, and Bullying: The PTA's Educational Response to School Gun Violence

To maintain their relevance, parenting groups strive to educate members about current issues. Not only does education amplify parenting groups' presence in a crowded social media landscape, but it contributes toward their common goal of educating and caring for parents. For the PTA, contemporary issues include programming around antibullying, social and emotional health, technology use, substance use and abuse, healthy eating and nutrition, and diversity, equity, and inclusion. These issues relate to some of the most challenging social problems today around mental and physical health and safety. Perhaps the issue that has received the greatest attention is school gun violence. Given their orientation and size, alongside a galvanizing tragedy, the PTA response to school gun violence provides an important case to examine for its scale, scope, and legacy.

Following the worst elementary school shooting in U.S. history, the national, state, and local PTA looked for ways to respond and help, like much of the country. The shooting took place on December 14, 2012, in Newtown, Connecticut, when Adam Lanza shot his way into the Sandy Hook Elementary School with a semiautomatic rifle (Office of the State's Attorney, Judicial

District of Danbury 2013). Once inside, he killed twenty first-grade children and six adults, among them the school's principal, a psychologist, two teachers, and two teachers' aides. He later killed himself. After police went to Lanza's home, they learned that he had also killed his mother.

This was not the first U.S. high-casualty school shooting. Before Sandy Hook, Columbine High School (1999) and Virginia Tech University (2007) suffered large student death tolls. "Columbine was kind of a wake-up call," said Ginny Markell, president of the National PTA. "Parents were realizing they don't know who their kids' friends are, or what the climate of their school was like" (Crary 2000). However, the school shootings and broader gun violence have kept coming. Parents have worried about both inaction and action surrounding school shootings, including the lack of comprehensive federal gun control legislation and the implementation of school-based active shooter and lockdown drills, for example.

One of the major ways the PTA has addressed school shootings is through informational campaigns, public dialogues, and podcasts, like those the PTA held for media consumption and substance use warnings from decades prior. Targeting parents and kids, in particular, contemporary PTA educational campaigns have urge parents to get involved, crafting national programs like a 2013 webinar, "Talking with Teens About Stress Management," with the American Psychological Association and clinical psychologist Dr. David Palmiter, and a 2016 webinar on "Bullying and Cyberbullying Prevention," with Caroline Knorr from *Common Sense Media* (Toney 2016). The PTA has also partnered with Sandy Hook Promise, in both its web resources and its programming. Six years after Sandy Hook, the National PTA organized a webinar, "School Safety—Mobilizing for Change" (National PTA n.d.-v). The panelists included Jackie Ball, national PTA director of government affairs, and Nicole Hockley, cofounder and managing director of Sandy Hook Promise. Hockley's six-year-old son Dylan was killed during the Sandy Hook shooting. Hockley focuses on violence prevention, informing parents how to "create safe schools and communities for all," through a better understanding of prevention, based on evidence from research (National PTA n.d.-v). PTA podcasts include "How to Talk to Your Kids About Gun Violence," a program from 2020 with guest speaker and pediatrician Dr. Edith Bracho-Sanchez on how parents can address children's questions and fears about school violence, safety, and lockdown drills (National PTA 2020a).

The national PTA has fostered broad conversations about how to implement local safety measures. In addressing school safety, the PTA wants to involve parents: "It is imperative that families are actively engaged in creating safe and supportive schools for kids. National PTA has developed resources for parents and PTAs to support you in becoming effective, successful school safety stakeholders" (National PTA n.d.-v). The national PTA has urged parents to educate themselves, communicate with their local school principals, help to organize local school safety events, and work to evaluate and develop safety policies at their schools (National PTA 2018a). These kinds of programs bring in experts and partner with other organizations to inform parents about the issues, connect members with additional resources they can consult to learn more, and empower them to be vigilant for kids at risk of self-harm or harm to others. Combined, these efforts promote education alongside care to potentially ease parents' fears, but these efforts never actually address the problem of gun violence itself.

Reproducing Individual-Level Solutions

While educational programming can raise awareness, many have felt the PTA and government interventions have not gone far enough. Responses from leadership and web-based information are paradoxical and lack clarity. James Accomando, who led the Connecticut State PTA in 2012, the year of the Sandy Hook shooting, became the national PTA president in 2017 (Barron 2012). Accomando's remarks specifically about gun violence are quoted on the PTA advocacy page for "Gun Safety and Violence Prevention": "We have all watched in horror as our country has experienced far too many gun-related tragedies. We need immediate change. It is urgent that we work together to enact bipartisan policy solutions and make meaningful change to keep our children safe. Every student deserves to learn and grow in a safe environment." PTA advocacy work emphasizes stricter gun laws through PTA position statements, policy briefs, press releases, and a national legislative conference in 2018 (National PTA n.d.-d). By contrast, the PTA's educational platform that addresses gun violence falls under a broader heading of "Safety" and "Students Deserve a Safe Environment." Though it is important to integrate gun safety and related topics, this web page organization makes gun safety far less prominent, under headings like "School Safety" and subheadings like "Know the Signs" (National PTA n.d.-v). Combined, these approaches show the ways in which idealistic approaches can muddy important issues and favor the status quo over social change.

Parenting groups take a collective form but predominately focus on individual solutions. They also tend to serve more narrowly and locally focused communities rather than broader ones. As such, parenting groups disproportionally benefit families who were already well-positioned and well-resourced, those who are best able to conform to and embrace their ideologies. These organizations could provide a web to educate families and communities horizontally and vertically, in far more ways than they do. We know that families cannot meet their needs or manage social crises alone and that they rely on their broader communities to make care ends meet. However, though education raises community-wide and nationwide issues, care solutions in these groups are often organized around individual member and family solutions designed to make participants feel better. Like the self-help literature, informing and comforting parents and families stops short of addressing collective care needs. By adopting such a narrow approach, parenting groups undermine their contributions to the care infrastructure they develop by failing to see where interconnections are broken, missing, or even possible.

Conclusion

Examining parent groups' information sharing, parental education, and care enables us to see and understand the strengths and limitations of their contributions to care infrastructure. Though sometimes contradictory, these groups advocate for a community approach to education and care across many families. One of the groups' major strengths is their understanding that education and care are intertwined for parents. Answering parents' vexing questions and offering resources can help foster parents' understanding, reduce their isolation, boost their self-esteem, and provide them with sense of community, to encourage better caregiving, for the parents *and* their children.

Another strength lies in their size and scope. National and international groups like the PTA, LLL, and City Dads Group provide outreach on multiple levels and involve great numbers of people in the human care infrastructure. The largest groups can assert themselves (or be invited) into educational opportunities and assert impact at state and federal levels that individual local groups, like the Oakwood babysitting co-op and local MOMS Clubs and dads' groups, may not have the influence or inclination to pursue. The PTA response to the Sandy Hook tragedy provides one well-known example and LLL's breastfeeding advocacy provides another. Long histories of name recognition enable both groups to enter national conversations on these important issues. Similarly, the large membership rosters and well-established organizational infrastructure enable national organizations like the PTA, LLL, and City Dads Group to easily reach a sizeable audience.

This chapter also demonstrates these groups' weaknesses. Although, as multilevel organizations, the PTA and LLL have spoken with one voice on a range of issues, their educational missions have been in the service of their membership and avoid addressing contentious issues. All the largest groups I studied—the PTA, LLL, MOMS Club, and City Dads Group—have organizations that continually default to a decentralized model that leaves each local group to produce its own educational content and decision-making. In the case of the dads' groups, a decentralized model enables the men to foreground their roles as fathers and support each other's search for like-minded men to express their vulnerability, admit their parenting concerns, and share their stories through parenting education.

The PTA, LLL, MOMS Club, and babysitting co-op's embrace of ideologies like maternalism, intensive mothering, and symbolic diversity hinder access and content. For both the PTA and LLL, embracing maternalism saddles mothers with a primary responsibility for care (Ladd-Taylor 1994; Weiner 1994). Rooted in intensive and collective-intensive mothering, moms in the PTA, LLL, MOMS Club, and babysitting co-op are encouraged to provide ever-increasing, ever-improving parental care. Rather than solving mothers' problems, these groups also add to them. The PTA and LLL's use of a diversity discourse makes strategic use of the faces and stories of people of color, while sidelining real social change. In the case of the PTA, parent education has focused, for example, on raising cultural awareness about diversity rather than on dismantling systemic racism, calling for large-scale economic restructuring to fully fund public education, or seeking to level the playing field across suburban, urban, and rural schools. As such, the PTA falls short of truly addressing the broader issues facing parents, particularly parents of color. Looking at the parenting groups' organizational issues alongside the needs of caregivers can make a comprehensive approach visible. The next chapter addresses these issues through an examination of parenting groups' provision of resources.

4

From Fundraising
to Respite Care

Broad Resource Goals
and Narrow Allocation

The cultural trope of the PTA mom is a powerful one. Rooted in stereotypes of overbearing, white, affluent stay-at-home mothers, this cliché plays on sexist ideas about women's leadership, unpaid labor, and community building. The lasting power of this stereotype and its kernel of truth comes from both the historical legacy of the group's founders described in the first chapter as well as contemporary members I examine in this chapter who maintain an outsized influence over local PTA groups. Media and popular reproductions exaggerate this stereotype and have a polarizing and obstructive effect, disparaging and sidelining parent groups and their leaders as irrelevant, out of touch busybodies. Captured by blog posts like "Not a 'PTA Mom'" (Rosenfeld 2014), "Can We Retire This PTA Mom Stereotype, Please?" (Diaz 2014), and "In Defense of the PTA Mom" (ParentCo. 2017), the PTA mom stereotype highlights the heavy workload members perform. As one blogger noted, "These PTA moms of my imagination . . . pulled off school functions like Martha Stewart on steroids" (Rosenfeld 2014). Invoking Martha Stewart implies labor-intensive homemade products, like baked goods and kids' craft projects. The 2016 comedy *Bad Moms* captured these ideas in a scene featuring the film's PTA president (played by Christina Applegate) directing volunteers for a "bake sale police force" to monitor and punish anyone who supplies foods with "toxic ingredients." The National PTA promoted the film's sequel, tweeting, "Many of you might be enjoying #BadMomsXmas at the theaters this week. We totally got the 'overachieving PTA mom' joke from the first movie!" Recasting this comedic representation as "overachieving" again emphasizes the work—selecting, organizing, and controlling the content of care provided by the group.

Parent groups' contributions to the care infrastructure include the provision of financial and in-kind resources. These diverse economic and material offerings give parents comfort, provide assistance in periods of crisis, and enable them to work and rest. To generate financial resources, parent groups rely primarily on membership dues, donations, and corporate sponsorships. Parent groups provide access to in-kind resources directly from members and leaders or through group collection. In-kind resources have included everything from parents' access to health checkups, vaccinations, school lunches, and technology for their children to meeting spaces, refreshments, financial resources, and caregiving relief for themselves. These resources often benefit group members but may also be collected by members to benefit parents and families in their broader community.

In the PTA example, the resources include food and fundraising alongside convening events in the service of their schools, families, and communities. The PTA puts funds raised from these events toward member recruitment, meetings, and education, as the previous chapters illustrate. Since their early fundraising days, PTAs have become a major source of financial support for schools facing budget constraints due to inequalities in federal, state, and local funding as well as in property taxes, which perpetuate inequalities across families and schools. Parents provide books, technology, and sports equipment that enable teachers to fill gaps when districts face resource shortages. Parents also support schoolwide programming and events (like dances, assemblies, and end-of-year fairs). The PTA's contribution in effect provides money for "projects and items that really ought to be part of the school budget" (National PTA n.d.-f). The PTA addresses inequalities collectively, providing access to classroom materials that parents might otherwise need to purchase individually for their children or, in the absence of other sources, their children might go without.

Fundraising is perhaps what parenting groups like the PTA are well known for. The PTA and MOMS Clubs also raise funds through membership fees (see Table 1). LLL does not charge for meetings or breastfeeding and chestfeeding support, though it does offer memberships and may charge application and accreditation fees for leaders, accept donations, and generate revenue from book sales. City Dads Group has built opportunities through corporate sponsorships. Locally, UES Mommas, individual dads' groups, and Oakwood babysitting co-op are volunteer-based and rely on no monetary or nominal contributions that go directly toward group activities or members' needs, rather than funding the organization per se. The Oakwood babysitting co-op, for example, asks for members to pay five dollars annually.

The PTA, LLL, MOMS Club, Oakwood babysitting co-op, and dads' groups all provide in-kind resources in a variety of forms. As an online group, UES Mommas provides in-kind resources through its members only on an ad hoc basis. When parenting groups organize a time and space for parents to be together at members' homes, libraries, restaurants, faith-based or local community centers, they give parents a way to share time and the responsibilities of organizing, preparing, cleaning, and hosting. Providing food may include light snacks or dinners for members, children, or entire families. Sharing supplies through book, clothing, and diaper swaps enables parents to receive items others in the group may no longer need or use. These items may be distributed to group members or to others outside of the group as part of wider group philanthropy. Perhaps most importantly, parenting groups can provide relief from child caregiving responsibilities that can be shorter or longer in duration. On the shortest terms, when children are included in meetings or events, having a host provide child-friendly snacks and entertainment (toys, books, crafts) enables parents to attend without needing to pack additional food and activities. For children's care provided by parenting groups and in the place of or absence of parents, I use the term "respite care." Respite care is a term typically associated with elder care; it refers to rest or relief from caregiving for a period of time by having someone else provide that care. Parents provide a form of respite care, but they do not refer to it in the same way, despite the similarities. The Oakwood babysitting co-op makes this kind of care for kids central to the group's care for parents.

Parent groups also use funds to provide direct financial support and in-kind resources to members in need. MOMS Club International provides a Mother-to-Mother Fund, "which helps members in crisis situations and in need of financial assistance" (MOMS Club Simi Valley n.d.-b). In local clubs, like the MOMS Club in Ridgefield, Connecticut, groups provide a "sunshine" fund to "step up to support fellow Moms whether it's a joyous occasion, such as welcoming a child, or the solace of a bereavement period or illness" (MOMS Club of Ridgefield n.d.). The MOMS Club of New London and Waterford, Connecticut, encourages chapters to support members by creating a "Supper Club" to offer nourishment and new recipes and to give members "make-it-and-take-it-home" meals for their families" (MOMS Club n.d.-h). To recruit new members and foster community outreach, the MOMS Club of Lehigh Valley, Pennsylvania, hosts a clothing swap for members and nonmembers to share "women's (maternity included!) and kids' (infant-school age) clothing and gear" (MOMS Club of Southwest Lehigh Valley 2025).

Beyond their members, local groups and individuals also provide community outreach. The Simi Valley MOMS Club website explains, "Our goal is singular: to give and receive support, because navigating motherhood is best done together. In addition to supporting each other, we support our community through fundraisers and community projects" (MOMS Club Simi Valley n.d.-a). Many groups have elaborate websites with sections titled "giving back" that list many group contributions. Among them, raising money, collecting new books and toys, providing food, and purchasing diapers are most often mentioned by groups. Some groups also volunteer members' time, for example collecting winter clothing and transporting it to a local donation center (MOMS Club of Greater Windsor 2021). Many groups host local diaper drives. Other groups collect toys and school supplies for foster children. One group hired a photographer to take mother and child pictures and donate some of the proceeds from those purchased to a local diaper charity. Audrey Symes recruited help with her diaper collection when she posted to UES Mommas, "I was hoping to get 500 diapers with that post . . . I got about 1,200" (ABC News 2018). Building from this initial support, Symes collected diapers in her neighborhood using her stroller, ultimately donating 20,000 diapers to local nonprofit Good+Foundation.[1]

Taken together, parent groups build care infrastructure and associated resources that can provide a lifeline for parents. But access is not distributed equitably. While resources are drawn and circulated in a variety of ways through international to local organizations, the use of those resources may necessitate membership that is not always open and accessible to all, as discussed in chapter 2. The group's structure and demographics shape how and from whom resources are drawn and allocated. As we have seen, the parenting groups under discussion are part of a wider context of gender exclusivity, racism, and economic inequality, which narrows the circulation of resources. If we examine the organization of the parenting groups' collection and allocation of goods and services over time, we can see how groups and campaigns are prioritized and implemented, who provides care and who does not, and how these groups enhance or inhibit access to care.

From Founder's Day to French Programs: Struggles over PTA Funding

The PTA has changed significantly in participation, fundraising, and outreach over time. Scholars have examined fluctuations in the group's membership, with rising and later declining numbers (Ladd 1999; Putnam 2000; Skocpol 2003). While membership has declined significantly from its 1950s heyday, the PTA still boasts approximately four million members (National PTA n.d.-m). The size and scope of the PTA is tied to the group's fundraising and the relative power it affords some of its members. Fundraising has a long history at the PTA, dating back to Founders' Day, an event members designed to celebrate the work that Alice Birney, Phoebe Hearst, and Selena Sloan Butler provided as founders. Held on February 17 each year, Founders' Day has also been called Child Welfare Day to underscore the importance of the group's broad commitment to children's needs. Festivities have included tree planting and "an important part of each Founders' Day has been the voluntary offering of monetary gifts by local units to help national and state congresses expand the PTA's outreach" (National PTA 1997, 33).

During the PTA's early years, "Phoebe Hearst personally funded a good deal of its expenses." Later, others in the PTA's leadership followed Hearst's practice and donated money toward certain activities or to assist with operations when the available funds ran low. Relying on donations inevitably led to shortages. Facing constrained resources, national PTA president Schoff "made a series of appeals to the membership . . . to increase the current funding . . . to plan for a stable financial future." Following this request, Mrs. George K. Johnson bestowed the organization with a significant gift. "Her example led to several other large donations, followed by a cascade of smaller gifts." By 1920, the group had amassed a sufficient monetary base from which to operate (National PTA 1997, 34–35). In the NCCPT, by contrast, raising funds was a "constant concern," and groups faced "years of financial struggle" to provide for their organization alongside classroom materials (Woyshner 2009, 117–118).

Historically, the PTA engaged in fundraising to support extraordinary goals—beyond those we typically see today—to provide many in-kind resources. Beginning in 1925, PTA president Margaretta Reeve initiated "Put Parents' Power to Work," to support a "Summer Round-Up" program, "an annual campaign to get each 1st-grader-to-be registered and examined by a doctor and dentist" (National PTA 1997, 50). Following the Great Depression through the mid-twentieth century, the PTA was a major advocate for school lunch "to assure that needy children would receive at least one good meal a day" (63). By the 1950s, the PTA health program was "a vigorous public relations campaign," instrumental in supporting widespread polio vaccine inoculation. The PTA's polio immunization campaign of 1954 included "thousands of PTA volunteer leaders [who] assisted in the mass vaccination of more than 1.8 million children" by "[volunteering] to help administer the vaccine" (100). Largely forgotten to history, these and other large-scale initiatives by parent groups have provided a range of support for many families.

Fundraising may be the PTA's most central and important task, laying the groundwork for nearly everything else the group does (Addonizio 2000; Lareau and Muñoz 2012). PTA fundraising has become increasingly technologically driven and sophisticated. Yesterday's bake sales are eclipsed by today's book sales, online pie and giftwrap sales, virtual auctions, purchased donations through online stores, and grant writing though the PTA. The time and energy devoted to fundraising has become a major thrust of PTA work; more and more student success is linked to the resources and spending from PTA coffers. To highlight the role PTA fundraising plays in the organization, the 2018–2019 PTA Annual Report, titled "Impact," lists the "hundreds of thousands of dollars in programs and advocacy grants to state and local PTAs" as the first substantive undertaking, following the president's introductory note (National PTA 2019, 3). But this fundraising has far-reaching effects that promote inequalities. Research on parent teacher groups broadly (including PTOs) suggests that those "raising at least $50,000 annually operate almost exclusively in homogenously white and affluent schools" (58). As such, the researchers concluded that "PTAs might be both a common good and a mechanism for opportunity hoarding among the advantaged" (58). Many schools have targeted their resources even more narrowly by moving to hyperlocal PTOs without state and national ties, as conservatives have encouraged, to avoid distributing resources beyond their own schools (Haar 2002).

The power dynamics of the PTA are visible through fundraising, highlighting the ways in which money is a powerful force, especially for the interest groups with the deepest pockets. Sociologist Jessica McCrory Calarco studied a suburban public elementary school, explaining the resource role of PTA fundraising that "regularly brought in more than $50,000 a year for the school. That money paid for laptop and digital 'Smart Boards,' science equipment, books, art supplies, and countless other resources that teachers relied on day-to-day" (Calarco 2018, 155). This high-tech horizon privileges particular PTA members' knowledge and resources. Educational policy researcher Linn Posey-Maddox studied an urban public elementary school PTA. She found that the "increased professionalization . . . helped to garner more funds for the school; however, the creation of positions requiring special skills, and the expansion of fund-raising changed the norms and structure of the organization in ways that privileged middle-class forms of parental engagement" (2014, 3). Journalists also emphasize resource disparities across PTA groups, with an article titled "Bake Sales and Tesla Raffles: The Unequal World of PTA Wealth" (Morton 2021). These inequalities across and within schools have led to struggles over PTA organization and control and mounting controversy over affluent white parents who provide financial resources and usurp local PTA control (Calarco 2018; Cutler 2000; Lareau and Muñoz 2012; Morton 2021; Murray et al. 2019; Posey-Maddox 2014; Quinlan 2016). Taken together, these pieces emphasize contested resources and allocation within the PTA.

PTA contributions can give parents considerable power. School administrators often come to rely upon affluent parents to provide much-needed resources, and those parents, in turn, use their leverage to influence school decision-making (Quinlan 2016). In 2022, journalist Chana Joffe-Walt's *New York Times* Serial Production podcast *Nice White Parents* examined how fundraising by parents in a New York City public school in Brooklyn fostered inequalities.[2] At the School of International Studies (SIS), Rob Hansen, a new white parent and professional fundraiser, entered the struggling minority school his child attended and, independent of the school's well-established PTA, raised thousands of dollars to launch a French language program. Traditionally, SIS parents' fundraising is organized and distributed within the school's PTA. The school's PTA leadership were dumbfounded that Hansen's fundraising plans would be carried out without any notice or consultation. Regardless of Hansen's intentions, his actions circumvented the school's process, organization, and broader population. In effect, Hansen's actions were not subject to the same rules; the school accepted his unauthorized plan because of his passion and good intentions, but perhaps most of all because of the privilege he enjoyed as a white professional. In the end, the SIS principal supported the French language program with the money raised outside of the PTA, where decisions were not made democratically. Since PTAs often operate somewhat independently on the local level, there was no indication that the state or national PTA were consulted for guidance by the SIS PTA.

Public schools often lack sufficient funds to pay for enough teachers, technology, and materials. Given their shortfall, schools turn to the PTA. Rather than advocating to fund schools fully by changing the way schools are financed, communities sidestep important structural economic changes. The path of least resistance makes education only partly the responsibility of government and partly the responsibility of individual parents (Posey-Maddox 2013). In practice, the contributions of PTAs have become an important source for schools' primary fiscal operations, rather than secondary funds to augment those resources. Research by Calarco found that affluent parents pave the way for their kids, "given all that parents contributed, teachers may have been reluctant to say 'no' to parents' or students' requests" (2018, 155). Researching gentrified schools, education journalist Casey Quinlan reported that when "white, affluent parents come into a school that has a high percentage of less-affluent students of color, the more advantaged group tends to take over parent organizations and unintentionally marginalize the parent community that was already there" (2016). These power dynamics can be especially problematic in exacerbating existing economic inequalities among parents. As Posey-Maddox argues, "Middle-class engagement, when unfettered, is likely to create new patterns of educational inequality and exclusion in districts and schools, often despite the best intentions of individual parents" (2014, 2). Rather than leveling the playing field, PTA fundraising has intensified inequalities. Parents and school staff get drawn into struggles over competing concerns and interests, including "conflicts over decisions about how the school would be run . . . and the character of fundraising projects" (Lareau and Muñoz 2012, 202).

Snowflakes and Fundraising: Infrastructure and Decision-Making for Sandy Hook

The provision of goods and services by the PTA was perhaps most visible in the aftermath of the Sandy Hook Elementary School shooting mentioned in the last chapter. The Connecticut State PTA began nationwide organizing the very same day as the tragedy to help families and schools support the kids who were displaced from their school and traumatized by the shooting. The PTA was able to step in and provide institutional support at the local and state levels when the families were in mourning, the school itself had lost its leadership, and both were in crisis. This kind of organizational positioning illustrates how parent groups are central to care infrastructure. Through the Sandy Hook response, one can see the ways in which a multilevel organization provides a mechanism for broader-based support, rather than a siloed approach, particularly when local support and individual families may not be as readily able to respond.

PTA president James Accomando recounted the central role of the PTA: "At the time of the Sandy Hook Elementary School tragedy, it was a tough time for our community, for sure. Sandy Hook Elementary was a PTA school. And Connecticut PTA mobilized that Friday evening, as a board, to support the families and the students impacted by the tragedy. That weekend, our board met with town officials, government officials, and more than a dozen parents of the Sandy Hook school. We wanted to act. We found out the school was not going to reopen for some time, and they were going to move to a neighboring town. So, the suggestion came up to create a welcoming environment. Being winter, snowflakes were the obvious, so we started a campaign called 'Snowflakes for Sandy Hook'" (National PTA n.d.-v).

While news and social media also amplified Snowflakes for Sandy Hook, the PTA was at the center of the outreach effort, connecting its networks and managing the donations that arrived. PTAs across the country sprang into action in support of Sandy Hook. Instead of purchasing teachers' gifts, the PTA at Ravena-Coeymans-Selkirk Elementary School in Ravena, New York, decided to send those funds two hours southeast to Sandy Hook (Wang 2012). On the opposite side of the country, in Washington State, Woodinville East Ridge Elementary School's PTA organized a card signing and made a donation from their own funds (Baumann 2012). The power of their expansive multilevel network reached thousands of families across the country through vast membership rolls, email distributions, and local chapter announcements. Former PTA president Betsy Landers explained in the month following the shooting, "Connecticut PTSA received so many snowflakes that they did not have the office space to accommodate them all. They have hung as many as possible in the school; the rest were used to decorate other schools in the community." The response was overwhelming. Mr. Accomando shared, "Within a few weeks, we had donations from all 50 states, and we had donations from 50 countries. Millions and millions and millions of snowflakes were coming in. . . . And we raised a little more than one million dollars within that year period of time; we stopped at the first anniversary. . . . So, the Sandy Hook Snowflakes campaign was a healing initiative by PTA for the state of Connecticut, but supported by PTAs throughout the United States."

The PTA quickly mobilized fundraising efforts to address the immediate and future emotional health and well-being of those impacted by the school shooting. Mr. Accomando explained the process: "We added a component of fundraising, and we determined, as a group, that the best place for those funds, because there were so many other groups donating monies for a variety of reasons, was to go into actually for mental health [*sic*]. To actually be there as a fund to track those children as they left elementary school, went to middle school and high school" (National PTA 2018b). Through their network of local groups affiliated at the state and national levels, the PTA was able to respond coast to coast, prioritize, and implement a plan to support the Sandy Hook students.

In the aftermath at Sandy Hook there were many other charities besides the PTA also receiving donations. Even higher profile charities like Sandy Hook Promise Foundation approached the same amount of contributions (over $793,000) in only five months of fundraising (State of Connecticut, Office of the Attorney General n.d.). The United Way raised more than $10 million within the first four months (*New York Times* 2019). Many of the victim's families also designated or started their own preferred charities (*Hartford Courant* 2020). Of course, relative to the biggest fundraisers, Snowflakes for Sandy Hook was a fraction of the size, raising $1 million in a calendar year (National PTA n.d.-v). To enter the *Forbes* list of the top one hundred U.S. charities in 2013, organizations had to raise $100 million (Barrett 2013). Nevertheless, given the many directions in which financial support was directed, for a short-term operation the PTA Snowflakes for Sandy Hook outreach was incredibly successful.

Once funds were raised, high-profile conflicts ensued over how those funds would be used within the Sandy Hook Elementary School PTSA. The PTA-raised funds were earmarked in advance to support school survivors' mental-health-related needs. However not all groups' fundraising guidelines were as clearly articulated. Sandy Hook funds were dispersed across many smaller groups and charities (as many as seventy-seven distinct fundraisers) (*New York Times* 2019). This broader context led to increased tensions among Sandy Hook School PTSA members. Remembering the aftermath, the school's library media center staff member Cindy Clement Carlson recalled, "When there was complaining at a PTA meeting about how donated goods were being distributed, one mom called out, 'If you have your kids, shut up!'" She explained, "And that's the crux of it. When to shut up, and when to speak up" (Kleinman and Archer 2018). These conflicts addressed whether funds belonged exclusively to the families of those who perished or to the broader Sandy Hook community (*New York Times* 2019).

Again, the question of voice emerges as a contested terrain within the PTA. The difference with Sandy Hook was that under emergent circumstances the PTA, as an organization, took charge of the planning and execution of the fundraising and allocated funds for survivors' mental health services. Organizations like the United Way raised money through "unrestricted gifts." In the end, the United Way decided to distribute more than two-thirds of the funds they raised to the families of the deceased and the remaining $3 million to the town of Sandy Hook. The process was contested, and survivors' families' outrage remains palpable. In the words of Robbie Parker, whose six-year-old daughter Emilie died at Sandy Hook, the United Way "used our children's names and photos to raise money, saying it was to support 'the families of Newtown,' and then they fought to give it to the entire community" (*New York Times* 2019).

In all, the PTA's response to Sandy Hook reveals much about the group's continued relevance. While the snowflakes symbolize an effort to make Sandy Hook survivors' new school more welcoming, the PTA's choice to address the aftermath of gun violence through school beautification demonstrates the PTA's attempt to appear nonpolitical. The other PTA component, fundraising for mental health, addresses an important issue facing Sandy Hook survivors. Though the organization eventually pressed for stronger gun control, in the aftermath of one of the country's worst school shootings, the PTA response to Sandy Hook provided a way out of really taking a stand (National PTA n.d.-k). When Accomando took over the national PTA president's office, he highlighted his perspective on the role of politics in the national PTA: "Our organization prides itself on being bipartisan and not political" (Lambeck 2017). Of course, being bipartisan is politics premised on compromise and cooperation. Though less divisive, this course of action centered primarily on fundraising and paper snowflake decorations rather than gun control. As such, the PTA's initial response favored consensus and a path of least resistance in response to the Sandy Hook Elementary School shooting.

The PTA's tremendous scale and scope is evident in the coordination of these fundraising and outreach efforts over time—from early health and school lunch to later school supplies, and tragedy-related mental health resources and school beautification. The support for parents and families across these diverse examples reveals the PTA's contributions to the care infrastructure, particularly in bridging education- and health-care-related resources. These efforts provide support for parents and families, connecting them with resources and facilitating their access. Inequalities, between and within schools, with regard to assets and decision-making are an ongoing challenge. Chapter 5 addresses how advocacy by some PTAs provides possibilities for social change. In addition to these larger scale initiatives, on a smaller scale local meetings often provide members with access to in-kind resources.

Group Care Initiatives to Provide In-Kind Resources

Parenting groups in this study regularly contribute goods to members (outlined in Table 1). These include arranging access to physical spaces in private family homes or local community spaces for meetings and providing food and refreshments. Members of the babysitting co-op frequently donate hand-me-down clothing, equipment, and toys to members with younger children. They also organize meal delivery for families experiencing a birth or illness. As the membership materials explain, "The [babysitting] co-op is supportive of its members. It provides dinners and encouragement to its members with new babies or a serious illness." These in-kind resources do more than provide access to support and nourishment; they constitute a form of care. To address limited resources during the pandemic, a PTA in Virginia made and distributed "Wellness Packs full of hygiene essentials including soap, hand sanitizer, toilet paper and paper towels" as well as "grocery store gift cards and masks." Local PTAs partnered with social media company TikTok to take similar actions in Florida, Maryland, and Tennessee. The Tennessee initiative included a "partnership with a local food bank and the support of other local businesses" to create "Little Free Pantries in several communities . . . [where] people can grab what they need anonymously" (National PTA n.d.-a). These kinds of COVID initiatives helped parents during a particularly vulnerable period. Parenting needs and parenting groups' contributions also extend to more routine experiences like following a birth, for example.

Providing space and nourishment alongside companionship and a helping hand can make all the difference to parents. Consider the following story from Julia Pelly's article, "How La Leche League Saved Me." After struggling to nurse her firstborn, Julia decided to attend an LLL meeting. She arrived late, with a fussy baby and was, herself, on verge of crying. In her words, "As the leader welcomed me—and oohed and aahed at my son's slate-blue eyes—the tears began to trickle. When another mom offered to hold my baby while I got settled and yet another offered me a 'lactation cookie,' I started to cry in earnest. . . . There were tales of exhaustion, tears and fights with partners, of pain and soreness, of wondering if motherhood would ever feel normal. They held my baby, showed me how to position him for a pain-free latch and told me that it was OK to cry and that this part would pass." Julia's reaction was palpable—by providing food, supporting her *and* her baby, and teaching her breastfeeding skills, LLL's care and support were sustaining. She explains, "These moms . . . were calm and gentle and soothed me as if I was theirs to take care of. When I left a few hours later, something had changed in me, just a little bit. Their support was simple, but it meant so, *so* much to me. I stumbled in on the unsteady fawn legs of motherhood and, with a lactation cookie and a spit-up-stained shoulder to cry on, they steadied me" (Pelly 2019). Stories like Julia's show how parent groups can provide care for parents.

The provision of in-kind resources regularly extends beyond attendees and members to their broader communities, as the City Dads Groups illustrate. City Dads Groups have organized different initiatives including diaper, clothing, and food drives for families throughout their communities and around the country. The Cincinnati City Dads Group partnered with a local diaper bank to collect open diaper donations and celebrate Father's Eve, the night before Father's Day, an annual celebration of dads connecting with other dads (City Dads Group 2024). Similarly, the Boston and Las Vegas City Dads Groups worked with Huggies to stock their local National Diaper Banks. The Philadelphia City Dads Group partnered with Cradles to Crayons to collect "clothes, school supplies and toys" for "children in need" (Samuels 2017; Zelenka 2017). Working with Good+Foundation, the New York City Dads Group created "Dad Toolkits" for fathers in need that include "diapers, diaper wipes, an infant front carrier, a car seat, a stroller, a high chair, and a safety gate" (APW 2018b). To provide support for children in foster care, the Cleveland City Dads Group organized backpack donations that were filled with "clothes, toiletries or personal supplies" (APW 2018a). For several years, in a major initiative across the United States including City Dads Groups from Chicago, Dallas, Denver, Los Angeles, Minneapolis, Saint Paul, New York City, and San Francisco, members worked with Plum Organics to organize their "[donation of] more than 41,000 [pouch] . . . meals to help children in need" (APW 2016; Bennion 2018). These common forms of outreach for City Dads Groups are a source of great pride, as reflected in their website's press coverage of their many group initiatives and corporate partnerships. Members are connected with their broader communities through the group's emphasis on service, collection, and distribution of resources. Through these initiatives, City Dads Groups build and connect care infrastructure by encouraging members' labor and their provision of resources, building bridges between corporations, national and local nonprofits, and parent groups. Through their contributions, member dads develop further into being both recipients and providers of care. In addition to providing in-kind resources, parenting groups also organize various kinds of supervision for kids.

Parenting Groups Provide Respite Care

"Respite care" is a term most often used to describe care for caregivers of elderly and disabled family members. The National Institutes of Health explains that "being a caregiver can be a labor of love, but it can also be stressful"; "respite care provides short-term relief for primary caregivers. It can be arranged for just an afternoon or for several days or weeks" (National Institute on Aging 2023, n.d.). The importance of respite care for caregivers has been well researched. In a meta-analysis, Sörensen, Pinquart, and Duberstein identified that elder caregiver respite and day care were "successful in alleviating burden and depression" and "increasing general subjective well-being" for caregivers (2002, 369). This description is apt for parents and children who benefit from access to additional caregivers and caregiving relief. For this reason, I use the term "respite care" to describe the work provided by parent groups, in particular the Oakwood babysitting co-op. During LLL and other parent group meetings, respite care might take the form of someone else holding a member's baby or arranging access to babysitting, both of which give parents a break from direct care. The babysitting co-op provides access to short-term caregivers outside of their meetings; the help enables parents to have time for themselves, complete household labor and paid work, and rest.

The babysitting co-op provides highly structured access to respite care. As its membership materials explain, the group "assists frazzled parents when they need to step away from parenting for a while." Respite care within the group is organized to trade brief duration babysitting, or "sits" as they are called (typically lasting less than four hours). These are designed for (1) carrying out short-term work, (2) filling scheduling gaps, (3) going to doctors' appointments, (4) performing household labor, (5) gaining leisure time, and (6) providing backup and last-minute emergency care. Members make care requests for their kids online with other co-op members and exchange coupons as compensation. Though moms' use of babysitting varies, on average they exchange care with three or more members. As children enter middle school and begin to provide self- and sibling-care, members reduce or end active membership.

The group's highly organized approach is reflected by their materials that include a handbook, membership list, babysitting coupons, coupon balance form, and dry erase "sit" sheet that must accompany children when they are dropped off for babysitting. The "sit" sheet outlines exhaustive information including a parent's location during the sit, their spouse's phone number, an emergency contact's phone number, their pediatrician's name and phone number, the family's health insurance provider (including name, identification, and phone number), and any relevant medical information. The form also contains a signed statement that reads, "In the event of an emergency, if neither I nor my spouse can be located, the sitter named above has my permission to make decisions regarding the medical care of my child(ren)." The level of detail and accounting required for the forms entails considerable preparation and labor.

For the babysitting co-op, respite caregiving is collective. Rather than relying on paid care through the growing service economy, participants choose a less individualistic solution. They face their care needs and labor-intensive parenting not by themselves but through a cooperative care solution that strengthens their resources, capitalizing on both direct and indirect care for themselves and their children. The group's approach provides an example of an intensive mothering ideology in its collective form that I call an *ideology of collective-intensive mothering* (Price-Glynn 2024). Co-op members provide this form of collective-intensive mothering—an ideology and practice that intensifies mothering, increasing the various mental, physical, and emotional aspects involved—through group membership, common beliefs, and collaborative practice.[3]

Comparatively, community mothering has long been in evidence in African American communities (see Collins 1994; Grusami 2019). For African Americans, patterns of othermothering relate to local engagement, to strategies for resisting racism and addressing poverty, and to celebrating women's contributions through motherhood, family, and cultural traditions, in the face of institutionalized discrimination (Collins 1994). The babysitting co-op's respite care, though much smaller, has some commonalities with community-oriented othermothering, particularly through its collective form.[4] By contrast, when looking at the fathers in this study—both in the dads' groups and those married to babysitting co-op members—the prospect of men providing respite care was a nonstarter.

Men's Caregiving Barriers

For many reasons, I thought examining caregiving among dads' group members might yield an ideal case to study. Situating fatherhood as a social relationship among men, dads' group members collectively challenge conventional expectations for fathering, masculinity, and caregiving. They actively support each other and exhibit vulnerability by questioning their parenting, confronting stigma they experience as caregivers, and resisting stereotypes of men and fathers. In other ways, however, dads' group members parent inside current norms, embracing conventional tenets of American masculinity that create barriers to fathers' caregiving. Dads' group members rely on essential and economic explanations for their decisions to foreground their identities as parents (both at home and working, part- to full-time). They hold essential understandings of parenting and gender alongside corresponding beliefs about fathers' fundamental differences from mothers in their parenting ideologies and practices. Even among this group of engaged care providers, dads' group members and their spouses were conflicted over whether men and boys should provide care more broadly. Their ambivalence stemmed from essential beliefs about men's predatory sexual behaviors that rendered men's caregiving problematic while simultaneously explaining its perversion and absence, a trope I also found among the Oakwood babysitting co-op members' husbands. Paradoxically, some of the commonalities I saw across men's narratives, in particular their embrace of negative stereotypes surrounding men's caregiving, simultaneously undermine dads' group scope and possibilities for care.

Despite acknowledging variation in masculinity, even in a group of men who foreground providing care, many participants I interviewed embraced stereotypes that men or boys providing care is atypical. For example, when I asked dads' group members if they trusted men or boys as caregivers for their kids, including men from their own dads' group, a majority said yes (62 percent), so long as the men or boys were well-known. However, a majority (52 percent) also expressed skepticism and worry over men and boys as care providers. Many responded with stereotypes—that seeing men or boys provide care is atypical. As Bryson explains, "I grew up babysitting kids . . . which is also sort of an odd thing to find like, you know, a high school boy watching kids. . . . like you don't see that go on very often either. It's usually like, you know, the baby-sitters club kind of deal. It's all made up of girls, that kind of thing." Alexander, a forty-four-year-old white healthcare technician employed part-time, considers scenarios in which he would feel comfortable hiring a boy to babysit his only child and those in which he might not:

It would be more important to me . . . if it's the son of a co-worker. And they are like "hey, you know, if you ever need a babysitter . . . my son is off for the summer. And you know his [mom], and [the] son could come over and he is looking for extra money." Saying [that would make me] . . . more comfortable with them. . . . [if] I call like a babysitter service . . . I would be more likely to go with the girl. I might, because I have a daughter and just because I think they would relate better. They should have more fun with the girl babysitter. And I don't know . . . if I have a son, I will be more likely to—I wanna say that it will be okay to think of a male babysitter—just because, again they will be more comfortable, have more fun together. It's hard to say because that's not something that I had to worry about. I certainly wouldn't disqualify somebody just based on the fact that they were male, and I don't think I would just naturally gravitate more towards a female just because they're more nurturing or because . . . [of] any of . . . the traditional . . . reasons why girls more often . . . fill that role.

Alexander's halting description reveals his uncertainty over whether he would hire a male babysitter; he stopped short of embracing the idea completely.

Dads' group members often rely on essential explanations of gender and care. Jacob argued that differences between dads and moms were due to evolution. "Oh, I mean, I think it's a natural dichotomy that the men are . . . aggressive. . . . I mean males' roles within primate groups, with the lions, . . . are predators. So, I don't know if that can necessarily shift, just because we haven't evolved. . . . Men do the protecting. They also do the most harm on the opposite end, you know, invading tribes, invading countries, you know, they historically rape and pillage. . . . I just don't know if it's . . . something that's evolutionary ingrained." Use of the word "predator" borrows from the metaphor of predator and prey from the animal kingdom in which women and children are cast as prey. Research suggests there are problematic outcomes in the use of these "metaphors [that] increase men's propensity for accepting sexual violence" (Block and Burkley 2019, 274). Drawing on evolutionary arguments to understand the base attributes of masculinity could be seen as distancing men from being fully accountable for transgressions committed today. When dads' group members and spouses use essential arguments to describe men broadly, they foster contradictions between men as connected care providers and men as disconnected and potentially too hazardous for caregiving.

Despite obvious normative patterns, there is something else lurking behind participants' responses about gender and care—namely, that the men have concerns about the content and risks associated with men's and boys' carework. Men like Paul decided, based on their lived experiences, that gender and safety were intertwined. "You know, I'm a father of a [young] girl. So, trust and safety . . . stick out to me because my mom, when she was a kid, she was assaulted . . . by a man. So, she . . . raised me to always be aware that you need to be safety first with little girls." Benjamin qualifies his concerns about men or boys providing care: "Because when you have a kid, you have to trust some of your instincts and some of them are just sort of prejudices. You are much more hardcore about indulging your hardcore prejudices if you are protecting a child. And even if it was unfair, I would say, any mom who gets a weird vibe from some man who is taking care of their kid should validate that and not ignore it." In both examples, the men share concerns over the safety of men and boys providing care.

Participants root their concerns over men's sexual violence in news reporting, crime statistics, and Catholic Church clergy sex abuse cases. As Jackson explains, "You know, looking at statistics, it is a fact that women are overwhelmingly the victims . . . the men are overwhelmingly the predators. . . . It is very far [from] the norm for a guy to be like, 'Yeah I'll watch all these kids.' [Those men are rightly met with] suspicion. . . . We have the studies now showing that kids are . . . most likely to be traumatized in various ways by somebody the family trusts. . . . Men are the overwhelming predators. [It makes sense for parents to think], I've never met this guy. I've only met this guy twice or three times. And I know the Catholic Church scandals come out and, you know, things like that." Likewise, Jacob argues that even general knowledge of crime statistics provided adequate evidence for concern over men as caregivers: "I don't know the stats on men, but men overwhelmingly are the most sexually deviant predators, you could say within the crime rate. Yeah, and I mean, for little girls, I know it's . . . something as high, like one in five . . . women will be sexually assaulted and you know [who] the perpetrator is going to [be] whether it's 90 percent, 95 percent, maybe even higher; it's going to be men. . . . But yeah, I'd probably be most likely to let a mom versus a man [babysit my child]." Men's use of reporting and crime statistics provides a way to further justify their perspective that men may not be fit for carework. Men's exclusion of other men from caregiving is based on normative assumptions about men's propensity for toxic masculinity and also their desire to protect their children. Men's descriptions of these issues enables them to position themselves as not being part of the problem, and it also exposes their fears.

Men's concern over other men's caregiving is not only directed at other men but also expressed about their own reputations—that they might be blamed for misconduct. Four dads' group respondents reported fears that they themselves or their spouses would be mistrusted or erroneously accused of wrongdoing. Paul elaborates, "You're not going to leave your kids alone with men. . . . [At] events with my kids [with] predominantly women . . . I felt very like I'm the bearded predator in the corner. Like, 'hey, you know, that's my kid. I swear I brought a kid here. I'm not just sitting and watching your kids!' . . . because I generally like to joke around with people . . . and I try that and [moms are] very standoffish, like I'm hitting on them . . . I'm like, '. . . [it] feels awkward being [here] alone and you guys are kind of looking at me like I'm a weirdo.' . . . If you look at . . . the crime statistics it's fair to be weary of, you know, random white guys . . . that's not an unfair thing to feel . . . if you're paying attention . . . you notice that the women or the mothers are kind of looking at you that way."

Similarly, Anita, a thirty-six-year-old white physician and mother of three, expresses worry that her husband might be targeted with allegations of misconduct: "But there's always this like same kind of fear . . . what if someone were to make an accusation? You know, if someone were to accuse a woman of improper behavior, it would require a great deal more evidence to make people believe that that could be true, then would be necessary if they made an accusation like that against [my husband]. Because our society has this idea that men alone with children might have impure motives. So, I don't know how to fix that. I mean, I think as parents that we just need to be mindful of making sure that we know the people that are taking care of our children. Because it is the case that that kind of behavior is more likely to come from a man, but it's also, like I said, . . . a man is more likely to be considered guilty until proven innocent in that case. Which is kind of a scary thing to think about." The challenges men (and their wives) have navigating their concerns over assumptions of men's propensity for sexual misconduct extend to both public and private settings. Randall tells a story about the rules at his church that limited men's solo caregiving: "I don't want to say it's funny but at the church we used to go to, I have no problem volunteering . . . for kids' care. . . . I was a little set back that one of the ladies made a comment that guys can't be alone in the room with the kids. There has to be a woman there too. And at first, I was a little bit offended by that, but I guess that's the way things go."

Concerns over men's intentions spill over and inhibit not just respite care but broader communities of care, which might not be separated by gender but include fathers as well as mothers within the same groups. As Benjamin explains, nursing mothers should be concerned that men might sexualize the sight of their breasts: "Breastfeeding, . . . you got to feel comfortable around the other dads if you are going to do that . . . and then if you could glimpse inside that dads' mind . . . some dads are still getting excited for a glimpse of someone's boob . . . it is just the way it works, so if you knew that, you would feel gross." LLL has long challenged women's worries that public breastfeeding will be titillating to men. They have urged women to "breastfeed in public places," reflect on their feelings about "discretion," and promote normalizing practices.[5] Nevertheless, Benjamin's comments align with typical expectations for men, particularly in groups. As sociologist Sharon Bird explains, "Among the forms of competitions in which men engage are those that involve the objectification of women" (1996, 128). While mothers might rightly find uninvited desire and objectification unwelcome and unwanted, it is telling how easily desire is cast as "gross."

The assumption of men's inappropriate behaviors is central to essentialist thinking about men and masculinity. Despite coming from different perspectives, across the interviews dads' group members, their spouses, and babysitting co-op members' spouses commonly link masculinity, amplified (and inappropriate) sexuality, and presumptions of men as predators—as part of broader cultural stereotypes and their own deeply held beliefs. In effect, these assumptions render men's caregiving problematic while they simultaneously rationalize its absence.

Babysitting co-op members' husbands also expressed fears and suspicions about men's caregiving. Two men questioned whether they would ever feel comfortable having their kids watched by one of the co-op member's husbands. As Travis, a thirty-eight-year-old white father of two employed in industry, says, "If I knew them, yeah. I'd feel uncomfortable leaving my little daughter with a dude I've never met. . . . There's some line that you cross somewhere, that it's odd. . . . Eventually there's a creepy factor to it. . . . [Laughs] That sounds horrible, doesn't it? . . . It sounds awful, but that's exactly how I see it; it's odd. . . . It's just the norms." Similarly, Jake responds with a pause, "Realistically, I . . .

would not be terribly comfortable with a father showing up to babysit my kids unless I really, really, knew him well. . . . One, it seems odd and out of place. Two, [pause] look, it's probably unfair to say it as a dad, but do I want some guy I don't really know putting my six-year-old [daughter] to bed? . . . I'm not comfortable with that, but for some reason I'm more comfortable with a mother because they're less apt to be creepy, predatory, [laughs] whatever. . . . You don't read a lot of articles about mothers preying on little kids. You read a lot of articles about men preying on little kids [laughs]." Like the dads' group members, the babysitting co-op fathers link masculinity, caregiving, and predatory behavior together. Tapping into normative understandings about gender, the men's constructions of masculinity fit within a complex framework of hegemonic masculinity, including "[men] engaging in toxic practices" (Connell and Messerschmidt 2005, 840). These actions make men's caregiving less likely while simultaneously explaining its absence (and perversion). In these cases, we see how incomplete and contradictory changing gender ideologies can be.

Conclusion

Parenting groups provide considerable resources to parents including material goods, like food, clothes, and financial resources for their children's schools. They also provide services like respite care, a care provision that is rarely named or acknowledged as such. Resources are distributed locally and at the state and national levels. Though some of the nationwide groups partner with corporations, many also operate independently. Given the organization of the PTA, LLL, City Dads, local dads' groups, and the babysitting co-op, each of these groups often reflects a narrower circulation of these resources due to the prevailing group organization and decision-making. Beyond specific charity events, like those sponsored by City Dads Group, the groups' regularly collected goods and services tend to benefit only those who are affiliated. In effect, the groups engage in opportunity hoarding that limits resources to those with the means to access them due to their flexible employment, geographic location, friendship network, and other mechanisms that restrict group membership.

Parenting communities expose the social problem of American individualism, in terms of both its myths and its realities. Families do not exist in isolation; nevertheless, they often get framed as independent entities. The web of community organizations that connect families to a care infrastructure do so in ways that can be seemingly disconnected. Outcomes could be different if care was organized in a less ad hoc way. We already know that families cannot meet their care needs on their own; we already know that parents rely on others in their extended families and nonfamilial networks to make care ends meet. Isolated thinking misses the opportunity to think about carework needs collectively. The groups I studied focused most often on more privileged parents with children who are not behaviorally, socially, or mobility challenged. As such, some of the parents most in need of networks of care, like disabled parents and parents of disabled children, are largely omitted from consideration by parent groups. The remote meetings example in chapter 2 is a case in point—the parent groups I studied did not prioritize how remote meeting access might help disabled persons participate before the pandemic brought so many aspects of life online. Parent groups' exclusion of disabled persons is rooted in ableism that is consistent with ableism in the broader culture. If parent groups can look at the intersecting needs of caregivers, that would make a more comprehensive approach possible. It could also make other related inequalities identifiable, like the ways in which carework is not evenly divided and disproportionately falls on women. Bridging state, community, and market-based support for parents and their children, parent groups provide evidence of the powerful contributions individuals and groups can make when they team up. However, the deeply gendered and idiosyncratic ways in which parent groups understand and identify care creates obstacles to parent groups' broader, more equitable, and sustainable care practices.

Participation in parenting groups is gendered and disproportionately includes women. Through an examination of interviews with both the dads' groups and babysitting coop members' husbands, we hear explanations for men's caregiving inequalities. The men I interviewed often held essential understandings of parenting and gender and corresponding beliefs about fathers' fundamental differences from mothers in their parenting ideologies and practices. These views act as a driving force behind their understandings of caregiving and parental group formation, fostering group separation by promoting essential gender differences as a central aspect of their comradery. These men are also often suspicious of other men's caregiving and see the cultural specter of men's sexual predation. Recognizing how men view other men's caregiving suggests how challenging it is to upend conventional ideologies.

Fathers' ideology of gender difference in some ways serves them—it limits their need to provide direct care for children beyond their own. Relatedly, these beliefs bolster an ideology of intensive mothering that increases mother's work. In other ways, men's ideology of fathers' differences from mothers, concerns over men as caregivers, and men's predatory tendencies undermine dads' group members' attempts to build membership and dismantle negative stereotypes of fathers and men. Continued gender stereotyping and essentialist thinking are thorny to unearth and continue to present obstacles to fostering greater equity in care. The *State of the Worlds' Fathers 2019* report identifies restrictive gender norms as a major barrier to men's involvement in carework. As the authors point out, one of the possible "catalysts for change" is to "promote men's allyship for gender equity." Yet, even among well-positioned, well-resourced, and well-intentioned possible allies, change presents real challenges. If we hope to understand the possibilities for men's caregiving, we need to examine where change is happening, as well as where it is not. We also need to consider the relationship between ideology and practice; changing ideology can precede a change in practice and vice versa. The next chapter addresses these issues through the parenting groups' advocacy—how they fight to change understandings and access.

5

Parenting Groups as Agents and Opponents of Social Change

Parent groups produce social action and public advocacy when they broaden gender norms, embrace economic equality, confront racism, and address ableism to challenge the status quo within and beyond their organizations. Among the most vulnerable groups to "discrimination and social exclusion" are parents and children with disabilities. Federal legislation like the Rehabilitation Act of 1973, the Americans with Disabilities Act (ADA) of 1990, and the Individuals with Disabilities Education Act (IDEA) of 2004 adopt a social model of disability that focuses on structural accessibility and demonstrates a "policy commitment to the social inclusion of people with disabilities." Though designed to provide protections against discrimination, the enactment of these laws has been "necessary, but not sufficient, for major institutional change" (Scott 2000, 216, 222). For parents and children with disabilities, navigating schools can be particularly challenging.

Over the past few decades, the PTA has issued statements, resolutions, and guidance to protect the rights and inclusion of people with disabilities (National PTA n.d.-j, n.d.-u). As part of this work, the PTA has developed and helped to implement special education PTAs (SEPTAs) (National PTA n.d.-w). In conjunction with state and local PTAs, parents can develop these groups as a committee within a school's PTA or as a district-wide SEPTA that is overarching and involves multiple schools. The idea behind SEPTA is to bring together parents of children with disabilities, better position them to address accessibility issues in their schools, and support their needs as parents. One year after the ADA, parents in New Rochelle, New York, "revived" their SEPTA to "[provide] emotional support to parents, [help] them understand their children's rights and the services available and [work] to erase some of the stigma that the children may feel" (Arnow 1991). As the PTA website explains, "One major benefit of a SEPTA is to offer support to other parents who have similar circumstances. Some SEPTA units have a business meeting then adjourn and offer a parent support time off the record. Sometimes parents like to speak on issues that concern their children and just listening to them can help other caretakers. During the support time, for instance, caretakers can learn about doctors and services that are a positive experience for their child such as a place to take your child for a haircut that is not stressful and a place of business that is understanding and patient" (National PTA n.d.-w). The PTA plan for these groups enables parents to gather information, receive support, and better navigate a complex process across institutions—local businesses, state and local government, health and social services, and schools—again providing and connecting care infrastructure. As stated on the website, advocacy is central to the PTA plan for these groups: "SEPTAs sponsor workshops and speakers on topics that can help better advocate for exceptional children and topics that can help parents better understand aspects of special needs and many diagnoses. Many SEPTAs start out with a general topic like understanding your child's IEP or 504 plan, the rights of your special needs child, and the parent's rights under IDEA" (National PTA n.d.-w). By facilitating and supporting groups with an "organizational structure, resources, and the opportunity to be a collective voice for their child and for all children," the PTA integrates mechanisms for collective care.

The PTA also promotes advocacy for persons with disabilities through national grants available to local PTAs. In 2022, the national PTA awarded the Swanson Elementary School (Arvada, Colorado) PTA with a diversity, equity, and inclusion (DEI) grant. The Swanson PTA used their funding to promote autism advocacy for families with children on the spectrum. In recognition of their work, the PTA website explains, "Understanding that meaningful DEI work starts with listening, the [Swanson] PTA surveyed families and educators of students with autism spectrum disorder (ASD) to determine how to create a more welcoming environment. They received two main pieces of feedback. First, there needs to be greater awareness of the autistic students within Swanson's community. Despite the fact that Swanson houses an autism center and a sizable population of students with ASD many families don't know that the classroom exists. Second the families and educators wanted PTA and school leaders to be more intentional and purposeful in including the ASD community in events and programming" (Colorado PTA 2022). By funding and showcasing the Swanson PTA, the National PTAs demonstrates its commitment to providing greater inclusion, awareness, and access alongside better information from data gathering.

As the PTA examples illustrate, parent groups contribute greatly to the North American care infrastructure, though their work is not recognized as such. Parent groups provide care and advocacy that is multifaceted, is provided for parents, facilitates parents' care and advocacy on behalf of their children, and enables parents' collective care within their organizations and broader communities. Parenting groups have much to teach us about how parenting organizations can expand and contract care access through political action. Though neither care nor parenting groups are typically seen as political, understanding their political relevance enables us "to think about care differently" and "situate it differently as an integral moral and political concept" (Tronto 1993, 124). In so doing, we can understand why a parenting group like the PTA is described as an "advocacy group" (Haar 2002, 5–6), a vehicle for "club activism," and an established part of community-based care infrastructure (Ladd-Taylor 1994, 59).

Existing parent groups, like the PTA, can and do provide networks of care for many parents. Looking at examples that expand that care on the local and national levels provides a chance to consider whether such care can be scaled up to better address parental care needs on an even larger magnitude. By focusing on parenting groups' advocacy to address social problems and spark organizational change, I examine what I call "strategic parenting," or parenting groups' individual and collective efforts to advocate for resources and social change. This concept is like Litt's (2004) notion of "advocacy carework," which centers on securing social service resources on an individual level. Strategic parenting is an approach for addressing inequalities parent to parent, by incorporating a broader range of political actions deployed inside and outside of groups. Parenting groups in the United States have a long history of advocating for broader access to resources and political causes. Advocacy examples include past and contemporary examples drawn from the national groups I studied: the MOMS Club International, City Dads Group, LLL, and PTA. Each of these groups has a lengthy history. Remember, the PTA began more than one hundred twenty-five years ago, LLL started nearly seventy years ago, MOMS Club was founded almost forty years ago, and City Dads Group was formed more than fifteen years ago. Their actions take a variety of forms. Run by leaders and members mobilized to address various issues, these groups act as agents of both progressive and reactionary goals. As such, they show both the opportunities for providing better care for parental caregivers through existing parenting groups as well as their limitations.

Early PTA Child and Family Advocacy

Through their organization, established presence, and lengthy membership lists, national parenting groups are in a strategic position to raise awareness about important social issues. PTA advocacy on behalf of children and parents dates back to the turn of the past century (1902–1920) when they promoted strategic parenting campaigns around the health of families. These campaigns include the abolition of child labor and the promotion of children's nutrition. Decades before child labor laws were enacted in the Fair Labor Standards Act of 1938, both the predominately white PTA and Black National Congress of Colored Parents and Teachers (NCCPT) worked toward change. The PTA organized against the use of child labor in the early 1920s and went "on record as actively in favor of a legislative, law-enforcement and child-welfare program which will get ... children back into schools, protect their health and restore them to the heritage of their childhood." Their efforts were not realized within the first decade of the century, and the group lobbied again in the early 1930s through "state branches ... for a basic minimum age of 16 for employment, a higher minimum age for employment in hazardous occupations, and minimum wage provisions for minors" (National PTA 1997, 42). Woyshner explains, "The NCCPT did not have the numerical or political force on its own to rally its members around legislation, which was one of the reasons black educational leaders remained as a segregated branch of the PTA for so long.... However, the NCCPT did not just publicize the white PTA's legislative agenda verbatim but amended each proposal, increasing its appeal to disenfranchised citizens and working to further racial equality" (2009, 131). Supporting parents' ability to protect their children's education, prohibit unsafe labor conditions, and secure minimum work renumeration, the PTA and NCCPT's advocacy helped bring about important social change.

Like child labor, school lunch was a galvanizing issue that brought white PTA and Black NCCPT members together in a 1950 Tuskegee meeting. Both groups were instrumental in advocating for kids' nutrition and access to school lunches through local actions and advocacy for federal funding. In the decade leading up to the School Lunch Act, the PTA was the only organization invited to participate in the National Cooperating Committee on School Lunches convened by the federal government. Locally, PTA members were instrumental in creating gardens and "serving lunches nationally" in "4,630 of the 40,309 schools serving lunches" nationwide (Woyshner 2009, 242). *Our National Family*, the NCCPT's publication, galvanized members through articles like "School Lunch Program Facing Crisis," urging members of "each unit to contact [their] representative in congress concerning saving the school lunch program with adequate appropriation," a program that "has meant much to our children, especially in Southern rural areas and in cities where many mothers go out to work" (*Our National Family* 1948, 22). The NCCPT "created its own network of state 'Health Chairmen,' who helped members sponsor health clinics and lunch programs" (*Our National Family* 1948, 136). Support for the School Lunch Act, passed in 1946, was the culmination of these organizing efforts led by the PTA and NCCPT (Woyshner 2009). School lunch does more than provide nutrition to children. Advocating for school lunches provides a way for parent groups to address hunger and food insecurity. These actions also offset the money and time for families (in particular mothers) that no longer have to plan, shop, purchase, and prepare school lunches for their children. These examples of early parent group advocacy demonstrate the range of issues tackled by parent groups.

Contemporary Parenting Group Advocacy

Fatherhood, Ideology, and Corporate Partnerships

City Dads Group was designed to advocate for dads. Lance Somerfeld and Matt Schneider founded the City Dads Group in 2013 to connect fathers with each other, offering access to online resources, parenting advice, and ways to meet and connect with other fathers face-to-face.[1] The group's founders focused on parents' inequalities and positioned the issue as gendered. As the City Dads Group website claims, "It's a mom, mom, mom, mom world of parenting. Mom-centric 'parenting' publications, blogs and advertisements. 'Mommy & Me' classes. Mom's Night Out parties. The 'maternal instinct' apparently needs lots of advice, support and nurturing from the media and society. So, what about dads?"[2] These remarks reflect tensions over who is included or excluded by parenting groups and who has access to power and resources. According to the City Dads Group founders, as dads "they often found themselves isolated. They'd be the only fathers at kiddie exercise or crafts classes, shunned by moms' groups, and ignored at the playground simply because of their gender." Similar sentiments were expressed in my interviews with City Dads Group leaders on the local level. Randall underscores the importance of prioritizing access for fathers to a dads-only group: "It's just a dads' group, you know, because there's mom groups everywhere . . . it's nice to have, you know, like dads . . . just to be with [dads], just like mindedness and like talking about different stuff." None of the men I interviewed claimed that any moms' groups specifically barred men from joining. Instead, they often pointed to their feelings of exclusion.

Fathering, like masculinity, is not fixed in men; rather, it is performed and shaped by the circumstances through which it is produced. Masculinity is often constructed as a binary concept in opposition to femininity, and fatherhood is considered part of dichotomous parenthood and normatively understood in opposition to motherhood. Of particular importance is "the extent to which adult masculinity is built on over-reactions to femininity, and the connection of the making of masculinity and the subordination of women" (Connell 1995, 11). Research suggests decades of contradictory cultural expectations for fathers. So when men provide care, it is often seen as contributing to changes in fatherhood. Sociologist Ralph LaRossa's historical study of fatherhood in the early twentieth century points out important myths. Contrary to popular beliefs, men of the 1920s and 1930s engaged in carework we mistakenly see today as new: "The belief, for example, that it is only in recent years that fathers have given any thought to the meaning of fatherhood, let alone spent any serious time with their children, creates a surreal world where almost anything fathers do in the way of childcare is prized" (LaRossa 1997, 200). Seeing contemporary fatherhood through this perspective enables us to better understand current contradictions and just how well established they are.

Locally, the dads' groups leaders I spoke with had contradictory views on politics and said they often shied away from political conversations. So although they want to build father's groups and engage in advocacy, they approach political differences with some apprehension. As a western dads' group leader, Jackson, explains, "I wanna keep politics far away from the Dads' Group because I know dang well, we have people on each end of the spectrum and, you know, everybody's in the middle, right, to some degree unless you're wearing a hood or a mask. You know, those are the psychos. But yeah, we're all in the middle but, you know, we can divide really easy if it gets brought up. So, I just want to keep the politics out of it. And as far as gender politics, I'd like to just have equality, you know, like, yeah, you have a dads' group for dads where we can talk about guy stuff and the husband stuff, you know?" Jackson's oversimplification is apparent when he denies that the mainstream middle includes all non-"psychos" who disavow the KKK but still "divide really easy" and equates gender equality with the presence of dads' groups. When asked about whether his group challenged cultural stereotypes about fatherhood, he offers critiques but still favors a hands-off approach toward social change: "I think that is good that we can get the nincompoop dad out of the public consciousness. . . . *The Simpsons* ruined a whole generation, you know, the [*Family*] *Guy* doesn't help either and *Married . . . with Children*. . . . As far as political stuff like that, I think I don't wanna take a direct approach to it. I just wanna be the consistent, constant, mature, steady, educated force that just continues on, right? Because if I . . . I think if we start getting into . . . the temporary hot-button topics then that's what we're gonna just shift to and then we got to find the next hot-button topic to advocate for, and then that's who we become." Similarly, as an East Coast dads' group leader, Randall, explains, in his group "we've talked about like stuff that's going on in the news and, you know, sports. . . . I don't really get into politics because . . . a lot of times people can't have the conversation . . . if they get all up in arms and offended and different kinds of things. So, I . . . stayed away from that . . . I'm not trying to make it a political group, but, um, yeah, I mean we have kind of." In part, of course, abstaining from "hot button" political conversations is de facto taking a position in support of the status quo. While the groups are still able to advocate for change, this kind of leadership perspective supports efforts that have widespread appeal.

Despite their awareness about the likely ideological differences in their groups, dads' group members are clear about the issues that matter. For example, Randall explains that his group is "trying to promote . . . fatherhood and . . . understanding" for dads, but missing key resources. Rhetorically he quips, "Like . . . why the hell there are no changing tables in the men's room . . . what's that about?" The lack of changing tables was apparent during a dads' group lunch he organized in which "four or five people came . . . and there was no . . . changing table in the bathroom and . . . I changed them on . . . the ledge above the toilet." These feelings of marginalization alongside a lack of resources have led national dads' groups to band together around key issues. One that has particularly energized dads involves negative stereotypes around fatherhood.

Over the past decade, the City Dads Group has mobilized hundreds of fathers to promote political initiatives related to men's health, recognition, and respect as fathers. Dads' groups have campaigned against negative "dadvertising" to address dumb dad tropes. They have also worked to expand access to changing tables in men's restrooms (D'Arcy 2012a, 2012b; Seligson 2013). They have worked in partnership with the national conference Dad 2.0 (modeled after Mom 2.0), a forum that began in 2012 to bring together "marketers, social media leaders, blogging parents and regular dads gather to discuss modern fatherhood" (City Dads Group 2020). At the Dad 2.0 Summit, the focus is entrepreneurial, promoting bloggers, social influencers, and dads' online presence as well as corporate activism—shaping the depiction of fathers in the promotion of products. Dad 2.0 is sponsored by brands like Dove Men+Care that contribute by offsetting the cost of tickets for attendees, advertising during conference events, and providing free products and related services, like shaves and haircuts (Steinmetz 2015; Chaitin 2016). Through these ongoing relationships, members have challenged corporate advertising to reflect the changing image of contemporary fatherhood—from slapstick bumbling dad to taken seriously skilled dad (Seligson 2013). Dad 2.0 and City Dads Group have cosponsored events like a National Dad's Day Out to "get fathers together outside" (City Dads Group 2021). The groundwork for corporate partnerships began in response to corporate advertising gone wrong.

In 2012, Huggies released a commercial that opens with mothers stocking household shelves with box after box of diapers. The commercial then cuts to those same mothers handing off their babies to their fathers. The ad's narrator says, "To prove Huggies diapers and wipes can handle anything, we put them to the toughest test imaginable: Dads, alone with their babies, in one house, for five days." On their Facebook page, Huggies asked readers to "nominate a dad. Hand him some [Huggies] diapers and wipes and watch the fun. Tell us how it went on Facebook!" (Meljax 2014). Numerous critiques resulted, including one dad who began a Change.org petition that received over thirteen hundred signatures, titled "We're Dads, Huggies. Not Dummies" (Change.org. 2012). Dads' group criticism of the Huggies campaign continued into the 2013 Dad 2.0 Summit, to which Huggies sent a representative to talk with participants and better understand where the ad campaign went wrong. Huggies also issued an apology on their Facebook page and promised to change their ad. A spokesman for Kimberly-Clark, the parent company, said, "We have learned that our intended message did not come through and we have made changes."

The expectation of father's incompetence is part of a normative trope. Mainstream media is full of failed fathers, from the bumbling Homer Simpson to the myriad of commercial advertisements featuring inept dads. Babysitting co-op members' husbands also confront these stereotypes, as Jake explains: "I hear that all the time—moms who make comments about their spouses not having the first idea of how to care for their kids. . . . Just in general, among [the] well-educated, well to do. As a dad, that's not something I haven't had aimed at me before. Moms, who assume I, because I'm the dad, have no idea how to take care of the kids! Which is utter nonsense! I take care of them all the time! I've been the target of comments like that all the time." When I asked Jake why these stereotypes exist, his explanation fell into two parts: "One, is some degree of traditional roles. . . . that stuff is still out there. And two, there are some dads out there who are clueless; I know them!" Jake's contradictory refusal and embrace of these stereotypes illustrates their power. As we saw from the mom's use of these stereotypes in chapter 4, distrust of men's caregiving also reinforces mothers' particular skills. Despite the costs to men of being negatively stereotyped, these characterizations also have the tangible benefit of decreasing men's workloads.

Perhaps due to the pervasiveness of these stereotypes, alongside corporations' willingness to pull adds and offer apologies as well as access to deep pockets, City Dads Group continues to prioritize corporate relationships, including with Huggies. The City Dads website lists twenty-five corporate brand partnerships, including Dove, Plum Organics, and BabyBjörn (City Dads Group n.d.-b). Dads' group members engaged in these partnerships around the country, as midwestern dads' group leader Bryson explains: "They've partnered with . . . Dove Men Plus Care and Pampers, and Plum Organics is a sponsor there. So they, they're constantly working with those groups in the bigger cities to host events, with Plum Organics or with Dove Men Plus Care, like [in] Chicago and San Francisco and New York and Charlotte and . . . the more established City Dads Groups . . . they're always doing work with that and activism. . . . I think it's like Pampers for [those who are] less fortunate or . . . they'll [distribute] Plum Organic to kids . . . go to the shelters and you know, where people are with their kids. . . . They'll do some work at soup kitchens and stuff." In 2017, City Dads chapters in Boston, Chicago, and Las Vegas partnered with Huggies' "No Baby Unhugged" program to supply diapers to families in need. The program both supports access to diapers and, playing on the word "hug," emphasizes the importance of skin-to-skin contact for newborns (Huggies n.d.). The Boston and Chicago chapter members volunteered to compile Huggies diapers into bags distributed by the nonprofit organization Cradles to Crayons. In Las Vegas, local City Dads Group members donated Huggies to the Las Vegas Diaper Bank (Zelenka 2017).

In 2019, City Dads collaborated with another large U.S. disposable diaper manufacturer, Pampers, to install five thousand men's restroom changing tables in the "US and Canada by 2021." Koala Kare provided the changing tables. In an interview about the initiative, City Dads Group cofounder Lance Somerfeld said, "We [are] extremely proud of this new City Dads Group partnership with Pampers and Koala Care because it gives [us] a change to make a positive impact on our communities and help other fathers who are committed to sharing the work as much as the fun of being an active, involved parent" (City Dads Group 2019).

How do we understand these advocacy actions? Corporate partners can do wrong, as Huggies did. Opposition to Huggies' high-profile mistake of stereotyping fathers' incompetence for profit was covered in the *Washington Post* and the *New York Times* (D'Arcy 2012a, 2012b; Seligson 2013). However, corporate partnerships also provide financial and media opportunities. The distribution of diapers and changing tables and the opportunity to raise awareness of fathers' needs provide meaningful resources and visibility. Corporate partnerships also have limitations. Driven by profit, the corporations' orientation and commitment differ from those of parenting groups that seek to provide and increase parental care. Corporations engage in what the Care Collective has called "carewashing" (Chatzidakis et al. 2020). There is a long history of similar corporate social and environmental attempts to "cleanse" themselves of wrongdoing, like greenwashing (in which corporate polluters promote environmentalism). This opportunistic use of care conceals past wrongs and is driven by profit. It commodifies care to sell products. For example, in 2019 Huggies got attention for featuring dads on their diaper boxes for the very first time. The company specifically designed their marketing to target fathers, as Huggies' North American brand director Kristine Rhode explained: "When you think about the important role that dads have in the family today and how that continues to grow, we wanted to make sure they were equally celebrated" (Tyko 2019). For a company that began in 1978, waiting over forty years to "equally celebrate" dads seems like a very long time. Despite mixed experiences, all of the national parent groups I studied engaged in corporate partnerships.

Parent groups see a usefulness in connecting with the broader set of resources corporations provide in advertising their groups and highlighting their work. For example, LLL has pursued at least two corporate partnerships, including a 2007 partnership with MamAmor Dolls, which produces colorful handcrafted dolls designed as sibling gifts and teaching tools. Each wears a dress and a baby in a wrap. Their other partnership is endorsing Joeyband, a company launched in 2012 that produces a "wrap for holding a sleeping baby" (La Leche League International n.d.-a). Joeyband highlights on their website their wrap's "exclusive" "endorsement" from LLL in their website's marketing details. What these parent group corporate relationships all have in common is that they are designed to expand available resources, boost exposure, and increase both buyers and members.

The next advocacy example moves away from corporate relationships that result from many different contributors across businesses as well as parent group leadership and members. It stems from a singular source—one man who in 2012 would almost single-handedly transform LLL's core mission and constituency. Though my research focuses on the United States, I incorporate this case from LLL Canada since it demonstrates how strategic parenting, even from a single member, can create widespread social change with global impact.

LLL's Struggle over Transgender and Nonbinary Inclusion

When Trevor MacDonald, a transgender man from Manitoba, Canada, became pregnant in his late twenties, he did not know whether he would breastfeed his baby. Since Trevor had undergone breast reduction surgery, he anticipated that he could no longer lactate or provide a way for his baby to latch and nurse. His preparations were aligned with formula feeding until he reached out to his friend, Simone, who is an LLL breastfeeding counselor. Simone suggested an LLL text by Diana West that addressed how to "breastfeed after reduction surgery" (2001). Though the book was written for an audience of women and makes no mention of men, transgender persons, or chestfeeding, it provided an invaluable resource for Trevor. Reading West's book made him aware that he might still lactate, opening the possibility for him to breastfeed his child: "Even a small amount of milk could be really valuable to my baby. . . . Breastfeeding is about more than the milk. . . . It can be a relationship too and a whole way of parenting" (CBC News 2015). Ready to advocate on her friend's behalf, Simone approached her coleaders and secured permission for Trevor to attend an LLL meeting.

As a leader, Simone had seen LLL meetings as a safe haven for nursing mothers. She explained to Trevor, "Women come in with their nipples cracked and bleeding. They sob uncontrollably while telling their stories. A La Leche League meeting is often the only place where they are comfortable to breastfeed without covering up. Sometimes even their husbands don't support them"

(MacDonald 2016, 72). Simone understood that Trevor's presence might not be welcome. "She worried that if [Trevor] were present at a meeting, the women there would behave differently. They might hide their breasts, and they might hesitate to discuss their problems openly" (73). Based on these factors, Simone was "undecided about asking the other leaders if [Trevor] could attend the group" (72). Where Simone saw challenges, Trevor and his partner saw exclusion. As Trevor understood LLL philosophy, "peer support is a major factor in breastfeeding success. . . . Except for [him]." Trevor was "surprised, elated, and petrified all at once" to receive word from Simone that he could attend her meeting held in a local church basement (73–74).

Arguably, it was Simone's position as a good friend, an LLL leader, and an advocate that facilitated Trevor's ability to attend his first meeting. Simone was instrumental in securing an agreement from her fellow leaders and encouraging Trevor's attendance. She also helped to run the meeting, so she was a source of support throughout this process. Studying transmen at work, sociologist Kristen Schilt found that transmen were sometimes included as "one of the guys" and actively incorporated into workplaces by management and coworkers. Her study showed how "gender boundaries can shift for individuals—former women can be accepted as men—without making workplace gender trouble and without causing a change to business as usual" (Schilt 2010, 17). Examining Trevor's writings, I wondered whether his story would parallel the one told by Schilt. The inclusion that Trevor sought was facilitated by LLL leaders and participants alike. The question remained whether his access to LLL would prompt only local or broader social change.

Trevor's first meeting was typical of LLL. As he describes, "Over the course of the meeting, people discussed their various nursing challenges and asked each other questions." He spent much of the time listening. After the meeting, he was approached by some of the attendees who told him "how impressed they were by [his] determination to breastfeed and that they hoped it would go well." Trevor describes being "ecstatic at their response"; since he was "initially unsure of whether [he would] even be allowed to attend an LLL meeting as a guy," he "certainly didn't expect to be welcomed with open arms." He credits his first LLL meeting as "the beginning of what became an incredible support system" that enabled him to breastfeed his "baby for his first year of life" (Milk Junkies n.d.). Trevor acknowledges that "without [LLL], I'm sure I would not have been able to have a nursing relationship with my kids" (Curtis 2016). Trevor's devotion to LLL is familiar to anyone who has followed LLL or read other testimonials; it is what compels some participants to become fierce advocates and LLL leaders.[3]

Reflecting on his experience, Trevor sought to become a leader. LLL declined his request. After conferring "with members of the Boards of La Leche League Canada and La Leche League International" the LLLC representative concluded that "policies do preclude men from becoming Leaders." The letter quoted specific LLLC policy: "4.14 MEN AS LEADERS: Since an LLLC Leader is a mother who has breastfed a baby, a man cannot become an LLLC Leader. . . . LLLI's policies and mission statement consistently speak of Leaders as mothers, giving mother-to-mother support." In lieu of providing full access to LLL participation, LLL directors referred Trevor to the "Concept Policy Statements" that delineated the character of the "mother/baby relationship and the father's role." The Concept Policy Statement on the father's role was based on an "understanding of the father's role, not as a mother substitute, but as a unique figure in the baby's life." The letter's author spoke directly to Trevor: "You told me that you do not identify as a mother. You are your baby's father. According to LLL philosophy the roles of mothers and fathers are not interchangeable. I think that this would make it difficult for you to represent LLL philosophy. You acknowledge that some women may not be comfortable working with a male Leader. A Leader needs to be able to help all women interested in breastfeeding. Fathers are able to help in other ways, for example an informed LLL father who is supportive of LLL philosophy might present a fathers' meeting" (Curtis 2016). The possibility of men participating in leadership was against LLL policy and culture, according to the board.

Later in 2012, Fiona Audy, LLL Canada board chair, released her own statement to address the group's rejection of Trevor's leadership request: "This is the first time in La Leche League's 56-year history that we have had an inquiry about leadership from a breastfeeding father, so we have had to consider carefully La Leche League's prerequisites for leadership, policies and the societal issues of gender identity." She attributed the group's decision to the broader organization, La Leche League International, and explained that "as an Affiliate of La Leche League International (LLLI) our foundational philosophy and policies originate with the central division of the organization. Our Leader Accreditation Department (LAD) also operates under LLLI, meaning that LLLC is not able to make a decision on such a complex issue without a process in which all parts of the international organization can participate." Opening up a possibility for change, Audy raised the question Trevor and others were asking: "Should these policies be reconsidered in light of our changing society? Many believe they should; however, it may take considerable time, effort and discussion to reach an international consensus" (Curtis 2016).

In the interim, Trevor continued to pressure for change through a letter-writing campaign started on his blog, MilkJunkies.net, where he provided a template letter, a link to send direct messages to LLL, and contact information for LLLI (*Milk Junkies* 2012b). Trevor's partner, Ian MacDonald, also sent his own letter to LLL as a "stakeholder," which Trevor posted to his blog. Ian wrote that "many have been skeptical of [Trevor MacDonald's] motives and have attacked what they imagine to be 'our way of life.' Transgendered and gay people are excluded from the veneration of family life that is easily afforded to all others. Many people believe that GLBT people should have no reproductive rights to parent and raise children. Perhaps that is starting to change as more people recognize that GLBT people are not separate from humanity in general, in our activities and aspirations." Ian pleaded with LLL to consider his partner's inclusion. He asked, "With that in mind, I am writing to request that you rewrite your policies so as not to exclude any breastfeeding family. Please allow Trevor and other GLBT people to participate in all levels of LLL." He stopped short of calling for full-scale social change, qualifying his request in the context of LGBTQI+ worldwide human rights abuses. He explained that he was focused on change within LLL that may also have a broader impact: "I am not asking LLLI to enter the fray and express an opinion about this worldwide struggle. However, I do believe that by emphasizing gender roles for parents, LLLI unwittingly facilitates discrimination against some breastfeeding families. This includes not only GLBT people, but also other cultural viewpoints and family circumstances" (*Milk Junkies* 2012a).

On April 23, 2014, Diana West, director of media relations for LLLI, issued a press release reversing their previous position. LLL would enable Trevor and other men to become full members, including leaders, within LLL. Her response again called on the organization's rules, "the preamble of La Leche League International bylaws states: 'La Leche League International (LLLI) is a worldwide, educational, nonsectarian, nondiscriminatory service organization which has been incorporated in Illinois as a general not-for-profit cooperation.' As a nondiscriminatory organization . . . applicants for volunteer breastfeeding counselor positions cannot be considered ineligible based on factors such as gender, race, religion, physical disability, marital status, financial or social position, or political or social views." In her statement, she highlighted the role of the group's Board of Directors in reviewing and ultimately changing LLL policy: "As the cultural understanding of gender has expanded, it is now recognized that some men are able to breastfeed. In the spirit of nondiscrimination and with this awareness, La Leche League International has refined the eligibility qualifications for its volunteer breastfeeding counselors to include men who otherwise meet the prerequisites for becoming a volunteer applicant." She concluded, "The expanded eligibility criteria demonstrate La Leche League International's commitment to assisting even more parents breastfeed their babies" (La Leche League International 2014).

LLL added website language that specifically addresses transgender, nonbinary, and adoptive parents who "may choose to breastfeed or chestfeed their babies. You do not need to have given birth to breastfeed or chestfeed, as we can also see in the experiences of those nursing adopted babies" (La Leche League International n.d.-k). LLL's policy notes that volunteer breastfeeding counsellor positions would not be restricted based on sexual orientation or marital status, among other factors (i.e., race, religion, or political views). LLL's decision exemplifies how reproduction is "inevitably bound up with the production of culture" (Ginsburg and Rapp 1995, 2). This change shows LLL's willingness to embrace, at least in writing, "the experiences of non-feminine, non-female chestfeeding parents and to queer reproduction more generally" (Walks 2017, 136).

Nearly two years after he helped transform LLL to "be inclusive of all gender identities," Trevor completed his training and became an LLLC leader. He wrote on his blog, "As a result of the rule change, I was able to apply, and I went through La Leche League Canada's (LLLC) thorough and fantastic training, becoming accredited as a Leader two weeks ago. I am grateful to the Leader who supported me and spent many hours answering my questions, and to the Leader at the Accreditation Department who guided me with patience and kindness and kept me on track" (La Leche League International n.d.-k). Trevor rebuilt his life around chestfeeding and has served not only as a La Leche League leader but also as a researcher and vocal advocate for chestfeeding awareness.[4] LLL's gender diversity is largely due to his activism.

Essentialism and exclusion are significant barriers to overcome, especially when core issues and divisions are left unaddressed organizationally. Trevor's story is one of grassroots social and organizational change. It represents an impressively fast turnaround for a multilevel international organization of this size—to transform LLL's rules in two years' time. This is precisely what makes the LLL decision so important. Their ability, as an organization, is potentially a powerful worldwide force to influence the global ideology and practices around LGBTQI+ inclusion. LLL added website language that specifically addresses transgender, nonbinary, and adoptive parents who "may choose to breastfeed or chestfeed their babies. You do not need to have given birth to breastfeed or chestfeed, as we can also see in the experiences of those nursing adopted babies." LLL has changed its website to include a link under "Breastfeeding Info" that is titled "Support for Transgender & Non-Binary Parents." It introduced LLL readers to the term "chestfeed," by affirming that "LLL supports everyone who wants to breastfeed or chestfeed in reaching their goals" (La Leche League International n.d.-k). In reaffirming their new constituents, LLL signals support for this change in membership. The extent of such change is best understood within the context of the group's gendered carework and contributions to care infrastructure.

An organization's capacity for change is complex and happens on multiple levels through rules, practices, and social norms (Acker 1990, 1992, 2006). While group rules define access for trans and nonbinary parents' chestfeeding, a rule change in and of itself does not necessarily usher in wider social change or inclusion. Taking a closer look at LLL's online materials reveals a story of narrow inclusion. A search for the terms "transgender" and "nonbinary" on the

LLL Canada and U.S. websites produces very few resources.[5] Both websites contain links to their "Joint Statement on the Use of the Term Chestfeeding." The statement is the first to appear in a transgender and nonbinary search on Canada's site. It is embedded with links to other resources on a general "Transgender and Non-Binary Nursing" page on the U.S. site, making it more challenging to locate. The statement provides a "response to some recent discussions on social media" in which the organizations "wish to clarify the use of the term 'chestfeeding'" in LLL Canada and LLL USA communications, materials, and counselling of parents by Leaders." The groups explain that "chestfeeding is a term used by many transmasculine and nonbinary parents to describe how they feed and nurture their children from their bodies. Some prefer the term nursing instead, while others prefer breastfeeding. We use all of these words, and our volunteer Leaders warmly accept whatever term a family chooses for their own experiences." They acknowledge that "including chestfeeding and nursing in our communications is one of the ways La Leche League Canada and La Leche League USA express support for parents of all gender identities and all family structures" (La Leche League USA 2018). While the educational and political intents are clear from these statements, the small amount of material on transgender and nonbinary inclusion suggests a modest shift in focus.

The majority of the LLL USA chestfeeding stories are found through the LLL New Beginnings blog, from which stories are also posted to the LLL website (Breimer 2020). MacDonald continues to be integral to this process, interviewing chestfeeding dads for a post titled "Support and Reassurance in Meeting Chestfeeding Goals" (Breimer 2017b). There is also a repost from U.S. dad Evan Joy's blog titled "My Journey: Non-binary Nursing," in which Joy briefly recounts his positive embodied experience over three and a half years breastfeeding his son (Breimer 2017a). Both stories are from 2017. The site includes another post from 2019 titled "Growing in LLLove: How La Leche League Helped Me Parent My Gender Non-conforming Child" (Breimer 2019). There are also posts about "Induced Lactation and Relactation" (La Leche League USA 2020b) and "Breastfeeding Under Special Circumstances" (La Leche League USA 2020a).

LLL Canada provides conference links and a 2020 Breastfeeding Week speaker list, including a keynote from MacDonald based on his book *Where's the Mother?*; a talk from Amanda Jetté Knox, author of *Love Lives Here: A Story of Thriving in a Transgender Family*; and another for a 2021 health professional conference also featuring Knox.[6] The other links include notice of a meeting in Saskatoon that "welcomes pregnant and chestfeeding transgender parents" and a link for a "Trans Nursing Tip Sheet."[7] The Saskatoon page also integrates inclusive messaging for all meetings: "You are always welcome to attend LLLC meetings before and after you have welcomed your baby. Bring your breastfeeding/chestfeeding questions and concerns, talk about your joys and challenges or come and just listen. Babies and young children are always welcome, and some Groups include father/partners and support persons in some or all of their meetings. All La Leche League Canada Leaders are volunteers. They are experienced breastfeeding/chestfeeding parents who have been accredited to provide up-to-date breastfeeding/chestfeeding information, encouragement and support."[8]

Taken together, both the U.S. and Canadian sites provide limited inclusion for transgender parents across public forums, local meetings, and written resources. The most sustained and detailed information is found in the "Transgender, Transsexual, Genderfluid Tip Sheet" and the "Tip Sheet for Assisting Trans Men," both compiled by MacDonald. The first tip sheet overviews "gender vs. sex," "gender identity vs. sexual orientation," "asking questions," "language," and "common terms." The second sheet, on assisting trans men, provides brief information on "language," but also includes "testosterone use," "top surgery," "chestfeeding goals," "gender dysphoria and chestfeeding," "binding," "providing lactation support," "supporting the decision not to nurse," "LLL meetings," and "other support and resources."[9] As designed, both sheets provide a brief introduction to various relevant topics. Since they are written without any citations, except for links to MacDonald's Facebook group and blog, it is difficult to evaluate whether the source of information was primarily drawn from his knowledge and experiences or whether he consulted other sources.[10] This more detailed reading of the resources suggests MacDonald's unique role in promoting transgender inclusion has been central to this change.

On the LLL International website, the same search for transgender and nonbinary produce the same overview on "Transgender & Non-Binary Parents," including links to several of the U.S. personal narrative posts and six pages available only to LLL leaders (La Leche League International n.d.-k). There is also a repost of an anniversary article by Teresa Pitman, "60 Years Later: Celebrating LLLI," in which Pitman praises the changes LLL has undergone: "The wisdom and insights the Founders put into developing the concepts is impressive. There have, though, been necessary changes over the years. I have, for example, used 'mother' throughout this essay to talk about the person who gave birth to and breastfeeds the baby, as the Founders did. I suspect that the Founders didn't even consider the possibility of transgender men giving birth and breastfeeding— yet today, I'm proud that a transgender man is now an accredited LLL Leader here in Canada." Alongside recognizing change, Pitman acknowledged the difficulties that lay ahead: "The emphasis on the father's role in another concept has also met with challenges, as we work with and accredit Leaders from other types of families: those with two mothers or two fathers, those with a single parent, and those with other situations and different types of support systems" (Pitman 2018).

As Pitman's comment suggests, LLL has faced disagreement over greater diversity. Disputes over LLL's inclusionary practices prompted Marian Thompson, a founding member of LLL, to resign from the Board of Directors in November 2024. LLL New Zealand's website reprinted Thompson's letter in which she explains, "I resigned . . . from LLL itself, an organization that has become a travesty of my original intent. From an organization with the specific Mission of supporting biological women . . . LLL's focus has subtly shifted to include men who, for whatever reason, want to have the experience of breastfeeding. . . . This shift from following the norms of Nature, which is the core of mothering through breastfeeding, to indulging the fantasies of adults, is destroying our organization" (La Leche League New Zealand 2024).[11] In response, an announcement posted to the LLLI website by the Board of Directors eschews Thompson's explanation and frames her departure as a retirement, mentioning that they "respect her decision" and honor her "contributions to creating and sustaining LLL over the past six decades" of service (La Leche League International 2024a).

Greater diversity also prompts questions about LLL's long-standing approach of supporting mother-to-mother counseling, like those Simone considered with Trevor and other LLL leaders. Namely, will mothers want to consult with transgender men about how to breastfeed? In the presence of men, will women reveal their anxieties about breastfeeding in public? While these questions may reflect women's concerns, they also contain embedded gendered assumptions. These questions assume that cross-gender interactions will be less comfortable, less supportive, or less informative. That kind of essentialist thinking supports the status quo. Just because two people share the same gender or anatomy does not mean they will get along or that they will provide the best care. LLL already encourages participants to inquire about the makeup of local meetings to find the best fit. Broadening LLL's base provides recognition and access to a marginalized group—having profound implications both within and beyond LLL for expanding understandings of gender.

What emerges across LLL's website language and images is a mixture of continuity and change. The mother-child dyad is overwhelmingly reflected by organizational materials, the group's logo, and the many images of mothers and nursing infants in their books and on the LLL international, U.S., and Canadian websites (La Leche League International 1963, 1991).[12] All of the LLL websites retain much of their "mothering through breastfeeding" language, and the organizations are still largely run by and made up of women. As outlined in the current *Leader's Handbook*, groups may include a "'diversity statement' to make it clear that participation is open to parents of any religion, ethnicity, work status, race, sexual orientation, etc." (La Leche League International 2022a, 128). Relatedly, developing more inclusivity for chestfeeding families is a strategic goal through 2025 to "establish a more welcoming culture" through group leader training, publications, website, social media, and publications (La Leche League International n.d.-c).

A major change is visible in their central manual's title, *The Womanly Art of Breastfeeding*, which has been updated to *The Art of Breastfeeding* (La Leche League International 2024b). Despite dropping "womanly" from the title, they are not expanding the manual's title to include chestfeeding. Instead, LLL explains in their promotion of the new edition, that their rationale results from current trends and marketing: "LLLI sent an internal survey to all its volunteers around the world. The survey gathered information about how the title is seen. The results of the survey were complemented by market insights given by the publisher. These gave us a strong case for changing the title of the new book to *The Art of Breastfeeding*. This allows us to keep brand continuity while sounding more appealing to the current generation of mothers and parents" (Williams and de Raad 2022). Though they mention LGBTQI+ families within an earlier paragraph on greater inclusivity, they do not explicitly link this change to the book's title. A more detailed reading of the resources suggests MacDonald's unique and central role in promoting transgender inclusion and LLL's challenges navigating these changes.

A charismatic leader can foster social change, as MacDonald demonstrates, and in the beginning of the PTA's economic advocacy, there were also charismatic leaders at the helm. In the next examples, PTA leadership in Evanston and Skokie, Illinois, and Brooklyn, New York, organized a coalition of other parents in pursuit of their vision. In the end, the two groups organized very different campaigns—a short-term program designed to help families in need and a three-year equity agreement that transformed PTA fundraising district-wide.

PTA Equity Actions and Economic Outreach

Well known for their bake sales, PTAs have developed very different modes and models of fundraising and distribution over time. Reporters have emphasized vast PTA inequalities across schools (Miller 2021, Quinlan 2016). Scholars have debated the trajectory of PTA membership and outreach over time (Ladd 1999; Putnam 2000; Skocpol 2003). News media and scholarly research have examined how affluent parents mobilize financial resources and control to benefit their child's school (Calarco 2018; Cutler 2000; Lareau and Muñoz 2012; Murray et al. 2019; Posey-Maddox 2014). As mentioned in chapter 4, journalists have emphasized PTA inequalities with articles like "Bake Sales and Tesla Raffles: The Unequal World of PTA Wealth" from *The Nation* in 2021. In 2022, journalist Chana Joffe-Walt's podcast *Nice White Parents*, a New York Times Serial Production, examined how white affluent parents fundraise and foster inequalities in the PTA at a New York City public school in Brooklyn.

Some PTAs have taken different approaches to inequality and have focused on outreach that addresses broader disparities across schools. The examples that follow provide different approaches to addressing inequality. The first is an equity action from the Evanston and Skokie PTA (PTA Equity Project 2020). The second is the "adopt-a-family" program from the PTA at a school in Brooklyn (Rembert 2020).

The Evanston/Skokie School District 65 is a school district headquartered in Evanston and a small neighboring section of Skokie, north of Chicago. The idea for the PTA Equity Project (PEP) was first proposed at a 2016 PTA Council meeting. Two parents with kids in the Evanston schools, Elisabeth "Biz" Lindsay-Ryan and Suni Kartha, were both serving on the school board. Biz is a self-described equity consultant who had both the knowledge and the skills to promote this work. Nearly one year later, Suni and Biz were instrumental in forming a PTA Equity Committee to pool financial resources into a single PTA fund district-wide and allocate funds equitably across all schools for three years (2020–2023). The core idea for the group was to "better equalize PTA fundraising by reallocating a portion of fundraising dollars from PTAs with the highest revenues to PTAs with lower revenues" (PTA Equity Project 2020). "PEP began by implementing a pilot intervention that divided PTAs into three earning categories: those that earned up to $70 per student, those that earned $71–90 per student and those that earned over $90 per student. The highest were asked to contribute 12%–15% of their earnings so that they could be redistributed to ensure every PTA had at least $65 per student" (National PTA n.d.-s). Several PTAs across the country have recognized inequalities across groups and instituted similar initiatives to address them like those by PTAs in Santa Monica, Malibu, and Palo Alto, California, and Portland, Oregon, with varying degrees of success.[13]

The PTA in Brooklyn created an Adopt-a-Family program in June 2020 in District 15, the same district but different schools from those that Joffe-Walt studied (Rembert 2020). Similar actions have occurred in other parent groups; for example, a Connecticut MOMS Club "adopted" two families for Thanksgiving by providing meals (MOMS Club of Greater Windsor 2022). The PTA initiative was led by two presidents and executive boards, with school administrations providing support; they drew on funds parents contributed through Amazon and a GoFundMe campaign. The plan was to have schools "adopt" other schools' families by creating two "teams"—one donor team that purchased items and a sponsorship team that received them. They provided school supplies and household goods (like diapers, food, and hand soap). The idea was that once the sponsorship team received the support, they would become a donor team for another school. The process by which that could happen was unclear, however.

There are differences in these approaches. PEP, though implemented with a trial period, was designed to transform PTA fundraising allocation. The Adopt-a-Family program was a limited, short-lived, COVID-related initiative. The Adopt-a-Family program took a savior-based approach—designed to help organizers feel better about themselves by providing resources, rather than working to address systemic problems—"Once PTA leaders agreed to share . . . their budgets, PEP led leaders through the data using visual storytelling. PEP leader Fuschia Winston emphasized that using charts to map out the funding disparities was crucial, 'because if you can see [the disparity], you can no longer ignore it.' PEP . . . leaders intentionally earned buy-in from PTA leaders and the larger community and made changes gradually" (National PTA n.d.-s). This makes it closer to mutual aid—built on a common understanding and longer-lasting, collective, and participatory action (Spade 2020). These PTAs are smaller parts of a larger organization, the National PTA, and this context matters. Local actions may appear isolated, however; since the organizations exist as part of a larger national group, they can influence much larger actions. As Skocpol argues, consider "the important role the state and national PTA leaders have traditionally played in connecting local school-support groups to state and national legislative campaigns; and . . . the many bridging ties that state and national PTA congresses fostered among parents and teachers from various local communities and disparate social backgrounds" (2003, 228). Annual PTA estimates range from $425 million to nearly $800 million (Morton 2021). Despite their differences, both parenting group initiatives are attentive to more equitable care practices, and this is where parenting groups make meaningful contributions.

These actions are not isolated. PTA attention to economic inequalities is also happening in other parts of the United States. Beginning in 2015, in Arlington, Virginia, the County Council of PTAs donated resources to create a grant fund that accepts applications for support for things like "books, furniture and field trips." In addition to providing economic outreach, they are also encouraging "inter-school activities so the relationship is not defined by charity" (DeVoe 2021). In Oakland, California, in 2018, a group of parents established Equity Allies for Oakland Unified School District, which works alongside but independently from the local PTAs from which they solicit support (Equity Allies for OUSD n.d.). In 2022, they used an equity index to donate five thousand dollars each to the "highest-stressed schools in the district" and sponsored several local political initiatives to address equity and segregation and to expand youth voting.[14] These kinds of actions both within and alongside PTAs show a range of possibilities for strategic parenting. Alongside possibilities for social change, parent groups' contradictions are among the most vexing challenges to parenting group advocacy. By examining both twentieth- and twenty-first-century examples, we can see how parent groups work against inclusion and in favor of the status quo.

Parenting Group Challenges

PTA, LLL, and Dads' Groups' Partisan Politics

Under Hannah Kent Schoff's leadership, the PTA established activist "committees, called departments . . . to study and advance positions on a wide range of child-related issues: child hygiene, organizational finances, good roads, rural school improvements, international outreach, kindergarten extension, marriage sanctity, and playground and social centers" (National PTA 1997, 44). This diverse set of issues reflects the group's contradictory and sometimes disciplinary actions around gender that may both expand resources and prescribe outcomes (like the sanctity of marriage). Leadership within the PTA has long oscillated between conservative and progressive orientations.

At the turn of the twentieth century, Schoff, national PTA president, cautioned that the group "cannot afford to risk antagonisms needlessly," noting that there are other outlets for partisan politics (Schoff 1916, 140). By 1943, national president Minetta Hastings made a statement to the UN that "the first step toward citizenship in an interdependent world must be the elimination of all prejudice and bias toward minority groups within our own border" (Woyshner 2009, 143). Despite ideological changes at the national level and annual PTA-NCCPT joint meetings to "[recommend] definite programs of cooperation," at the local level PTA and NCCPT groups often operated independently (National PTA n.d.-r). "While their objectives needed to match the platform of the national level, the flexible federated infrastructure of the PTA allowed them the freedom to interpret those objectives according to their own interests and local contexts." Most local PTAs "carried on with business as usual" (Woyshner 2009, 143). Writing about Virginia's PTA meetings in the late 1950s, Elizabeth Gillespie McRae argued that "parliamentary procedure and politeness . . . disguised what was really a way through for open school advocates and segregationists. Those who embraced moderate rather than absolute resistance continued their grassroots work for some racial segregation and integration" (2018, 191). So despite progress on important issues, the inability and unwillingness of white PTA members to address racism kept broader progress at bay.

Like the PTA, LLL's beginnings reflect the group's privilege and exclusivity. For LLL founders, reaching out to mothers and providing community support for breastfeeding was their core mission toward greater cultural acceptance and associated natural mothering practices. Though their goals are cast broadly, the founders expressed a very particular set of worldviews related to their position as affluent, white, Catholic, married, heterosexual women. LLL's advocacy for breastfeeding, especially breastfeeding on a long-term basis, is predicated on a parent's broader access to socioeconomic, familial, and cultural support that is often lacking especially for employed women (and more so those employed in low-income jobs). Rather than addressing these issues head-on, LLL simply "recognizes that misinformation and social pressures may cause difficulties that require breastfeeding mothers to seek outside assistance" (La Leche League International n.d.-g). Organizationally, LLL has remained politically neutral on issues beyond, but related to, breastfeeding. As Hausman explains, "The organization follows a strict policy of not mixing causes, since to align itself to a specific political cause might alienate women who would otherwise seek breastfeeding advice from LLL" (2003, 163). LLL "would not take an official position on the Nestle boycott [over formula marketing in the global south], nor on feminist reproductive rights issues. Journalists, nonetheless, credit LLL activism for the rising popularity of breastfeeding" (Blum 1999, 44–45). For LLL and the PTA, gender, race, and social class have shaped the groups' exclusivity. Parenting groups continue to operate as deeply gendered, raced, and classed organizations. Dads' groups are no exception.

Dads' groups also have a history of promoting inequality. The organization Promise Keepers provides one such example of an earlier dads' group that fostered inequalities within families. It began over three decades ago as an evangelical Christian faith-based organization, started by former University of Colorado Boulder football coach Bill McCartney, who founded the men's only group in 1990 to call "on men to . . . bond together with other men to retake responsibility for caring for and leading their families, their communities and their nation" (Messner 2000, 92). By ministering conservative evangelical Christian teachings, the Promise Keepers have brought many men together to promote men's participation in families as heads of households (Heath 2003). The group believes that "men's problems today result largely from departures from men's natural roles" seen in biblical terms (Messner 2000, 27). At the height of their popularity in the late 1990s, Promise Keepers packed stadiums with men who came together to reassert their commitment to Christian values and encouraged men to connect with each other as well as their wives and families. As sociologist Melanie Heath explains, "The men's collective identity is bound by practices that reaffirm hegemonic masculinity and heterosexuality through references to essential gender differences, a focus on heterosexual family relationships, and the absence of women and gay men from rallies" (2003, 440). The relationship between men connecting emotionally with other men as well as their families, alongside men simultaneously reasserting their dominance as men, serves as a reminder that political action and social change are often uneven and contradictory. These challenges carry over into current groups as this example from MOMS Club International captures.

Racism and MOMS Club International

Following the murder of George Floyd, the Rancho Santa Margarita MOMS Club, based in Orange County, California, a local chapter of the global twenty-thousand-member MOMS Club International, posted a photo collage to their Facebook page (Cummins 2020; "MOMS Club of Rancho Santa Margarita" n.d.). The collage presented colorful photographs of demographically diverse parents and children holding signs with individual words that read, "We stand with all moms and pledge that racial discrimination will stop with our kids." The president and organizer of the post explained that the image provided support for other moms, referring to the group's acronym MOMS, or Moms Offering Moms Support (Ludwig 2020). Since posts require permission from the administrator, she contacted the International MOMS Club corporate nonprofit leadership, asking them to further share the image on their Facebook page.

The MOMS Club leadership replied that they would not post the image on Facebook because its message was "political" and in conflict with the group's nonprofit status (Cummins 2020).[15] In response, leadership posted the following message: "Anytime anyone is killed by brutality or neglect, it is a tragedy for everyone. The right to life, liberty and pursuit of happiness are not just words, they are rights. Everyone needs to give other people the same respect—of the other's dignity, property, and profession—that they would expect for themselves. The Golden Rule is perfect: Treat other people as you would have them treat you. . . . We stand for all mothers-at-home and will be judged by how we treat them all equally" (Cummins 2020). While the Rancho Santa Margarita MOMS Club's post declared a commitment to help moms and kids end racism, leadership's response that "everyone needs to . . . respect . . . the other's dignity, property, and profession" directly connects the conversation back to events in the spring of 2020. Analogous to invoking an "all lives matter" response to "Black Lives Matter," it dismisses systemic racism and police violence against Black Americans and actively excludes Black people and their allies. In effect, the MOMS Club leadership made their politics of denial known, while strongly advising members to be apolitical, at least on issues related to racism.

In response, the MOMS Club of Rancho Santa Margarita produced a final post, dated June 6, 2020: "The MOMS Club of Rancho Santa Margarita would like to announce its formal disbandment from the International MOMS Club. We refuse to associate ourselves with an umbrella organization that will not support anti-racism" ("MOMS Club of Rancho Santa Margarita" n.d.).[16] In solidarity with the Orange County members, several hundred local MOMS Club chapters withdrew from the organization in protest, and nearly six thousand persons signed a Change.org petition asking Mary James, the longtime International MOMS Club chairperson, to resign (Change.org 2020). At the time of this writing, Mary James is still listed on the MOMS Club website as "chairman of the board" (MOMS Club n.d.-d). Divisions like those seen in MOMS Club International are not isolated, nor are they new. Struggles over racism were common in the summer of 2020, particularly on Facebook (Dixon and Dundes 2020). These struggles within parenting groups are contemporary examples of long-standing challenges, as the previous chapters have detailed; however, they are not always this well documented from both sides. This kind of visibility matters because it enables us to understand and recognize the conditions under which advocacy can thrive and, for the MOMS Club, whom to hold accountable when advocacy is undermined. Perhaps paradoxically, this example also reveals parents' deep investments that lead them to struggle for change within, against, and beyond parenting groups.

Conclusion

Parenting groups in the United States provide a vehicle for parents' advocacy. These networks constitute another path toward expanding parents' access to care—not through the family, professional organizations, or the state, but through local and national community and largely parent-to-parent groups. Through their organization and work in conjunction with other groups, they build and contribute their unique branch of the care infrastructure. By focusing on advocacy by the PTA, LLL, and the City Dads Group, I document some of the more successful actions I found in my research. Despite limitations, there are important commonalities across these groups. All provide evidence of care beyond individual or self-care to collective nonfamilial groups. When civic engagement has been waning in the United States, these collective possibilities provide an existing path toward caring for unpaid carers. Members mobilized these large groups to address gender, transphobia, and economic inequalities, advocate for inclusion, address social problems, and spark organizational transformation. With the Biden administration, discussion of care infrastructure entered the national parlance (Federal Register 2023). Despite important executive actions, the broader policy objectives Biden campaigned on never came to fruition, showing the limitations of relying solely on government support to solve care problems (White House n.d.). Parenting groups constitute an existing resource, a possibility that could be better developed. Although these actions depend on the power of charismatic individuals to enact social change, the impact and influence of autonomous reformers and activists rest upon a group's local autonomy with leadership's support. PTA autonomy enabled movement on equity and adopt-a-family actions, whereas LLL's interdependence almost thwarted MacDonald's gender inclusion actions.

Parenting groups have much to teach us about how existing organizations can expand or contract access to care infrastructure. By focusing on parenting groups' advocacy actions, I examine what I am calling "strategic parenting," or the potential for parenting groups to use their collective efforts to push for resources and social change, across parents, groups, and organizations. The strategies and outcomes are divergent. Dad groups' corporate partnerships have the benefit of vast corporate media and dollars allocated toward fathers' issues and resources, but they exist primarily in the service of "carewashing" rather than social change. As stakeholders, dads' groups' role in advocacy is mediated by corporate interests. In other words, dads' groups and corporations have different motivations and influence to shape the issues and initiatives they address. In the LLL example, one future member's decisive goals for trans and nonbinary inclusion were almost rejected by leadership. Though LLL instituted a meaningful rule change, the trajectory of that change is not yet clear. The PTA examples demonstrate how equity and charity advocacy models produce different kinds of change. The charity (adopt-a-family) model was shorter lived, smaller in scope, and indicative of more reactive approaches. The equity model led to a longer (at least three years) and broader (across many schools) progressive change. In this analysis, the concept of "strategic parenting" is best captured through SEPTA and PTA accessibility work, Trevor Macdonald's work to make LLL inclusive of trans and nonbinary parents, and the PTA Equity work to address parents' economic needs. All of these examples advocate for broader social change, and their work exemplifies how caring is activism when parenting groups address ableism, embrace gender inclusivity, and challenge economic inequalities (Ramsey 2012).

There are important limitations and opportunities in these examples. All of these groups operate independently and are somewhat siloed in their approaches. Even when they engage in coordinated advocacy efforts, the relationships are often dyads. If parent groups could better coordinate and collaborate, there might be occasions to scale up their advocacy and share networks and resources, not just through corporate partnerships but through alliances between parent groups and across various community organizations. Participation in local groups with national reach engages members in broader organizational networks and issues. Within groups, interdependency on the local and national levels connects parents and provides evidence of how advocacy actions can bring parents together, reduce isolation, and foster social change, both for the groups of parents and for their broader communities.

Conclusion

Building Strategic Parenting Groups

To answer the question posed in the title, *Who Cares About Parents?*, the short answer is, of course, parent groups do. Parent groups are significant and often underutilized resources for parental care in the United States. Parent groups' internal care infrastructure includes their leaders, members, organization, mission, ideology, and initiatives, but also the connections they build to the broader care infrastructure including educational and healthcare institutions as well as corporations. These groups have a long history of organizing membership, meetings, education, material resources, and advocacy to provide for parents' needs. Most importantly, these groups know that alongside all of these resources, parents need emotional support as caregivers.

I have focused on the content of care from mainstream established parent groups operating on a local to an international scale, drawing on data from the PTA, LLL, City Dads Group, a set of local dads' groups, MOMS Club International, UES Mommas, and the Oakwood babysitting co-op. Among these parent groups are those with vast networks—some with thousands or even millions of members—that mobilize to provide integral forms of care for their members and their members' families. Their influence, therefore, is both highly focused and widespread. The resources drawn together by different parent groups show how interconnected participating families are and make clear the needs these groups fill. Beyond this, they show how group care models are different from individualistic models of care based in the family using private care resources. Although parenting groups provide a cautionary tale for how they marginalize prospective members, parenting groups also provide existing models for greater care access.

Drawing on economist Shahra Razavi's care diamond, we can see that care provision typically falls within four categories: "families/households, state (federal/local), markets, and not-for-profit care" (Razavi 2007, 21). While parenting groups fall within a nonprofit care sector, they also provide a bridge across family-, state-, and market-based care. Given their outreach, they make scalability possible—sharing resources and ideas, promoting and expanding parental care. Parenting groups' actions include work on public health and safety campaigns, addressing economic inequality, promoting nutrition, fostering gender inclusion, and providing resources to families in need. Add to these examples parent groups' large-scale corporate partnerships and smaller-scale provision of respite care and the local transmission of resources. Parent groups' expectations of participation and reciprocity—an implicit agreement to provide care in exchange for receiving it—also broaden members' access to care (Hansen 2004a).

Parenting groups build collective resources, mutual obligation, and connection—all of which go a long way toward seeing parenting differently through interdependence. They emphasize the groups' responsibility for parents' care as a collective problem. Seeing parents' care as a social obligation also reinforces parenting groups' outreach to other families beyond their membership, especially more vulnerable ones. Consider the PTA and NCCPT's early campaigns to abolish child labor and establish school lunches. These goals enabled parents to care for families and children beyond their own to promote a "caring activism" that uses care as a key source to address economic inequalities and racism (Ramsey 2012, 245). Many decades later, PTAs in various cities have developed equity initiatives designed to redistribute resources and better-democratized power by directly engaging with members, instead of centralizing power and applying a top-down approach to achieve their equity program (Skocpol 2004). Through these kinds of fundamental issues, the parent groups cast a broad net across families to provide more community-based care for parents and their families. These actions, like mutual aid, are a way to build group-based parent-to-parent support (Spade 2020).

Possibilities for Transformation

These groups employ different strategies that do not all lead to success. Nevertheless, they are instructive. Some parenting groups' actions provide resources within and beyond the groups' members to address social problems and foster social change—working to dismantle racism, promote gender inclusion, address economic inequality, and foster a parenting community. Joan Tronto writes that "care is a complex process, and it also shapes what we pay attention to, how we think about responsibility, what we do, how responsive we are to the world around us, and what we think of as important in life" (2015, 8). LLL's story represents a profound transformation, from their struggle to establish breastfeeding as an accepted practice to expanding their work to integrate recognition of chestfeeding. LLL's inclusion of transgender and nonbinary parents represents a major ideological shift from the group's conservative Catholic beginnings to reflect a more diverse set of beliefs and constituents. The City Dads Group and local dads' groups have sought both the resources and normative changes required to better recognize and enable men's caregiving. Both groups challenge innate and essentialist understandings of gender and care, supporting a broader understanding of parental caregivers to include men and nonbinary and transgendered persons.

Among these often well-positioned, well-resourced, and well-intentioned parent groups, change can present real challenges. I found parenting groups' ideologies and practices historically and contemporarily often endorse broad goals but produce exclusion. I also found that alongside possibilities for advocacy and social change, groups foster narrow inclusion. Parenting groups are indicative of how often caregiving is siloed by care-related issues, populations, and locations (Folbre 2012). Parenting groups also reflect how challenging it is to work toward more sustainable and equitable care practices. As a result, their stories and scope of change are uneven.

Parenting groups' organization often reproduces essentialist ideologies around gender, family, and parenthood. Because of this, they limit broad access by engaging in gendered, racist, and economically exclusionary ideologies and practices. As they are products of their local communities and a broader U.S. context that reproduces gendered segregation, institutional racism, and economic inequalities, this is not surprising. However, it is important to understand the mechanisms by which this happens—namely through their origin stories, organization, recruitment practices, and outreach. Across the groups, their founders' ideologies, practices, and membership often reinscribe and perpetuate social inequalities, resulting in a narrow circulation of care resources. Even when groups cast a broad set of goals, in practice they tend to reach those most demographically like themselves.

Questioning Organizational Ideologies

Parenting group ideologies—shaped greatly by their belief in gender difference and their disregard of racism—drive their operations on multiple levels. All groups embrace to some extent an essentialist ideology around gender. Gender-based camaraderie among caregivers is particularly visible in parenting groups, and it often blocks participants from seeing beyond gender. LLL is the only group that was compelled to really address gender essentialism directly, a change that happened only recently because of strong advocacy. By expanding their community to include trans and nonbinary parents, LLL successfully challenged their gender essentialist roots. Though this change is ongoing, expanding their rules formally provides a measure of protection around increased access. Increasing chestfeeding's visibility in their materials can help foster a sense of growth and belonging in a group that has struggled to broaden its organization beyond its womanist breastfeeding origins.

Expanding access to care can also have unintended consequences. The gendered inequalities of caregiving already position women to perform a disproportionate amount of the work within parenting groups that is exacerbated by the cultural valorizing of motherhood and intensive practices. Collective-intensive mothering fosters women's particular skills and resources and at the same time sidelines men. By separating women from men and simultaneously making women's gendered labor less visible and men's contributions less likely, parent groups outsource to other women labor that might also be shared (or at least negotiated) with men.

Parenting groups' essentialist thinking about men and masculinity contributes toward villainizing men's caregiving, which underscores the ideological obstacles to broader communities of care and collaboration across parents and parenting groups. Since the dads' groups include men who share care and identify as caregivers among men, I imagined that within them I would find more support for men's caregiving generally. However, alongside celebrating fathers and their own care, dads' group members and their spouses express fears about men's predatory behaviors and worries that allegations of impropriety might be waged against them; they had experienced precautions put in place to ward off the dangers associated with men's caregiving. Similar concerns were raised by the babysitting co-op members' husbands. The distrust expressed by both groups led men to consider other men's caregiving only in the narrowest circumstances, with fathers who were very well acquainted. Of course, these men are not alone. Overcoming men's barriers to caregiving is a problem that extends beyond parenting groups to the broader culture. Even among well-positioned, -resourced, and -intentioned families, change presents real challenges that cannot be overcome by a single strategy. There needs to be a coordinated effort to challenge caregiving's gendered inequalities.

Parenting groups' approach to racism reflects the struggle, resistance, and often ineffective strategies seen elsewhere in the United States. Parenting groups often lean toward tokenism, when inclusion is prioritized. All the groups use images featuring diverse membership but shy away from controversial topics that might alienate current members. In short, parenting groups often take a path of least resistance. In a sense, they strive for decorum in place of the struggle that might ultimately foster change in place of the status quo.

Addressing Organizational Processes

My analysis shows that despite parenting groups' organizational diversity, including small-scale local and large-scale multilevel forms, similar organizational processes stifle progressive goals. Parent groups have a tendency toward overpowering leadership with too little membership input or a horizontal organization that allows individual groups to operate with significant independence that makes them prone to leadership overreach. Across LLL, the PTA, MOMS Club International, and UES Mommas, the scope of change or political action is constrained by the organizations' leadership. This was the case initially for trans and nonbinary inclusion that was almost denied by LLL's leadership. Many of the parenting group actions began through charismatic individuals with decisive goals, but also revealed problems that individuals alone could not solve. Solutions were also dependent on broader organizational change.

Creating transparency in the group's guiding principles and processes may help participants understand how the organizations are supposed to operate and provide members with access to making changes. However, as we saw in chapters 1 and 2, parenting groups' missions often fail to match their practices. To solve exclusionary practices, groups need to address leadership's power in the process. Among the advocacy examples are leaders who thwarted voices and shut down dialogue, rather than striving to facilitate, and they were unwilling to share power. Opening groups to dialogue, transparency, accountability, and representation may enable the groups to recruit and empower diverse members into positions of authority. These changes would benefit the organization as parenting groups earn the trust of their members and recruit new membership.

Situating Parenting Groups Within a Culture of Individualism

Individualism, as an ideology, has defined the United States for decades, and arguably its importance has only increased (Cherlin 2009; Hacker and Pierson 2010; Harding 1981). Since the 1980s, neoliberalism has infused U.S. policies with the deregulation of capitalist markets, increased privatization, shrinking government spending, increasing austerity measures, and a greater dependence on unpaid family caregiving (Kotz 2017; Tronto 2017). Individualism is reflected in the lack of government policies that fund and provide care for young, old, ill, and disabled Americans, resulting in many people having to fend for themselves while they craft their own care solutions. As political scientists Jacob Hacker and Paul Pierson argue, "More than most societies, Americans believe that people rise or fall because of their own efforts, and therefore get what they deserve. . . . We distribute blame and praise to individuals because we believe that it is their individual actions, for better or worse, that matter" (Hacker and Pierson 2010, 103). When applied to parents, these messages include that we value your privacy and your family is ultimately your responsibility, both of which undermine parents' lives and quality of care. Parent groups expose the social problem of America's individualist ideology around care, especially when their care for parents and membership are expansive. Due in part to the ethic of individualism, families in the United States are typically understood as individual units, despite considerable evidence that they participate in broader care networks (Hansen 2004b). The privileged status ascribed to the nuclear family alongside American individualism wreaks havoc on our ability to see the potential of collective and community-based solutions to parents' care needs and obscures the collective work of parenting groups.

Using a carework lens to study parenting groups' care for parents makes the broader care infrastructure visible to see the groups' objectives, organization, accomplishments, and potential. We can observe parent groups' contributions, across membership that is often time-limited, concentrated on support of parents while their children are young. We also see parent groups' complexity; they stand in contrast to the normative tendency to think about care relationships in dichotomous terms—paid and unpaid, private and public, household and institution, family and nonfamily, provider and recipient. Parent groups make the needs and work of parents visible, as unpaid private household family providers and in their relationship to paid, public, institutional, nonfamily care of which they may be a recipient.

There are many care myths that persist and underlie understandings of parenthood and care, perhaps most importantly that parents are normatively understood as providers rather than recipients of care. However, as we know from care scholarship, no one exists outside of care (Tronto 1993). As Tronto argues, "The assumption that such people care for themselves, and that 'care' is only a concern for the dependent and infirm—the young the unhealthy and the old" is false (2013, 102). As a corrective, taking a more integrated approach to care enables us to see how we can better see and meet parents' care needs. Rethinking how parents and their families can access their broader communities' care infrastructure provides an important start toward understanding both the care we have and the care we need.

Parenting groups have long seen the need to provide care for parents. Parents need more—more time, more help, and more support. Sometimes parents will benefit from something as simple as a kind word—"you will figure this out" and "take it one day at a time." Other times, parents' needs are more complex, like the need for in-kind care, respite from a challenging childhood stage, or support through a medical emergency. Parent groups are ideal for providing this kind of care, but without expanding their understandings of care providers, such groups tend to draw from already overburdened mothers. In short, the tactic of strategic parenting through group engagement needs further development to be effective (rather than onerous).

While too often marred by exclusionary ideologies and practices, parenting groups can (and some already do) offer a compelling model for parental care and social change. Collective nonfamilial care possibilities can expand care for caregivers. Care infrastructure is part of an ongoing national conversation, and parent groups constitute an existing resource, a possibility that could be transformed and harnessed. Based on this research, we see that parent groups can develop a better understanding of parents' needs and how best to meet them by building collective resources and senses of shared responsibility, mutual obligation, and connection, especially when they broaden access and address inequalities.

Despite their many challenges, I remain hopeful about the possibilities for nonfamilial and collective care infrastructure like that performed by parent groups. Recent Pew Center research underscores Americans' optimism toward collective care: "More adults embrace collaboration than individualism. Asked about the best way to navigate life, 71% say it is better in most situations for people to work together with others, compared with 29% who say it is better to be self-reliant" (Rainie, Keeter, and Perrin 2019, 8). In parent groups, we see clear evidence of this collaboration—joining and working together with others to provide the care parents so desperately want and need. Families, government, and private paid providers do not have to be the disproportionate sources of care for parents—we have a broader care infrastructure. I hope this research takes us steps closer to understanding how parenting groups' care can develop to provide more comprehensive care for parents.

Appendix A

Research Methods

Comparative analysis enables researchers to examine groups' organizational practices, like the small-scale interactions among members to their overarching ideologies, reflected by group mandates and texts, on local and national levels (Acker 1990, 1992). We can also situate these groups within broader social and cultural patterns, to examine the processes of caring for parents across the various groups and data sources. The primary cases under study include large-scale parenting organizations—the PTA, La Leche League, City Dads Group, and MOMS Club International—and several smaller-scale local parenting groups—including the Oakwood babysitting co-op made up of moms, a set of dads' groups, and UES Mommas. In addition to their relative size variation, all but one of the groups (the babysitting co-op) includes broader international, national, and city as well as local organizations. UES Mommas operates primarily through its Facebook group. The dads' groups are affiliated with the broader City Dads Group, but each operates relatively independently on a local level.

PTA and LLA

I studied the PTA and LLL through an examination of primary and secondary sources, including a range of texts, organizational websites, and group publications. Both organizations have been the subject of several wonderful book-length investigations that pushed my research forward. Drawing on these sources, I mapped both organizations' overarching histories and contemporary practices. PTA and LLL data were collected between 2019 and 2024. PTA data include historic texts beginning in 1916 through contemporary books, websites, magazines, and annual reports (National Congress of Parents and Teachers 1944; National PTA 1997, 2019, n.d.-g, n.d.-h, n.d.-n, n.d.-t; NCCPT 1961; Schoff 1916) as well as secondary sources that address the group's inner workings (Addonizio 2000; Calarco 2018; Lareau and Muñoz 2012; Posey-Maddox 2014; Woyshner 2009). LLL data begin with self-authored books from the 1970s and extend through contemporary books, websites, and annual reports (La Leche League International 2003; Lowman 1978; Wiessinger, West, and Pitman 2010); many secondary sources were helpful in documenting the group's ideology and practices (Blum 1999; Hausman 2003; Koerber 2013; La Leche League International n.d.-b, n.d.-d, n.d.-f, n.d.-g, n.d.-j; Ward 2000). Through textual analysis of nationwide PTA and LLL online and print publications I was able to document these parenting groups as organizations with normative ideologies, rules, and structures. I explore the history of the PTA and LLL as emblematic of a collective approach to care.

MOMS Club International and the UES Mommas

I studied both MOMS Club and UES Mommas through their online materials and secondary resources. MOMS Club International data include their overarching website (www.momsclub.org) and individual club sites with elaborate details on leadership, membership, ideology, and outreach. I collected information from more than twenty club websites in states nationwide, including Alabama, California, Colorado, Connecticut, Florida, Georgia, Iowa, Maryland, Massachusetts, Minnesota, Nevada, New Jersey, North Dakota, Pennsylvania, Ohio, Oregon, and Tennessee. Most states include at least one MOMS Club, and many have several located in various regions. All data collected were publicly available. I did not join MOMS Club to access member materials, though I did participate briefly several years ago in my local group when my children were preschool-aged. The national MOMS Club website, including training materials from their eLearning course (MOMS Club n.d.-b), and news articles provided me with additional details on the group's history, leadership, and membership. I collected data from 2015 through 2024.

The UES Mommas leadership limits outreach to mothers with online information confirming residence on the Upper East Side of Manhattan. Despite being unable to join this Facebook group, I included it due to the tremendous popular and news media attention to the group (e.g., *ABC News* and the *New York Post*), particularly following allegations of racism in response to members' reactions to George Floyd's murder (Coleman 2020; Klein 2020; Kreth 2023; Lorenz 2020; Sucharov 2017).[1] I began studying UES Mommas in 2020 but collected data on this group between 2017 and 2024. In part, the popular and news media attention to the UES Mommas is due to their location and privilege, living on Manhattan's Upper East Side. They are also known for members openly engaging in challenging dialogues in a well-documented forum. Though they are distinctive in some ways—holding more ad hoc gatherings and accessibility only through their Facebook site (rather than a stand-alone website or in person meetings)—in other ways they provide data that are difficult to access. In particular, the visibility of their disputes facilitated my study. In effect, this group shows what other groups may hide behind local privacy and in-person decorum.

The Oakwood Babysitting Co-op

Many ethnographers conduct studies that intersect with their biographies. As a method that often incorporates taking part in the activities under study, ethnography comingles the researcher with those being researched. I was both an outsider and an insider in my research (Naples 2003). My position was demographically like those I studied, and I have benefitted from being a member of the co-op, but my position was also unique as the only researcher within the group. I became a co-op member in 2010 and began research four years later. Interviews and observations were conducted beginning in the summer of 2014 through the spring of 2018. In all, data sources for the babysitting co-op include four years of participant observation, twenty-eight interviews—eighteen with babysitting co-op members and ten with their partners/spouses—and an analysis of co-op organizational texts and online materials. With the babysitting co-op I also conducted over a hundred hours of observation, including nine months of monthly meetings, playdates, and adult events, like members' nights out. Over these years, I took field notes during and following meetings as well as after playdates and events.

Babysitting co-op members were open to my research since I was already an established member. I proposed the idea at a co-op meeting to gauge openness and received very supportive responses from the members in attendance. Before I began interviewing, I sent follow-up emails to all members. Since husbands were not members, their participation was requested via an email sent to their wives. As I had completed four years of membership, the research was well received and I recruited members easily. Not only did participants give of their time to interview, but they were also helpful in recruiting their husbands to participate. I explained consent as an ongoing process that could be withdrawn by participants at any time, and I encouraged participants to stop and ask questions during and outside of formal interviews. I relied on a volunteer sample of participants that includes nearly three-quarters of the members (eighteen of twenty-four) and approximately half of the spouses (ten of eighteen to twenty-four) who reflect broader co-op demographics. Members who did not volunteer to interview cited lack of time as their primary explanation. If some were uncomfortable with the research, they did not share their concerns with me. Interviews with co-op members lasted between thirty minutes and two hours. Interviews with co-op members' partners/spouses lasted between thirty minutes and one hour. Participants often described the interviews as a meaningful way to explore issues they hold dear. Being a member of the co-op has enabled me to maintain dialogue with participants who have offered suggestions and revisited questions and answers throughout the research.

City Dads Groups

I used online networks to recruit participants drawn from three City Dads Groups, located in the eastern, central, and western United States. I draw upon twenty-four interviews to conceptualize comparative aspects of dads' groups and their members. My goal was to seek a variety of informants, to get an idea of the scope of dads' group experiences, and to generate theory about the relationship of dads' groups' organization to the practices and ideologies of their members. It was more important to give myself the freedom with my research design to seek a deeper understanding of the process—to look for regularities as well as outlying cases. Given the sample size, this research is not representative of fathers or of men. It would not be possible to access a list of all dads' group members from which to generate a representative sample. Instead, I used several data sources to provide detailed descriptions of the dads' groups. I rely on twenty-four interviews, including eighteen interviews with dads' group members, three of whom were interviewed twice, both as members and as leaders, and six of their spouses. I also conducted an analysis of dads' group texts like website pages, blogs, interviews, and conference images, materials, and transcripts.

Given the dads' groups' general prohibition of women's or moms' active membership, I could not join and carryout participant observation with the dads' groups as I did for the babysitting co-op. I had to figure out how to gain access to my chosen comparison group, to get my "in." Research is often a combination of very hard work and lucky breaks. This study is no exception. My "in" with the dads' group began when I was able to capitalize on a lucky break. I developed a connection with a charismatic local dads' group leader who connected me with dads in his group and two other charismatic leaders in the midwestern and western United States. Given these introductions, I was able to network with participants and their wives who took part in telephone interviews. These introductions were key to gaining access and trust before establishing my own telephone presence. I encouraged participants to ask questions of me, and many of the men did, often asking what I thought about dads' groups. Having previously conducted interviews with male patrons and workers in the sex work industry for my book *Strip Club*, I had experience discussing very intimate life details with men (Price-Glynn 2010). Also, drawing on my identity as a parent and caregiver, I easily established rapport in conversations about how exhilarating and exhausting caring for kids can be.

Qualitative Methods

This analysis brings together evidence from several qualitative methods—interviews, participant observation, and textual analysis of historical and contemporary books, organizational print and online materials, videos, blogs, and conference materials. Drawing on multiple data sources enables a broader analysis that situates findings from one source with information from the others. The ethnographic research includes fifty-two interviews, observations, and an examination of text, audio, and video materials. Textual data collection began in 2014 and continued through 2024. I analyzed group texts, like membership materials, online posts, and newsletters, alongside dads' group website information and conference video transcripts. Ethnographic data collection was conducted over five years, beginning in the summer of 2014 until the summer of 2019. Exploring *thick descriptions* from parents' experiences in caregiving communities, I can provide parents' detailed accounts of their experiences with these groups (Geertz 1973).

Members and spouses from the babysitting co-op and City Dads Groups were interviewed using a semistructured instrument. Both member and spouse interviews were conducted separately. Babysitting co-op members were interviewed in person. Babysitting co-op spouses, dads' group members, and dads' group spouses were interviewed by phone via Webex. Phone interviews enabled the greatest flexibility in terms of scheduling and spanning geographic distances between myself and research participants. Interviews were digitally recorded and transcribed verbatim. Questions covered babysitting co-op and dads' group perceptions and experiences, parenting practices and ideologies, as well as household organization of paid and unpaid labor. To enable comparability across groups, the semistructured instrument followed the same structure for members and spouses. I opened by asking members how and what they learned about their group and why they joined. These questions directed the conversation toward the groups and not parenting generally. I then turned to participation, in particular activities and events, and a discussion about everyone's involvement—members, spouses, and kids.

Once I had built some familiarity and rapport, I turned to more intimate questions related to their caregiving and care-receiving philosophies. These questions provoked the most interest and pushback from respondents. I asked, "If you had to choose between caregiving philosophies like *it takes a village to raise a child* or *family is best for raising children*, which better describes your perspective and why?" Participants had so many strong reactions to the choices and juxtaposition in this question. One parent even probed the politics around capturing a collective approach with the title of Hillary Clinton's book. The connection with Clinton's book was unintentional, and the phrase certainly predates her work. Rather than putting participants off, these strong reactions fostered lively and supportive exchanges.

Another question asked parents to respond to four words—support, community, trust, safety—related to care for kids. Though not explicitly instructed, many participants began by trying to rank order the terms. Rank ordering pushed parents to consider what was most and least important and why. I also asked participants to reflect on the terms "stay-at-home parents" and "working parents" and to reflect on the work and family futures they envisioned and wanted for their child(ren). This juxtaposition enabled parents to move from their lived experience to their hopes and dreams for their kids. Across both groups, the moms answered this question easily, while the dads often struggled.

The final section of the interview schedule asked about the relationship between home and work. I asked parents to detail how they organized care for their child(ren) and whether membership in a parenting group provided a source of support and direct care. For the babysitting co-op members, care was central to group membership but produced different results for moms than for dads. Across both groups, men and sometimes women questioned men's ability to provide care and expressed their fears over men's predatory behaviors including other men's actions and allegations that might be wrongly directed at dads' group members. To get a broader sense of how care for kids fit with their broader household organization, I asked them to describe how they divided household tasks (e.g., scheduling, cleaning, laundry, meal planning, shopping, cooking, home maintenance) and who did what in their household. I concluded by asking how they navigated demands between home, paid, and unpaid work. Participants often described the interviews as a meaningful way to explore issues they hold dear.

Textual data include field notes from co-op observation and organizational materials from parenting communities, group web and Facebook pages, member podcasts, and dads' group conference video transcripts. Information collected from texts, observations, and interviews was analyzed using a grounded theory approach (Glaser and Strauss 2012; Strauss and Corbin 1994). Grounded theory allows concepts to emerge directly from the data. Following this approach, I coded the texts to identify patterns and concepts within and across materials using the qualitative research software NVivo (QSR International 2018). Using NVivo's thematic coding trees, I organized and grouped patterns together to map out central ideas and theoretical propositions in the research. NVivo enables an analytical process that allows researchers to easily test and retest research questions across the data and to capture both major themes as well as minor threads across research findings. I identified the main themes based on their overarching frequency and importance across the data. In doing so, I paid careful attention to both agreement and divergence regarding relationships between particular concepts and themes. Moreover, drawing on different data sources allowed me to evaluate the accuracy and consistency of my findings and make informed decisions regarding the use of multiple research methods (Denzin 1989).

Appendix B

Parenting Group
Interview Guide

Member/Partner Questions:

How did you learn about the babysitting co-op/dads' group? Briefly, what did you learn?

How did you get involved in the babysitting co-op/dads' group? Please describe the recruitment process.

Why did you (or your partner) join the babysitting co-op/dads' group?

Have you encouraged others to join the babysitting co-op/dads' group? If so, who and why?

Ideology and Practice:

How have you participated in the babysitting co-op/dads' group? What activities/events have included you? Would you please describe those activities/events?

Does the babysitting co-op/dads' group encourage partners' and kids' participation?

If you had to choose between caregiving philosophies like "it takes a village to raise a child" or "family is best for raising children" which better describes your perspective and why?

How do the following words relate to your beliefs about caring for kids—support, community, trust, safety? Do these beliefs relate to the babysitting co-op/dads' group?

What do you think about the terms "stay-at-home"/"working" dads and moms?

What work/family futures do you envision or want for your children?

Relationship Between Home and Work:

How do you organize care for your kids?

Does the babysitting co-op/dads' group provide a source of support and/or direct care?

Please describe how you organize household tasks (e.g., scheduling, cleaning, laundry, meal planning, shopping, cooking, home maintenance).

If partnered, which tasks do you do, which does your partner do, and which do you share?

How do you navigate demands from home and paid work?

Dads' Group Leader Questions:

Why did you start a dads' group?

What are your goals for the dads' group?

How have you encouraged men's participation in the dads' group?

What are the biggest successes and challenges you have faced in organizing a dads' group? Why?

Does your dads' group encourage partners' and kids' participation? Why or why not?

Relationship with Caring Labor:

How do the men in your group organize care for their kids? Does the dads' group provide support for this care?

Do the men talk about the care they provide for their families? If so, what do they say? What do they emphasize?

Prompts:

Being financial providers?

Providing of love and emotional support?

Involvement in their child(ren)'s lives on a day-to-day basis?

Providing discipline?

Being a teacher-guide and coach?

Doing day-to-day care-related tasks?

Other care?

Appendix C

Parenting Group
Demographic Survey

1. Please list your date of birth (month/day/year):
2. Are you: single, dating, married, divorced (list all that apply)?
3. Do you live with a partner?
4. If so, please identify your partner's gender:
5. Please identify your partner's racial/ethnic background:
6. How many children do you have?
7. Please list your child/children's age/s?
8. Please identity your child/children's gender:
9. Please identify your gender:
10. Please identify your racial/ethnic background:
11. Please identify your religious background:
12. Please identify your highest educational degree completed (HS, associate's, BA/BS, MA, PhD):
13. Are you employed (no/yes, part-time/yes, full-time):
    a. How many hours per week are you employed (hours/week)?
14. Do you volunteer (no/yes):
    a. Where do you volunteer (e.g., community organization, school, faith-based institution)?
    b. How many hours per week do you volunteer?
15. Do you own or rent your home?
16. In what town do you live?

17. Please list your babysitting co-op/dads' group activities (e.g., hosting/ attending events and all related tasks).

18. Please list with whom you have shared care in the babysitting co-op/ dads' group.

Acknowledgments

This book has been years in the making, produced through several iterations, with support and contributions from so many along the way. I am deeply grateful for the generous access I had to the babysitting co-op and dads' groups, their members, their partners/spouses, and their kids. Protecting everyone's confidentially prevents me from naming them, but I can honor them with these first sentences of recognition. The many conversations we had about parenting, carework, and gender were refreshingly honest. The groups welcomed my many questions and gave of their time selflessly. This book would not exist without them.

Amy Armenia and Mignon Duffy—a huge thanks to both of you. Working with brilliant and thoughtful friends like you makes me a better scholar and a happier person. In addition to being my sounding board throughout this process, both Amy and Mignon read draft chapters and provided detailed editing on the entire manuscript. I take full responsibility for the research and writing, but recognize the importance of their contributions.

At Rutgers University Press, my manuscript benefitted from the tremendous support of executive editor Peter Mickulas, production manager Daryl Brower, the external reviewers, including Markella Rutherford, and feedback from Margaret Nelson and Karen Hansen. Thanks to you all. Thanks also to Regina Higgins for your careful review and editing of the entire manuscript, and to Westchester Publishing Services production editor Brian Ostrander.

The Carework Network, an international organization of researchers, policymakers, and advocates involved in various domains of carework, has nurtured me and my research—connecting me with a global community of scholars and activists who have provided comradery and feedback throughout the research process. While at the Carework Network's 2018 Eastern Sociological Society Carework Mini Conference, I presented a talk on the Oakwood babysitting co-op research. In 2019, at the Carework Network Global Summit in Toronto, Canada, I presented a talk on the dads' groups research. Finally, at the 2023 Carework Network Global Summit in San José, Costa Rica, I presented a paper on parenting groups and social change that provided the building blocks for chapter 5.

At the University of Connecticut, I appreciate the many colleagues who have provided encouragement and advice, chief among them Mary Bernstein, Alaina Brenick, Manisha Desai, David Embrick, Ken Foote, Davita Glasberg, Vicki Magley, Christin Munsch, Nancy Naples, Mark Overmeyer-Velázquez, Bandana Purkayastha, Ingrid Semaan, and Fumilayo Showers. I received generous financial support for transcription, editing, and indexing from the University of Connecticut Scholarship Facilitation Fund and the Women's Gender and Sexuality Studies program. I also received support on the Hartford Campus from Mark Overmeyer-Velázquez and Kim Schwarz, who helped me build a monthly Research Café that has provided a distraction-free writing space, delicious meals, and camaraderie among my esteemed colleagues.

I appreciate the support I have received over the years from University of Massachusetts faculty and alumni. Robert Zussman, Naomi Gerstel, Joya Misra, Lynette Leidy Sievert, and Nathalie Goubet have shaped my thinking and influenced my work directly and indirectly in so many ways. Alice Julier and Ingrid Semaan read drafts of early chapters and provided detailed comments. I thank Alice for her helpful suggestions on literature and writing. I am fortunate to also have Ingrid as my colleague at UConn; her friendship, honesty, and wisdom have time and again provided a safe haven for me.

I am deeply indebted to my faculty and friends from Ohio Wesleyan University, including Margaret Caldwell, Theodore Cohen, John Durst, Mary Howard, Alice Miller, and Amy Rathbone. You have nurtured my work over years as an undergraduate student, graduate student, and years later as a faculty member. Thank you for your continued friendship and for providing such collegial roots.

I joined three book clubs during this project. I am thankful for the amazing women who made up these groups, including (in alphabetical order) Elizabeth Ahlstrand, Edith Barrett, Jessica Borden, Vicky Connors, Manisha Desai, Sue Gibson, Golda Ginsburg, Davita Glasberg, E. J. Greenspan, Liz Gustafson, Paula Guy, Artisena Hill, Elizabeth Keifer, Sarah Kopp, Jill Pollack Lewis, Bandana Purkayastha, Katherine Ratcliff, Nancy Savage, Lynn Sherman, and Audrey Walker. Reading so many different books has given me new outlets to reflect and improved my writing. The groups have also provided a much-needed space for relaxation and camaraderie.

My final thanks are for my family. Eric, Lucas, and Lilly, I cannot thank you enough for respecting my work and for being the people I most want to be with. Eric, thank you for your kind words and sage advice about this research, for reading drafts along the way, and for all of the extra caring labor you did that enabled me to write. I love you and the kids more than I can ever say. My parents, Ronald and Christina, I am so thankful to have you as supporters and role models; you always lift me up with your love, pride, and encouragement. Diana and Cindy, who are far away but would be by my side at a moment's notice (as I would for you), thanks for always looking out for me as sisters and best friends. Thanks to my brother-in-law (who is more like a brother), Doug, my nieces, Maria and Christina, and my nephews, Nathaniel, Kyle, Alex, and Zachary. Thanks also to my Glynn family, Patricia, Michael, Lisa, Ava, Gavin, Patrick, Lynn, Ashley, and Leah. I look forward to our visits and family togetherness; thanks for always working so hard to keep us connected across so many miles.

Notes

Introduction

1 I located at-home care providers through carework websites like care.com and sittercity.com.

2 None of our local schools had PTA affiliations; they all had independent, unaffiliated PTOs.

3 La Leche League has many abbreviations. For simplicity I use LLL to represent the group as a whole. LLLI refers to the group's international organization; LLLC is Canada's acronym; and LLL USA is the short version for groups in the United States. This analysis focuses mostly on the United States, where LLL began and developed. I specify a different acronym when examining groups outside of the United States or placing specific groups in comparison.

4 The primal scream hotline began in December 2020. See Carmel (2021).

5 From the City Dads Group, https://citydadsgroup.com. Their website reads, "Dads come in all stripes: stay-at-home and working, single and married, gay and straight, and from different races, nations and religions."

6 See the home pages of MOMS Club (www.momsclub.org), Jack and Jill of America (https://www.jackandjillinc.org), Mocha Moms (https://www.mochamoms.org/i4a/pages/index.cfm?pageid=1), and Jewish Community Center of Greater Baltimore (www.jcc.org).

7 Looking at PTA leadership from 2018 to 2020, almost 60 percent of the members of boards of directors are women (seventeen of twenty-nine). Only three of the past ten national presidents have been men since the first man took office in 2009. In the decades prior, all presidents were women. For more information, see National PTA (n.d.-e). In Connecticut, for example, only 10 percent (three of thirty) of the members of boards of directors are men. For more information, see Connecticut PTA (n.d.).

Chapter 1 Parenting Group Beginnings

1 Schoff (1916) was published under the name Mrs. Frederic Schoff.

2   To adopt the name La Leche without knowing its origins or how to pronounce it seems a clear case of cultural appropriation. One might have guessed, especially given the members' Catholic religious beliefs, that taking another culture's name for a sacred Catholic shrine as one's own might raise more than passing questions.

3   International MOMS Club is a public 401(c)3 nonprofit organization based in Santa Clarita, California. Their employee identification number is 77-0125681. I obtained copies of their IRS Form 990 from https://www.irs.gov.

4   Conference 2 includes the central United States from Illinois to Nevada and south to Texas. Conference 3 includes southeastern states from West Virginia to Florida, north to south all the way to Arkansas and Louisiana to the west. Conference 4 includes New England states through New York and Pennsylvania. Finally, Conference 5 includes Southern California. See MOMS Club (n.d.-b).

5   Only one stay-at-home dad has been a member. His membership ended several years before I joined the organization and began my research.

6   Each script bill counts for thirty minutes of care for one child.

7   The organizers do not explain why outreach is concentrated in metropolitan areas.

Chapter 2   Belonging and Exclusion

1   Austin Council PTA Facebook page, May 18, 2021 ("Austin Council PTA" n.d.).

2   Since women cannot be dads' group members, I relied on the generosity of dads' group members to share available resources, accompanied by research of my own. Dads' group members provided links to online materials that feature not only presenters but, in some cases, other men in attendance. Conference sponsors and attendees also posted their own articles and videos on conference websites, blogs, and YouTube, for example. Some of the data, for example information from publicly available websites, include original names and credit the authors. I have not identified locations or conferences by name to ensure confidentiality for research participants and use pseudonyms for all identifying information from interviews to protect confidentiality.

3   There are several national dads' conferences. The following is written about a national dads' group conference that I named Dads Collaborate and about a session during that conference about dads' group recruitment. To provide additional scope and obscure identifiable information, the excerpt merges transcripts from several different conference dates and presentations. The descriptions are taken from podcast, video, photo, website, blog, and interview sources.

4   Dads Collaborate sessions were video recorded and available on YouTube. The following description comes from one such session.

5   Including students can provide local possibilities for student involvement; however, it is not mandatory, and the number of PTSAs is not promoted in PTA materials. National PTA simply provides member organizations with some resources and explanations of PTSA functioning. As such, PTSAs seem to operate on mostly the local level.

6   An IRS Form 990 search (www.irs.gov) of organizations with name combinations including "babysitting," "parents," "care," and "cooperative" turned up preschools, homeschools, and playgroups, co-ops designed to provide free clothes to foster kids, and unrelated co-ops.

7 The LexisNexis newspaper search of North American English-language publications included the terms "babysitting cooperative" (37 articles, excluding an advertisement, duplicate, and calendar entry) and "babysitting co-op" (591 are from newspapers, out of 1,388 across all publication types including blogs, press releases, and web-based publications). Fifty of those articles addressed economist Paul Krugman's retelling of Joan and Ricard Sweeney's cautionary tale of a babysitting co-op in recession. The search was conducted May 29, 2020.

8 Economist Paul Krugman's first piece, "Babysitting the Economy," from *Slate*, which reproduced the Sweeneys' babysitting co-op example, emerged in 2008; references to this work account for fourteen news articles from 2007 to 2009.

Chapter 3   Educating Parents

1 See What to Expect's home page, https://www.whattoexpect.com.

2 *Our Children* began in 1906 as the *National Congress of Mothers Magazine* (National PTA n.d.-l).

Chapter 4   From Fundraising to Respite Care

1 See the Good+Foundation website, https://goodplusfoundation.org.

2 *Nice White Parents* is a five-part *New York Times* and Serial Productions podcast, reported by Chana Joffe-Walt (available at https://www.nytimes.com/2020/07/23/podcasts/nice-white-parents-serial.html). The series addresses the relations between white parents and their sixty-year history with the racially diverse New York City public schools in Brooklyn. Over the course of five episodes, Joffe-Walt uncovers patterns of interaction that promote white privilege, economic privilege, and systemic racism. She recounts the ways in which white parents meddle with social change, always favoring their own children's interests and their own sense of self over the good of the Black, Latino, and Hispanic majority. They embody white privilege and thwart racial integration at almost every turn.

3 Collective-intensive mothering shares an affinity with the related concept of extensive mothering. Extensive mothering is a form of care performed by mothers who merge intensive mothering with employment by overseeing and delegating intensive caregiving responsibilities to their children's caregivers while they are at work (Christopher 2012). By contrast, collective-intensive mothering is unpaid work, not mediated by the market, a direct personal exchange that is mutually constructed and enacted. Members do not include paid providers. Instead, within the babysitting co-op, mothers privilege their own identity within a community of like-minded moms.

4 Co-op moms resemble the middle- and upper-middle-class Black moms in sociologist Dawn Marie Dow's *Mothering While Black*, for whom "community members were viewed as the preferred source of childcare in the absence of mothers" as well as sources of important advice and support (2019, 18). Co-op members also view each other as preferable caregivers and confidants. However, unlike participants in Dow's study who shared resources more organically with family and friends, co-op moms embrace intensive mothering through an organized group.

5 See Wiessinger (2018) and La Leche League USA (2024).

Chapter 5   Parenting Groups as Agents and Opponents of Social Change

1   In 2008 they started the New York City group and in 2013 brought the concept nationwide with the City Dads Group network (City Dads Group n.d.-a).

2   This link is available through the Internet Archive, March 30, 2019, https://web.archive.org/web/20190330092932/https://citydadsgroup.com/about-us/.

3   As Trevor prepared for his LLL debut, he described in a blog post his nervousness in approaching the group as a man. In particular, he wanted to be clear about how and why he was there. He gave a "carefully prepared" introduction: "My name is Trevor and I am able to be pregnant because I am transgender. This means that I was born female but transitioned to male by taking hormones and having chest surgery. When my partner and I decided to start a family, we got advice from my doctors, and I stopped taking my testosterone. My baby is due in April. Because my surgery removed most of my breast tissue, I don't know how much I'll be able to breastfeed, but I really want to try." As it turns out, his fears were alleviated when he "looked up to see many of the women in the room nodding their heads and smiling" at him. At the time that he attended the meeting, his pregnancy was "quite far along," and looking back, he assumed that lent him some credibility that he "was the real thing." The meeting format, with participant introductions and breastfeeding stories, has been scripted through LLL's formal organization.

4   MacDonald started the blog (*Milk Junkies* 2012c). He works with the University of Ottawa on research (*Milk Junkies* 2013). He also founded the Facebook group "Birthing and Breast or Chestfeeding Trans People and Allies," with over six thousand members.

5   This count does not include the Spanish translation of the "Transgender and Non-binary Nursing" information page on the LLL USA site.

6   See two links available through the Internet Archive: https://web.archive.org/web/20200929140855/https://www.lllc.ca/news/world-breastfeeding-week and https://web.archive.org/web/20210620040519/https://www.lllc.ca/2021-hpc-speakers. See also Penguin Random House (n.d.) and La Leche League Canada (2021).

7   See two links available through the Internet Archive: https://web.archive.org/web/20210418081735/https://www.lllc.ca/lllc-saskatoon-daytime-series-meeting and https://web.archive.org/web/20210303031011/https://www.lllc.ca/sites/default/files/REVISED-Trans-Nursing_Tip-Sheet.pdf.

8   See this link available through the Internet Archive, https://web.archive.org/web/20210418081735/https://www.lllc.ca/lllc-saskatoon-daytime-series-meeting.

9   See this link available through the Internet Archive, https://web.archive.org/web/20210303031011/https://www.lllc.ca/sites/default/files/REVISED-Trans-Nursing_Tip-Sheet.pdf.

10 The Facebook group is named "Breastfeeding Transmen and Allies," and MacDonald's blog is www.milkjunkies.net.

11 Mirian Thompson makes the connection with transgender members clear in interviews with Helen Joyce for *The Times* (Joyce 2024) and for season 4 of the podcast *Gender: A Wider Lens* (December 20, 2024, https://www.widerlenspod.com/p/episode-198).

12 See www.llli.org, www.lllc.ca, and www.lllusa.org.

13 The Santa Monica–Malibu Unified School District changed its equity program in 2014 to separate staff and program funding into a districtwide pool while

maintaining individual schools' and parents' ability to fund their own school activities and resources. For more information, see Palo Alto Partners in Education (2025), Goldstein (2017), and Fund for Portland Public Schools (n.d.).

14 For a news article, see Oakland Ed Fund (2020). See also Equity Allies for OUSD (2019) and Equity Allies for OUSD (2022).

15 Bylaws for all MOMS Club Local Chapters (MOMS Club 2013) state that "group[s] shall not support, affiliate with or participate in any political party or campaign, nor with any religious group or cause. Nor shall [they] participate in any cause not directly related to children, homemaking or the family."

16 The MOMs Club of Rancho Santa Margarita elaborated their reasoning on their Facebook page: "International MOMS Club refused to share the collage on their Meta (Facebook) page, stating that their 501(c)(3) status prohibited them from posting something so political. According to the IRS website, this is simply untrue and we have seen numerous non-profits make strong anti-racism statements. As other chapters across the US learned about this situation it created an uproar among MOMS Club members. Hundreds of emails were sent to International and rather than opening a dialogue with us, the leadership doubled down on their stance that anti-discrimination is a political act. We cannot stand by and be part of an organization whose views do not align with our own. Currently there are over 200 chapters across the US that have also disbanded and thousands of members have resigned. Know better, do better. We will forever be passionate about supporting caregivers in our community and if you are interested in joining an inclusive mothering group, please email rsm@wearemaeve.org, #MOMSagainstRacism #racismisnotpolitical #internationalmomsclub #momsclub."

Appendix A

1 For long-term coverage, see ABC News (2018), Kreth (2023), and Klein (2021).

References

AARP and National Alliance for Caregiving. 2020. "Caregiving in the United States 2020." May 14. https://doi.org/10.26419/ppi.00103.001.

ABC News. 2018. "Mom Uses Stroller to Collect 20,000 Diapers for Families in Need." January 19. https://abcnews.go.com/Lifestyle/mom-stroller-collect-20000 -diapers-families/story?id=52441494.

Abel, Emily K., and Margaret K. Nelson, eds. 1990. *Circles of Care: Work and Identity in Women's Lives.* State University of New York Press.

Accomando, James L. 2018. "Relevant, Responsive, Revitalized." *Our Children* 44 (2): 5.

Acker, Joan. 1990. "Hierarchies, Jobs, Bodies: A Theory of Gendered Organizations." *Gender & Society* 4 (2): 139–158.

———. 1992. "Gendering Organizational Theory." In *Gendering Organizational Analysis*, edited by Albert J. Mills and Peta Tancred. Sage.

———. 2006. "Inequality Regimes." *Gender & Society* 20:441–64.

Adams, Gina, and Monica H. Rohacek. 2010. "Child Care Instability: Definitions, Context, and Policy Implications." Urban Institute, December 27. https://www .urban.org/research/publication/child-care-instability-definitions-context-and -policy-implications.

Addonizio, Michael. 2000. "Private Funds for Public Schools." *Clearing House* 74:70–74.

Alam, Ashraful, and Donna Houston. 2020. "Rethinking Care as Alternate Infra-structure." *Cities* 100 (May): 102662. https://doi.org/10.1016/j.cities.2020.102662.

Andrews, Florence Kellner. 1991. "Controlling Motherhood: Observations on the Culture of the La Leche League." *Canadian Review of Sociology & Anthropology* 28 (1): 84–98.

Angeles, Domingo. 2018. "Share of Women in Occupations with Many Projected Openings, 2016–26." *Career Outlook*, March. https://www.bls.gov/careeroutlook /2018/data-on-display/dod-women-in-labor-force.htm.

APW. 2016. "Watch City Dads Give Back to Those in Need." City Dads Group, December 15. https://citydadsgroup.com/giving-tuesday-city-dads.

———. 2018a. "Cleveland Dad Collects Backpacks for Foster Care Kids in Need." City Dads Group, January 11. https://citydadsgroup.com/cleveland-dad-backpacks -foster-care.

———. 2018b. "Your Donations Can Help Low-Income Fathers with Dad Toolkits." City Dads Group, November 27. https://citydadsgroup.com/dad-toolkits-good-foundation/.

Arendell, Terry. 2000. "Conceiving and Investigating Motherhood: The Decade's Scholarship." *Journal of Marriage and the Family* 62 (4): 1192–1207.

Armstrong, Jo. 2006. "Beyond 'Juggling' and 'Flexibility': Classes and Gendered Experiences of Combining Employment and Motherhood." *Sociological Research Online* 11 (2): 94–106.

Arnow, Ina. 1991. "Special Education P.T.A. Is Revived." *New York Times*, February 10. https://www.nytimes.com/1991/02/10/nyregion/special-education-pta-is-revived.html.

Arxer, Steven L. 2011. "Hybrid Masculine Power: Reconceptualizing the Relationship Between Homosociality and Hegemonic Masculinity." *Humanity & Society* 35:390–422.

Attanasio, Valentina. 2019. "Black Breastfeeding Week Celebrations." *Breastfeeding Today*, October 24. https://llli.org/news/black-breastfeeding-week-celebrations/.

"Austin Council PTA." n.d. Facebook. Accessed April 8, 2025. https://www.facebook.com/AustinCouncilPTA.

Barrett, William P. 2013. "The Largest U.S. Charities For 2013." *Forbes*, November 25. https://www.forbes.com/sites/williampbarrett/2013/11/25/the-largest-u-s-charities-for-2013/?sh=1653894439e3.

Barron, James. 2012. "Nation Reels After Gunman Massacres 20 Children at School in Connecticut." *New York Times*, December 14. https://www.nytimes.com/2012/12/15/nyregion/shooting-reported-at-connecticut-elementary-school.html.

Baumann, Lisa. 2012. "Woodinville PTA to Send Donation to Sandy Hook Elementary." *Patch*, December 17. https://patch.com/washington/woodinville/woodinville-school-pta-to-send-card-donation-to-sandy5d4cc9837e.

Bazelon, Emily. 2008. "Founding Mothers: Edwina Froehlich b. 1915." *New York Times Magazine*, December 28. https://www.nytimes.com/2008/12/28/magazine/28froelich-t.

Beatty, Barbara, Emily D. Cahan, and Julia Grant. 2006. *When Science Encounters the Child: Education, Parenting, and Child Welfare in 20th-Centry America*. Teachers College Press.

Bennion, Eric. 2018. "Giving Tuesday 2017: Putting Food Where Hungry Mouths Are with Plum Organics." City Dads Group, January 11. https://citydadsgroup.com/giving-tuesday-2017.

Bernard, Jessie. 1982. *The Future of Marriage*. 2nd ed. Yale University Press.

Bianchi, Susan M. 2000. "Maternal Employment and Time with Children: Dramatic Change or Surprising Continuity?" *Demography* 37 (4): 401–414.

Bianchi, Susan M., Liana C. Sayer, Melissa A. Milke, and John P. Robinson. 2012. "Housework: Who Did, Does or Will Do It, and How Much Does It Matter?" *Social Forces* 91 (1): 55–63.

Bird, Sharon R. 1996. "Welcome to the Men's Club: Homosociality and the Maintenance of Hegemonic Masculinity." *Gender & Society* 10 (2): 120–132.

Block, Jarrod, and Melissa Burkley. 2019. "On the Prowl: Examining the Impact of Men-as-Predators and Women-as-Prey Metaphors on Attitudes That Perpetuate Sexual Violence." *Sex Roles* 80 (5–6): 262–276.

Blum, Linda. 1993. "Mothers, Babies, and Breastfeeding in Late Capitalist America: The Shifting Contexts of Feminist Theory." *Feminist Studies* 19 (2): 290–311.

———. 1999. *At the Breast: Ideologies of Breastfeeding and Motherhood in the Contemporary United States*. Beacon.

Blum, Linda, and Elizabeth A. Vandewater. 1993. "'Mother to Mother': A Maternalist Organization in Late Capitalist America." *Social Problems* 40 (3): 285–300.

Bobel, Chris. 2002. *The Paradox of Natural Mothering*. Temple University Press.

Boggs, Leslie. 2019. "A Call to Courage." *Our Children* 45 (2): 5.

Breimer, Yael. 2017a. "My Journey: Non-binary Nursing." La Leche League USA, December 5. https://lllusa.org/my-journey-non-binary-nursing/.

———. 2017b. "Support and Reassurance in Meeting Chestfeeding Goals." La Leche League USA, June 6. https://lllusa.org/support-and-reassurance-in-meeting -chestfeeding-goals/.

———. 2019. "Growing in LLLove: How La Leche League Helped Me Parent My Gender Non-conforming Child." La Leche League USA, June 18. https://lllusa.org /growing-in-lllove/.

———. 2020. "2020: Voices from New Beginnings." La Leche League USA, December 29. https://lllusa.org/2020-voices-from-new-beginnings/.

Brenton, Joslyn. 2017. "The Limits of Intensive Feeding: Maternal Foodwork at the Intersections of Race, Class, and Gender." *Sociology of Health and Illness* 39 (6): 863–877.

Bridgman, Ralph P. 1930. "Ten Years' Progress in Parent Education." *Annals of the American Academy of Political and Social Science* 151 (1): 32–45.

Brown, Debbie-Marie. 2022. "Local PTA Council Revitalizes Local Ecosystem While Redistributing Funds." *Evanston RoundTable*, March 12. https://evanstonround table.com/2022/03/12/local-pta-council-revitalizes-local-ecosystem-while -redistributing-funds.

Brown v. Board of Education, 347 U.S. 483 (1954).

Bureau of Labor Statistics. 2017. "Economic News Release: Employment Characteristics of Families Summary." Accessed April 19, 2018. https://www.bls.gov/news .release/famee.nr0.htm.

———. 2019. "Labor Force Characteristics by Race and Ethnicity, 2018." Accessed April 23, 2021. https://www.bls.gov/bls/blswage.htm.

———. 2020. "News Release: Employment Characteristics of Families 2019." Accessed December 31, 2020. https://www.bls.gov/news.release/pdf/famee.pdf.

———. 2024a. "Licensed Practical and Licensed Vocational Nurses." August 29. https://www.bls.gov/ooh/healthcare/licensed-practical-and-licensed-vocational -nurses.htm.

———. 2024b. "Security Guards and Gambling Surveillance Officers." August 29. https://www.bls.gov/ooh/protective-service/security-guards.htm.

Cahill, Mary Ann. 2001. *Seven Voices, One Dream*. La Leche League International.

Cain Miller, Claire. 2020. "'I'm Only One Human Being': Parents Brace for a Go-It-Alone School Year." *New York Times*, September 8. https://www.nytimes .com/2020/08/19/upshot/coronavirus-home-school-parents.html.

Calarco, Jessica McCrory. 2018. *Negotiating Opportunities: How the Middle Class Secures Advantages in School*. Oxford University Press.

———. 2024. *Holding It Together: How Women Became America's Safety Net*. Portfolio.

Carmel, Julia. 2021. "To Hear America's Mothers, We Let Them Yell." *New York Times*, February 7, A2.

Carse, Ashley. 2017. "Keyword: Infrastructure: How a Humble French Engineering Term Shaped the Modern World." In *Infrastructures and Social Complexity:*

A Companion, edited by Penny Harvey, Casper Bruun Jensen, and Atsuro Morita. Routledge.

Catania, Sara. 1995. "Club Dedicated to Helping Moms Survive Rigors of Childhood." *Los Angeles Times*, May 29. https://www.latimes.com/archives/la-xpm-1995-05-29-me-7218-story.html.

Cazenave, Noel A. 2015. *Conceptualizing Racism: Breaking the Chains of Racially Accommodative Language*. Rowman & Littlefield.

CBC News. 2015. "Manitoba Father Who Breastfeeds Shares Story to Promote Tolerance." September 28. Accessed May 22, 2025. https://www.cbc.ca/news/canada/manitoba/manitoba-father-who-breastfeeds-shares-story-to-promote-tolerance-1.3246720.

Centers for Disease Control and Prevention. n.d. "Parent Information." Accessed April 8, 2025. https://www.cdc.gov/parents/index.html.

Chaitin, Mitchell A. 2016. "Dove Men+Care, Dad 2.0 Title Sponsor Extraordinaire!" *Gay NYC Dad*, February 24. https://www.gaynycdad.com/2016/02/dove-mencare-dad-2-0-title-sponsor.html.

Change.org. 2012. "We're Dads, Huggies. Not Dummies." March 3. https://www.change.org/p/we-re-dads-huggies-not-dummies.

———. 2020. "Call for International MOMS Club Founder, Mary James, to Resign amid Racism Scandal." June 17, https://www.change.org/p/moms-club-call-for-international-moms-club-founder-mary-james-to-resign-amid-racism-scandal.

Chatzidakis, Andreas, Jamie Hakim, Jo Littler, Catherine Rottenberg, and Lynne Segal. 2020. *The Care Manifesto: The Politics of Interdependence*. Verso.

Chen, Wei-ting. 2016. "From 'Junk Food' to 'Treats': How Poverty Shapes Family Food Practices." *Food, Culture & Society* 19 (1): 151–170.

Cherlin, Andrew J. 2009. *The Marriage-Go-Round: The State of Marriage and the Family in America Today*. Knopf.

Christopher, Karen. 2012. "Extensive Mothering: Employed Mothers' Constructions of the Good Mother." *Gender and Society* 26 (1): 73–96.

City Dads Group. 2019. "City Dads Helps Pampers' Mission to End Diaper Changing Table Inequity." October 11. Accessed May 22, 2025. https://citydadsgroup.com/city-dads-helps-pampers-changing-table/.

———. 2020. "Dad 2.020 Conference Gathering Fathers in D.C. on Feb. 27–29." January 13. Accessed May 22, 2025. https://citydadsgroup.com/dad-2-020-conference-gathering-fathers-in-d-c-on-feb-27-29/.

———. 2021. "National Dads' Day Out to Get Fathers Together Nov. 6." October 25. Accessed May 22, 2025. https://citydadsgroup.com/national-dads-day-out-to-get-fathers-together-nov-6/.

———. 2024. "Fathers Eve 2024: Dads Celebrating Fatherhood, Each Other." June 10. Accessed May 22, 2025. https://citydadsgroup.com/fathers-eve-2024-dads-celebrate-fathers-day/.

———. n.d.-a. "About Us." Accessed March 8, 2019. https://citydadsgroup.com/about-us/.

———. n.d.-b. "City Dads Media Kit." Accessed April 8, 2025. https://citydadsgroup.com/media-kit/.

———. n.d.-c. "Start a Group." Accessed March 8, 2019. https://citydadsgroup.com/start-a-group/.

Clawson, Dan, and Naomi Gerstel. 2014. *Unequal Time: Gender, Class and Family in Employment Schedules*. Russell Sage Foundation.

Cohen, Philip N. 2018. *Enduring Bonds: Inequality, Marriage, Parenting, and Everything Else That Makes Families Great and Terrible.* University of California Press.

Coleman, Oli. 2020. "The 'UES Mommas' Facebook Group Is Not Handling the Discourse Well." *Page Six*, June 4. https://pagesix.com/2020/06/04/ues-mommas -facebook-group-not-handling-the-discourse-well/.

Collins, Caitlyn. 2019. *Making Motherhood Work: How Women Manage Careers and Caregiving.* Princeton University Press.

Collins, Patricia Hill. 1994. "Shifting the Center: Race, Class, and Feminist Theorizing About Motherhood." In *Mothering: Ideology, Experience, and Agency*, edited by Evelyn Nakano Glenn, Grace Chang, and Linda Rennie Forcey. Routledge.

Colorado PTA. 2022. "President's Message." *Children's Voice*, July. https://copta.org /wp-content/uploads/2022/07/COPTA-July-2022-Newsletter.pdf.

Connecticut PTA. n.d. "Meet the 2023–2025 CT PTA Executive Committee & Board of Directors." Accessed April 8, 2025. https://www.ctpta.org/board-of-dir.

Connell, Raewyn, and Rebecca Pearse. 2015. *Gender in World Perspective.* 3rd ed. Polity.

Connell, R. W. 1995. *Masculinities.* University of California Press.

———. 2000. *The Men and the Boys.* University of California Press.

Connell, R. W., and James W. Messerschmidt. 2005. "Hegemonic Masculinity: Rethinking the Concept." *Gender & Society* 19 (6): 829–859.

Cooley, Charles H. 1998. *On Self and Social Organization.* University of Chicago Press.

Crary, David. 2000. "Parents Confused About Columbine's Lessons as Anniversary Nears." *Los Angeles Times*, March 26. https://www.latimes.com/archives/la-xpm -2000-mar-26-me-12997-story.html.

Croake, James W., and Kenneth E. Glover. 1977. "A History and Evaluation of Parent Education." *Family Coordinator* 26 (2): 151–158.

Crowder, Kyle, and Liam Downey. 2010. "Inter-neighborhood Migration, Race and Environmental Hazards: Modeling Micro-Level Processes of Environmental Inequality." *American Journal of Sociology* 115 (4): 1110–1149.

Cummins, Tori Masucci. 2020. "Inside the Racial Justice Scandal That Erupted in Our International Moms Club." *Huffington Post*, July 23. https://www.huffpost .com/entry/international-moms-club-racial-controversy_n_5f1863e5c5b6296fbf 3c8a3d.

Curtis, Rachel. 2016. "Breastfeeding Dad: 'There Is More to Breastfeeding Than Just the Milk.'" *Mamamia*, June 1. https://www.mamamia.com.au/breastfeeding-dad -on-birthing-and-chestfeeding.

Cutler, William W. 2000. *Parents and Schools: The 150-Year Struggle for Control in American Education.* University of Chicago Press.

Damaske, Sarah. 2011. *For the Family: How Class and Gender Shape Women's Work.* Oxford University Press.

D'Arcy, Janice. 2012a. "Bumbling Dad vs. Super Dad: Advertisers Try to Find the Right Image." *Washington Post*, June 14. https://www.washingtonpost.com/blogs /on-parenting/post/bumbling-dad-vs-super-dad-advertising-try-to-find-the-right -image/2012/06/14/gJQAoCXncV_blog.html.

———. 2012b. "Huggies Revamps 'Dad Test' Campaign After Complaints." *Washington Post*, March 12. https://www.washingtonpost.com/blogs/on-parenting/post /huggies-revamps-dad-test-campaign-after-complaints/2012/03/12/gIQAHQng7R _blog.html.

Delisio, Ellen R. 2007. "National PTA Taps First Man to Serve as President-Elect." *Education World*, August 16. https://www.educationworld.com/a_issues/chat /chat215.shtml.

Denzin, Norman. 1989. *The Research Act: A Theoretical Introduction to Sociological Methods*. Prentice Hall.

DeVoe, Jo. 2021. "Arlington PTA Leaders Consider Ways to Distribute Funding More Equitably." *ARL Now*, July 15. https://www.arlnow.com/2021/07/15/arlington-pta -leaders-consider-ways-to-distribute-funding-more-equitably/.

Diaz, Stephanie. 2014. "Can We Retire This PTA Mom Stereotype, Please?" *Fearless Volunteer*, October 23. https://fearlessvolunteer.com/2014/10/23/can-we-retire-pta -mom-stereotype/.

Dixon, Patricia J., and Lauren Dundes. 2020. "Exceptional Injustice: Facebook as a Reflection of Race and Gender-Based Narratives Following the Death of George Floyd." *Social Science* 9 (12): 231. https://doi.org/10.3390/socsci9120231.

Dow, Dawn Marie. 2019. *Mothering While Black: Boundaries and Burdens of Middle-Class Parenthood*. University of California Press.

Dowling, Daisy. 2021. *Workparent: The Complete Guide to Succeeding on the Job, Staying True to Yourself, and Raising Happy Kids*. Harvard Business Review Press.

Duvisac, Sara, and Maria del Rosario Castro Bernardini. 2024. "Care as Essential Infrastructure: Definitions of and Debates on Care Infrastructure from Kenya, Mexico, Peru, the Philippines, the United States and Zimbabwe." Oxfam, June 10. www.oxfam.org.

Edgley, Alison. 2021. "Maternal Presenteeism: Theorizing the Importance for Working Mothers of 'Being There' for Their Children Beyond Infancy." *Gender, Work & Organization* 28 (2): 1023–1039.

Elliott, Sinikka, Rachel Powell, and Joslyn Brenton. 2013. "Being a Good Mom: Low-Income, Black Single Mothers Negotiate Intensive Mothering." *Journal of Family Issues* 15 (36): 351–370.

Equity Allies for OUSD. 2019. "Equity Fund." Accessed April 8, 2025. https://www .equityalliesforousd.org/equity-fund.

———. 2022. "Equity Index 2022." Accessed April 8, 2025. https://drive.google.com /file/d/1gKfgVDs8A4SDCnvYt4Tjw27-YAvKWcja/view.

———. n.d. "Equity Allies for OUSD." Accessed May 22, 2025. https://www .equityalliesforousd.org/who-we-are.

Essed, Philomena. 1991. *Understanding Everyday Racism: An Interdisciplinary Theory*. Sage.

Fathers Eve. 2025. "What Is Fathers Eve." Accessed April 8, 2025. https://fatherseve .com/about/what-is-fe/.

Federal Register. 2023. "Increasing Access to High-Quality Care and Supporting Caregivers." April 18. Accessed May 22, 2025. https://www.federalregister.gov /documents/2023/04/21/2023-08659/increasing-access-to-high-quality-care-and -supporting-caregivers.

Feinberg, Lynn, Sysan C. Reinhard, Ari Houser, and Rita Choula. 2011. "Valuing the Invaluable: 2011 Update. The Growing Contributions and Costs of Family Caregiving." AARP Public Policy Institute. Accessed December 5, 2020. http:// assets.aarp.org/rgcenter/ppi/ltc/i51-caregiving.pdf.

Folbre, Nancy, ed. 2012. *For Love and Money*. Russell Sage Foundation.

Fomon, Samuel J. 2001. "Infant Feeding in the 20th Century: Formula and Beikost." *Journal of Nutrition* 131 (2): 409S–420S.

Foss, Katherine A. 2017. *Breastfeeding and Media: Exploring Conflicting Discourses That Threaten Public Health*. Palgrave Macmillan.

Fraser, Nancy. 2016. "Contradictions of Capital and Care." *New Left Review* 100 (July/August): 99–177.

Fund for Portland Public Schools. n.d. "PPS Parent Fund & LSF History." Accessed May 22, 2025. https://fundforpps.org/ppsparentfund.

Garey, Anita Ilta. 1999. *Weaving Work and Motherhood*. Temple University Press.

Geertz, Clifford. 1973. *The Interpretation of Cultures: Selected Essays*. Basic Books.

Gerstel, Naomi, and Sally K. Gallagher. 2001. "Men's Caregiving: Gender and the Contingent Character of Care." *Gender & Society* 15 (2): 197–217.

Ghezzi, Simone, and Enzo Mingione. 2007. "Embeddedness, Path Dependency and Social Institutions: An Economic Sociology Approach." *Current Sociology* 55 (1): 11–23.

Ginsburg, Faye D., and Rayna Rapp, eds. 1995. *Conceiving the New World Order: The Global Politics of Reproduction*. University of California Press.

Glaser, Barney G., and Anselm L. Strauss. 2012. *The Discovery of Grounded Theory: Strategies for Qualitative Research*. 7th printing. Aldine Transaction.

Glenn, Evelyn Nakano. 2010. *Forced to Care: Coercion and Caregiving in America*. Harvard University Press.

Goldberg, Eleanor. 2020. "A 38,000-Person Facebook Group for New York Moms Briefly Shut Down After Members Asked for a Black Moderator." *Insider*, June 6. https://www.insider.com/manhattan-mom-facebook-group-shut-down-over -demand-black-moderator-2020-6.

Goldstein, Dana. 2017. PTA Gift for Someone Else's Child? A Touchy Subject in California." *New York Times*, April 8. https://www.nytimes.com/2017/04/08/us /california-pta-fund-raising-inequality.html.

Goodrich, Marcia. 2014. "For the Kids." *Michigan Tech Magazine*, Fall. Accessed July 27, 2024. https://www.mtu.edu/magazine/fall14/stories/for-the-kids.

Granja, Rafaela, Manuela Ivone P. da Cunha, and Helena Machado. 2015. "Mothering from Prison and Ideologies of Intensive Parenting: Enacting Vulnerable Resistance." *Journal of Family Issues* 36 (9): 1212–1232.

Grant, Julia. 1998. *Raising Baby by the Book: The Education of American Mothers*. Yale University Press.

Gray, John. 1992. *Men Are from Mars, Women Are from Venus: A Practical Guide for Improving Communication and Getting What You Want in Your Relationships*. HarperCollins.

Grayson, Jennifer. 2016. *Unlatched: The Evolution of Breastfeeding and the Making of a Controversy*. Harper.

Greer, Frank R., and Rima D. Apple. 1991. "Physicians, Formula Companies, and Advertising: A Historical Perspective." *American Journal of Diseases of Children* 145 (3): 282–286.

Grose, Jessica. 2020. "Parenting Was Never Meant to Be This Isolating: Nuclear Families Have Always Relied on a Community for Practical Support." *New York Times*, October 7. https://www.nytimes.com/2020/10/07/parenting/childcare -history-family.html.

Grusami, Susila. 2019. "Motherwork Under the State: The Maternal Labor of Formerly Incarcerated Black Women." *Social Problems* 66 (1): 128–143.

Haar, Charlene K. 2002. *The Politics of the PTA*. Transaction.

Hacker, Jacob S., and Paul Pierson. 2010. *Winner-Take-All Politics: How Washington Made the Rich Richer—and Turned Its Back on the Middle Class*. Simon & Schuster.

Hall, Sarah Marie. 2020. "Social Reproduction as Social Infrastructure." *Soundings* 76 (Winter): 82–94. https://muse.jhu.edu/article/776495.

Hallett, Tim. 2003. "Symbolic Power and Organizational Culture." *Sociological Theory* 21 (2): 128–149.

Hansen, Karen V. 2004a. "The Asking Rules of Reciprocity in Networks of Care for Children." *Qualitative Sociology* 27 (4): 421–437.

———. 2004b. *Not So Nuclear Families: Class, Gender, and Networks of Care.* Rutgers University Press.

Harding, Sandra. 1986. *The Science Question in Feminism.* Cornell University Press.

Harding, Susan. 1981. "Family Reform Movements: Recent Feminism and Its Opposition." *Feminist Studies* 7 (1): 57–75.

Hartford Courant. 2020. "Foundations Honor Sandy Hook Victims Six Years Later." February 29. https://www.courant.com/2018/12/14/foundations-honor-sandy -hook-victims-six-years-later/.

Harvard Business Review. 2020. *Taking Care of Yourself.* Working Parents. Harvard Business Review Press.

Hausman, Bernice L. 2003. *Mother's Milk: Breastfeeding Controversies in American Culture.* Routledge.

Hays, Sharon. 1996. *The Cultural Contradictions of Motherhood.* Yale University Press.

Heath, Melanie. 2003. "Soft-Boiled Masculinity: Renegotiating Gender and Racial Ideologies in the Promise Keepers Movement." *Gender & Society* 17 (3): 423–444.

Henly, Julia R., and Sandra Lyons. 2000. "The Negotiation of Child Care and Employment Demands Among Low-Income Parents." *Journal of Social Issues* 56 (4): 683–706.

Hochschild, Arlie. 1995. "The Culture of Politics: Traditional, Postmodern, Cold-Modern, and Warm-Modern Ideals of Care." *Social Politics* 2 (3): 331–346.

Huggies. n.d. "Skin Essentials: Baby Butts, Rejoice!" Accessed April 8, 2025. https:// www.huggies.com/en-ca/why-huggies/about-us/no-baby-unhugged.

Ishizuka, Patrick. 2019. "Social Class, Gender, and Contemporary Parenting Standards in the United States: Evidence from a National Survey Experiment." *Social Forces* 98 (1): 31–58.

Johnston, Deirdre D., and Debra H. Swanson. 2006. "Constructing the 'Good Mother': The Experience of Mothering Ideologies by Work Status." *Sex Roles* 54:509–19.

———. 2007. "Cognitive Acrobatics in the Construction of Worker-Mother Identity." *Sex Roles* 57:447–59.

Joyce, Helen. 2024. "Why I Quit the Breastfeeding Charity I Founded over Trans Ideology." *The Times*, November 26. https://www.thetimes.com/life-style /parenting/article/la-leche-league-trans-ideology-x37b82bcr.

Kamenetz, Anya. 2022. "Parents and Caregivers of Young Children Say They've Hit Pandemic Rock Bottom." National Public Radio, January 20. https://www.npr.org /2022/01/20/1074182352/unvaccinated-young-kids-child-care-parents-omicron -disruptions.

Kantor, Jodi. 2005. "Expecting Trouble: The Book They Love to Hate." *New York Times*, September 15. https://www.nytimes.com/2005/09/15/fashion /thursdaystyles/expecting-trouble-the-book-they-love-to-hate.html.

Klein, Melissa. 2020. "Upper East Side Moms Facebook Group Implodes After Intense Diversity Fight." *New York Post*, June 6. https://nypost.com/2020/06/06 /nyc-moms-facebook-group-implodes-after-intense-diversity-fight.

——. 2021. "Upper East Side Facebook Group for Moms Has Strict Entry Require-ments." *New York Post*, November 27. https://nypost.com/2021/11/27/nyc-moms-facebook-group-requires-documentation-for-entry/.

Kleinman, Loren, and Amye Archer. 2018. "I'm a Survivor of Sandy Hook. This Is What the Past Six Years Have Been Like." *Marie Claire*, December 14. https://www.marieclaire.com/politics/a25575665/sandy-hook-anniversary/.

Koerber, Amy. 2013. *Breast or Bottle? Contemporary Controversies in Infant Feeding Policy and Practice*. University of South Carolina Press.

Kotz, David M. 2017. *The Rise and Fall of Neoliberal Capitalism*. Harvard University Press.

Kreth, Kelly. 2023. "'Unhinged' Ma Accused of Bullying Moms in Infamous UES Facebook Group." *Upper East Site*, March 22. https://www.uppereastsite.com/ues-mommas-tiffany-ma-bullying-allegations/.

Kroeker, Jo. 2018. "Ham Ave School Revamps the PTA to Meet Parents' Needs." *Greenwich Time*, November 26. https://www.greenwichtime.com/local/article/Ham-Ave-School-revamps-the-PTA-to-meet-parents-13422986.php.

Ladd, Everett Carll. 1999. *The Ladd Report*. Free Press.

Ladd-Taylor, Molly. 1994. *Mother-Work: Women, Child Welfare, and the State, 1890–1930*. University of Illinois Press.

Lake, Eleanor. 1950. "Breast Fed Is Best Fed." *Reader's Digest*, June 15–18.

La Leche League Canada. 2021. "Amanda Jetté Knox—The Art of Unlearning." May 11. https://www.facebook.com/LaLecheLeagueCanada/photos/a.374445019266717/4191227164255131/?type=3.

La Leche League International. 1963. *The Womanly Art of Breastfeeding*. 1st ed. La Leche League International.

——. 1991. *The Womanly Art of Breastfeeding*. 5th ed. Ballantine Books.

——. 2003. *La Leche League International Leader's Handbook*. 4th ed. La Leche League International.

——. 2010. *The Womanly Art of Breastfeeding*. 8th ed. Ballantine Books.

——. 2014. "La Leche League International's Post." Facebook, April 23. https://www.facebook.com/lalecheleagueinternational/posts/la-leche-league-international-llli-is-a-worldwide-educational-nonsectarian-nondi/10152410468254603.

——. 2016. "Passionate Journey of LLLI Founder." October. https://www.llli.org/passionate-journey-of-llli-founder/.

——. 2019. "Annual Report." Accessed October 27, 2019. https://www.llli.org/wp-content/uploads/Annual-Report-FYE-2019.pdf.

——. 2020a. *La Leche League International Leader's Handbook*. Accessed October 27, 2019. https://www.llli.org/wp-content/uploads/Leaders-Handbook-Aug-2020.pdf.

——. 2020b. "2020 Annual Report." Accessed April 8, 2025. https://llli.org/wp-content/uploads/FINAL-LLLI-Annual-Report-2020.pdf.

——. 2022a. *La Leche League International Leader's Handbook*. Accessed April 26, 2025. https://www.lllc.ca/sites/default/files/Leader%27s%20Handbook%20March%202022.pdf.

——. 2022b. "Welcome." Accessed April 8, 2025. https://llli.org/breastfeeding-today/.

——. 2023. "A Brief History of La Leche League." September. https://llli.org/about/our-story/.

——. 2024a. "Announcement." November 15. https://llli.org/news-from-llli/.

———. 2024b. *The Art of Breastfeeding: Completely Revised and Updated*. 9th ed. Ballantine Books.

———. 2024c. "LLL Today #5—Why Attend LLL Gatherings?" January 28. https:// llli.org/news/lll-today-5-why-attend-lll-gatherings/.

———. n.d.-a. "Associations." Accessed April 8, 2025. https://llli.org/about /associations/.

———. n.d.-b. "Bylaws." Accessed July 15, 2019. https://llli.org/about/bylaws/.

———. n.d.-c. "LLLI Strategic Plan 2021–2025." Accessed April 29, 2025. https://llli .org/about/llli-strategic-plan-2021-2025/.

———. n.d.-d. "LLL Today." Accessed July 15, 2019. https://llli.org/about/what-we-do /llli-today/.

———. n.d.-e. "*LLL Today* from La Leche League International." Accessed April 8, 2025. https://llli.org/breastfeeding-info/online-support/#Today.

———. n.d.-f. "Our Story." Accessed July 15, 2019. https://llli.org/about/our-story/.

———. n.d.-g. "Philosophy." Accessed April 8, 2025. https://www.llli.org/about /philosophy/.

———. n.d.-h. "Policies and Standing Rules." Accessed July 15, 2019. https://llli.org /about/policies-standing-rules/.

———. n.d.-i. "Steps to Accreditation." Accessed April 8, 2025. https://llli.org/get -involved/steps-to-accreditation.

———. n.d.-j. "Structure of LLL." Accessed April 8, 2025. https://llli.org/about/https -newsite-llli-org-about-board-of-directors/structure-of-llli/.

———. n.d.-k. "Support for Transgender & Non-binary Parents." Accessed April 8, 2025. https://www.llli.org/breastfeeding-info/transgender-non-binary-parents/.

La Leche League New Zealand. 2024. "LLLNZ Alumnae Association." Accessed May 22, 2025. https://lalecheleague.org.nz/wp-content/uploads/2025/02/Alumnae -News-5-Dec-2024.pdf.

La Leche League of Connecticut. n.d. "What Happens at La Leche League Meetings?" Accessed April 8, 2025. https://www.lllct.org/meetings.

La Leche League USA. 2018. "Joint Statement on Use of the Term Chestfeeding." July 8. https://www.lllusa.org/wp-content/uploads/2018/08/Joint-Statement-on -use-of-the-term-Chestfeeding.pdf.

———. 2020a. "Breastfeeding Under Special Circumstances." January. https://lllusa .org/special-circumstances/.

———. 2020b. "Induced Lactation and Relactation." May. https://lllusa.org/induced -lactation-and-relactation/.

———. 2021. "Our Mission." Accessed September 19, 2020. https://lllusa.org/about-us/

———. 2024. "Resource Roundup: Nursing in Public." September 10. Accessed May 22, 2025. https://lllusa.org/resource-roundup-nursing-in-public.

———. n.d. "Blog." Accessed April 8, 2025. www.lllusa.org/blog/.

Lambeck, Linda Conner. 2017. "Fairfield Dad Leads National PTA." *Connecticut Post*, September 6. https://www.ctpost.com/local/article/Fairfield-dad-leads-national -PTA-12168221.php.

Lareau, Annette. 2011. *Unequal Childhoods: Class, Race, and Family Life*. 2nd ed. University of California Press.

Lareau, Annette, and Vanessa Muñoz. 2012. "'You're Not Going to Call the Shots': Structural Conflicts Between the Principal and the PTO of a Suburban Public Elementary School." *Sociology of Education* 85 (3): 201–218.

LaRossa, Ralph. 1997. *The Modernization of Fatherhood: A Social and Political History.* University of Chicago Press.

Li, Meng, and Corrina Laughlin. 2023. "Care as Infrastructure: Rethinking Working Mothers' Childcare Crisis During the COVID-19 Pandemic." *Gender, Work & Organization* 31 (6): 2511–2526. https://doi.org/10.1111/gwao.13107.

Lipman-Blumen, Jean. 1976. "Toward a Homosocial Theory of Sex Roles: An Explanation of the Sex Segregation of Social Institutions." *Signs* 1 (3): 15–31.

Litt, Jacqueline. 2004. "Women's Carework in Low-Income Households: The Special Case of Children with Attention Deficit Hyperactivity Disorder." *Gender & Society* 18:625–644.

Lockman, Darcy. 2019. *All the Rage: Mothers, Fathers, and the Myth of Equal Partnership.* HarperCollins.

Lorenz, Taylor. 2020. "Upper East Side Mom Group Implodes over Accusations of Racism and Censorship." *New York Times*, June 9. https://www.nytimes.com/2020/06/09/style/ues-mommas-facebook-group-racism-censorship.html.

Lowman, Kaye. 1978. *The LLLove Story.* La Leche League International.

Ludwig, Ashley. 2020. "In Time of Trouble, Send Mothers: MOMS Club Chapters Seek Change." *Yahoo! News*, July 24. https://news.yahoo.com/time-trouble-send-mothers-moms-230826937.html.

MacDonald, Trevor. 2016. *Where's the Mother? Stories from a Transgender Dad.* Trans Canada Press.

Marinelli, Kathleen. 2017. "An interview with La Leche League Founders Marian Thompson and Mary Ann Kerwin, JD." *Journal of Human Lactation* 34 (4): 14–19.

Marjoram, Sarah. 2019. "Parent Talk: 5 Things I Learned as a PTA Volunteer." *Our Children* 45 (2): 18–19.

Martin, Joyce A., Brady E. Hamilton, Michelle J. K. Osterman, and Anne K. Driscoll. 2019. "Births: Final Data for 2019." *National Vital Statistics Reports* 70 (2): 1–50.

Martucci, Jessica. 2015. *Back to the Breast: Natural Motherhood and Breastfeeding in America.* University of Chicago Press.

McCorkell, Lisa, and Sara Hinkley. 2018. "The Great Recession, Families, and the Social Safety Net." University of California Institute for Research on Labor and Employment, Policy Brief, December 19. https://irle.berkeley.edu/publications/irle-policy-brief/the-great-recession-families-and-the-safety-net/#note10.

McKay, Beth. 2016. "Thank You, La Leche League." *Aptly Said: Parenting with Attachment in Mind*, August 3. https://attachmentparenting.org/blog/2016/08/03/thank-you-la-leche-league-international.

McKenzie, Sarah K., Sunny Collins, Gabrielle Jenkin, and Jo River. 2018. "Masculinity, Social Connectedness, and Mental Health: Men's Diverse Patterns of Practice." *American Journal of Men's Health* 12 (5): 1247–1261.

McRae, Elizabeth Gillespie. 2018. *Mothers of Massive Resistance: White Women and the Politics of White Supremacy.* Oxford University Press.

Meetup. n.d. "City Dads Group." Accessed May 22, 2025. https://www.meetup.com/pro/citydadsgroup.

Meljax. 2014. "'Ultimate Test: Dad' Campaign Puts Huggies to the Test." *Imperfect Working Mama*, December 1. https://imperfectworkingmama.wordpress.com/2014/12/01/ultimate-test-dad-campaign-puts-huggies-to-the-test.

Merrill, Elizabeth Bryant. 1987. "Learning to Mother: An Ethnographic Investigation of an Urban Breastfeeding Group." *Anthropology & Education Quarterly* 18 (3): 222–240.

Messner, Michael. 1992. *Power at Play: Sports and the Problem of Masculinity*. Beacon.

———. 2000. *Politics of Masculinities: Men in Movements*. AltaMira Press.

Michels, Robert. 1962. *Political Parties: A Sociological Study of the Oligarchical Tendencies of Modern Democracy*. Free Press.

Milk Junkies. 2012a. "Ian's Letter to LLLI." September 1. http://www.milkjunkies.net /2012/09/ian-letter-to-llli.html.

———. 2012b. "LLL to Revisit Policies: Write Letters!" August 26. http://www .milkjunkies.net/2012/08/lll-to-revisit-policies-write-letters.html.

———. 2012c. "My LLL Rejection Letter." August 16. http://www.milkjunkies.net /2012/08/my-lll-rejection-letter.html.

———. 2013. "Research Study." Accessed April 8, 2025. http://www.milkjunkies.net/p /research-study.html.

———. n.d. "My Story." Accessed May 22, 2025. http://www.milkjunkies.net/p/my -story.html.

Miller, Stephen. 2008. "Edwina Froehlich, 93, La Leche League Founder." *New York Sun*, June 12. https://www.nysun.com/obituaries/edwina-froelich-93-la-leche -league-founder/79854/.

Miller, Tina. 2007. "'Is This What Motherhood Is All About?' Weaving Experiences and Discourse Through Transition to First-Time Motherhood." *Gender & Society* 12 (3): 337–358.

Minkin, Rachel. 2023. "Diversity, Equity and Inclusion in the Workplace." Pew Research Center, May 17. https://www.pewresearch.org/social-trends/2023/05/17 /diversity-equity-and-inclusion-in-the-workplace/.

Minkin, Rachel, and Juliana Menasce Horowitz. 2023. "Parenting in America Today." Pew Research Center, January 24. https://www.pewresearch.org/social-trends /2023/01/24/parenting-in-america-today.

Mintz, Steven. 2004. *Huck's Raft: A History of American Childhood*. Belknap.

———. 2015. "American Childhood as a Social and Cultural Construct." In *Families as They Really Are*, 2nd ed., edited by Barbara Risman and Virginia Rutter. Norton.

Mintz, Steven, and Susan Kellogg. 1988. *Domestic Revolutions: A Social History of American Family Life*. Free Press.

Misra, Joya. 2012. "Care Work and Women's Employment: A Comparative Perspective." In *Women Who Opt Out*, edited by Bernie Jones. New York University Press.

MOMS Club. 2013. "Bylaws for All MOMS Club Local Chapters." March. https:// fvmcblog.wordpress.com/wp-content/uploads/2017/06/bylaws-3-13-pdf.pdf.

———. n.d.-a. "Area Coordinator: Board of Directors." Accessed April 8, 2025. https://momsclub.org/elearning/courses/area-coordinator/lessons/area -coordinator-board-of-directors/.

———. n.d.-b. "Area Coordinator: The Chapter's Role." Accessed April 8, 2025. https://momsclub.org/elearning/courses/area-coordinator/lessons/area -coordinator-the-chapters-role/.

———. n.d.-c. "Area Coordinator: Legal Organization." Accessed April 8, 2025. https://momsclub.org/elearning/courses/area-coordinator/lessons/area -coordinator-legal-organization.

———. n.d.-d. "Area Coordinator: Mary's Role." Accessed April 8, 2025. https:// momsclub.org/elearning/lessons/area-coordinator-marys-role/.

———. n.d.-e. "How We Support Our Chapters." Accessed April 8, 2025. https:// momsclub.org/start-a-chapter/.

———. n.d.-f. "International MOMS Club." Accessed April 8, 2025. https://momsclub .org/about/.

———. n.d.-g. "A MOMS Club Chapter." Accessed April 8, 2025. https://momsclub .org/chapters/.

———. n.d.-h. "What Is Supper Club?" Accessed May 22, 2025. https://momsclub.org /what-is-supper-club/.

MOMS Club Maple Grove. n.d. "Activities." Accessed April 8, 2025. https://sites.google .com/site/momsclubmaplegrove/activities?authuser=0.

MOMS Club of Birmingham-East, AL. n.d. "Welcome to the MOMS Club of Birmingham-East, AL!" Accessed April 8, 2025. https://momsclubbham.com/.

MOMS Club of Copley/Fairlawn. n.d. "Activities." Accessed April 8, 2025. http:// momsofcopley.com/activities/.

MOMS Club of East Lyme. n.d. "History." Accessed April 8, 2025. https://www .momsclubofeastlyme.org/history/.

MOMS Club of Greater Windsor. 2021. "Clothing Donation to the Village for Families and Children." November 8. https://www.momsclubofgreaterwindsor .org/post/women-overtake-men-in-college-degrees.

———. 2022. "Adopt a Family for Thanksgiving." November. https://www .momsclubofgreaterwindsor.org/post/adopt-a-family-for-thanksgiving.

MOMS Club of Las Vegas Summerlin Central. 2019. "MOMS Club Las Vegas Summer-lin Central Club Benefits." Accessed April 8, 2025. https://www.momsclublasvegas .com/moms-club-benefits.

"MOMS Club of Rancho Santa Margarita." n.d. Facebook. Accessed April 8, 2025. https://www.facebook.com/MOMSClubofRanchoSantaMargarita/.

MOMS Club of Ridgefield. n.d. "Member Benefits." Accessed April 8, 2025. https:// www.momsclubofridgefieldct.com/memberbenefits.

MOMS Club of Southwest Lehigh Valley. 2025. "Join Us for Our Meet and Greet & Clothing Swap!" Accessed May 22, 2025. https://www.instagram.com/momsclub swlv/reel/DG1chIJO-DL/.

MOMS Club of Stamford. n.d. "Frequently Asked Questions." Accessed April 8, 2025. http://www.momsclubofstamford.com/faqs.

MOMS Club of the White Mountains. n.d. "History." Accessed May 22, 2025. http://www.momsclubwm.org/history.html.

MOMS Club Simi Valley. n.d.-a. "About Us." Accessed April 8, 2025. https://www .momsclubsimivalley.com/about.

———. n.d.-b. "Frequently Asked Questions." Accessed April 8, 2025. https://www .momsclubsimivalley.com/faq.

"Moms of ADHD, Anxiety, ASD, ODD Kids (Support Group)." n.d. Facebook. Accessed April 8, 2025. https://www.facebook.com/groups/1203074073044010.

Mong, Sherry N. 2020. *Taking Care of Our Own: When Family Caregivers Do Medical Work*. Cornell University Press.

Morton, Neal. 2021. "Bake Sales and Tesla Raffles: The Unequal World of PTA Wealth." *The Nation*, June 14. https://www.thenation.com/article/society/pta -schools-education.

Mose, Tamara R. 2016. *The Playdate: Parents, Children, and the New Expectations of Play*. New York University Press.

Murkoff, Heidi. 2016. *What to Expect When You're Expecting*. 5th ed. Workman.

Murray, Brittany, Thurston Domina, Linda Renzulli, and Rebecca Boylan. 2019. "Civil Society Goes to School: Parent-Teacher Associations and the Equality of

Educational Opportunity." *Russell Sage Foundation Journal of the Social Sciences* 5 (3): 41–63.

Naples, Nancy A. 2003. *Feminism and Method: Ethnography, Discourse Analysis, and Activist Research.* Routledge.

National Center for Education Statistics. 2019. "National Household Education Surveys." Accessed April 8, 2025. https://nces.ed.gov/nhes/data/2019/pfi/cbook _pfi_pu.pdf.

National Congress of Colored Parents and Teachers (NCCPT). 1948. *Our National Family.* University of Kansas Libraries Exhibit. Accessed July 2, 2023. https:// exhibits.lib.ku.edu/items/show/7168.

———. 1961. *The Coral Anniversary History of the National Congress of Colored Parents and Teachers.* National Congress of Colored Parents and Teachers.

National Congress of Parents and Teachers, ed. 1944. *The Parent Teacher Organization: Its Origins and Development.* National Congress of Parents and Teachers.

———. 2020. "2020 National PTA Membership Dashboard." Accessed May 22, 2025. https://www.wastatepta.org/wp-content/uploads/2020/11/Membership -Dashboard_FINAL.pdf.

National Institute on Aging. 2023. "What Is Respite Care?" October 12. https://www .nia.nih.gov/health/what-respite-care.

———. n.d. "Caregiving." Accessed April 8, 2025. https://www.nia.nih.gov/health /caregiving.

National PTA. 1997. *The PTA Story: A Century of Commitment to Children.* National PTA.

———. 2018a. "Safe and Supportive Schools: Mobilizing Family Stakeholders." Accessed April 8, 2025. https://www.pta.org/docs/default-source/files/programs /health/safe-and-supportive-schools---mobilizing-family-stakeholders.pdf.

———. 2018b. "School Safety: Mobilizing for Change—WEBINAR." YouTube, November 6. Accessed May 22, 2025. https://www.youtube.com/watch?v =PbXBP3RVTCk.

———. 2019. "Impact: 2018–2019 Annual Report." Accessed November 8, 2020. https://www.pta.org/home/About-National-Parent-Teacher-Association/PTA -Reports-Financials.

———. 2020a. "How to Talk to Your Kid About Gun Violence." Accessed April 8, 2025. https://www.pta.org/the-center-for-family-engagement/podcast/notes-from -the-backpack/how-to-talk-to-your-kid-about-gun-violence.

———. 2020b. "How We PTA, 2019–2020 Annual Report." Accessed March 23, 2021. https://www.pta.org/home/About-National-Parent-Teacher-Association/PTA -Reports-Financials.

———. 2022. "Say Their Names: Addressing Institutional or Systemic Racism." https://www.pta.org/docs/default-source/files/advocacy/position-statements/say -their-names-addressing-institutional-or-systemic-racism_u.pdf.

———. n.d.-a. "Addressing Food Insecurity." Accessed April 8, 2025. https://www.pta .org/home/run-your-pta/how-we-pta/addressing-food-insecurity.

———. n.d.-b. "Building a Community (Family Engagement)." Accessed April 8, 2025. https://www.pta.org/home/run-your-pta/how-we-pta/building-a -community.

———. n.d.-c. "Charles J. Saylors." Accessed May 22, 2025. https://www.pta.org/home /About-National-Parent-Teacher-Association/PTA-Leadership/Past-National -PTA-Presidents/Charles-J-Saylors.

———. n.d.-d. "Gun Safety and Violence Prevention." Accessed April 8, 2025. https://www.pta.org/home/advocacy/federal-legislation/Public-Policy-Priorities /gun-safety-and-violence-prevention.

———. n.d.-e. "History." Accessed May 22, 2025. https://www.pta.org/home/About -National-Parent-Teacher-Association/Mission-Values/National-PTA-History.

———. n.d.-f. "Is Your PTA an ATM for Your School?" Accessed April 8, 2025. https://www.pta.org/home/family-resources/Our-Children-Magazine/Is-Your -PTA-an-ATM-for-Your-School.

———. n.d.-g. "Leadership." Accessed April 8, 2025. https://www.pta.org/home /About-National-Parent-Teacher-Association/PTA-Leadership.

———. n.d.-h. "Mission Statement." Accessed April 8, 2025. https://www.pta.org /home/About-National-Parent-Teacher-Association/Mission-Values.

———. n.d.-i. "Past National PTA Presidents." Accessed April 8, 2025. https://www .pta.org/home/About-National-Parent-Teacher-Association/PTA-Leadership/Past -National-PTA-Presidents.

———. n.d.-j. "Position Statement—The Education of Students with Disabilities." Accessed April 8, 2025. https://www.pta.org/home/advocacy/ptas-positions /Individual-Position-Statements/position-statement-education-of-students-with -disabilities.

———. n.d.-k. "Position Statement—Gun Safety and Violence Prevention." Accessed April 8, 2025. https://www.pta.org/home/advocacy/ptas-positions/Individual -Position-Statements/Position-Statement-Gun-Safety-and-Violence-Prevention.

———. n.d.-l. "Position Statements." Accessed April 8, 2025. https://www.pta.org /home/advocacy/ptas-positions/Individual-Position-Statements.

———. n.d.-m. "Presence of PTA." Accessed April 8, 2025. https://www.pta.org/home /About-National-Parent-Teacher-Association/join/presence-of-pta.

———. n.d.-n. "PTA History." Accessed July 15, 2019. https://www.pta.org/home /About-National-Parent-Teacher-Association/Mission-Values/Nan.dtional-PTA -History.

———. n.d.-o. "PTA History: 1900–1909." Accessed April 8, 2025. https://www.pta .org/home/About-National-Parent-Teacher-Association/Mission-Values/National -PTA-History/PTA-History-1900-1909.

———. n.d.-p. "PTA History: 1910–1919." Accessed April 8, 2025. https://www.pta .org/home/About-National-Parent-Teacher-Association/Mission-Values/National -PTA-History/PTA-History-1910-1919.

———. n.d.-q. "PTA History: 1920–1929." Accessed May 22, 2025. https://www.pta .org/home/About-National-Parent-Teacher-Association/Mission-Values/National -PTA-History/PTA-History-1920-1929.

———. n.d.-r. "PTA History: 1950–1959." Accessed April 8, 2025. https://www.pta.org /home/About-National-Parent-Teacher-Association/Mission-Values/National -PTA-History/PTA-History-1950-1959.

———. n.d.-s. "PTAs Leading the Way in Diversity, Equity and Inclusion." Accessed April 8, 2025. https://www.pta.org/docs/default-source/files/cfe/2023/ptas-leading -the-way-in-diversity-equity-and-inclusion.pdf.

———. n.d.-t. "Reports & Financials." Accessed July 15, 2019. https://www.pta.org /home/About-National-Parent-Teacher-Association/PTA-Reports-Financials.

———. n.d.-u. "Resolution on Inclusive Schools Build Stronger Communities." Accessed April 8, 2025. https://www.pta.org/home/advocacy/ptas-positions/Individual-PTA -Resolutions/resolution-on-inclusive-schools-build-stronger-communities.

———. n.d.-v. "School Safety." Accessed April 8, 2025. https://www.pta.org/home/family-resources/safety/School-Safety.

———. n.d.-w. "Start a Special Education PTA." Accessed April 8, 2025. https://www.pta.org/home/About-National-Parent-Teacher-Association/Governance/Types-of-PTAs/Start-a-Special-Education-PTA.

National Woman's Christian Temperance Union. 2022. "History of the WCTU." Accessed April 8, 2025. https://www.wctu.org/history.

Nelson, Margaret K. 2010. *Parenting Out of Control: Anxious Parents in Uncertain Times*. New York University Press.

New York Times. 2019. "A Lesson of Sandy Hook: 'Err on the Side of the Victims.'" May 25. https://www.nytimes.com/2019/05/25/us/politics/sandy-hook-money.html.

NYU Furman Center. 2024. "Upper East Side MN08: Demographics." May 21. https://furmancenter.org/neighborhoods/view/upper-east-side#demographics.

Oakland Ed Fund. 2020. "Equity Fund Helps Level the Playing Field for Oakland Students." July 20. https://www.oaklandedfund.org/2020/07/20/equity-fund-helps-level-the-playing-field-for-oakland-students/.

Office of the State's Attorney, Judicial District of Danbury. 2013. "Report of the State's Attorney for the Judicial District of Danbury on the Shootings at Sandy Hook Elementary School and 36 Yogananda Street, Newtown, Connecticut on December 14, 2012." November 25. https://portal.ct.gov/dcj/-/media/dcj/sandyhookfinalreportpdf.pdf?rev=6c8abcf638a74151b13e96bd4913e638&hash=1EF0371D4C1C776A16BC8D66B0718474.

Osterman-Davis, Heather. 2021. "I'm a Disabled Parent. It Took a Pandemic to Let Me Join the PTA." *New York Times*, February 2. https://www.nytimes.com/2021/02/02/well/family/im-a-disabled-parent-it-took-a-pandemic-to-let-me-join-the-pta.html.

Ostrander, Susan A. 1984. *Women of the Upper Class*. Temple University Press.

Our National Family. 1948. "School Lunch Program Facing Crisis." February. Accessed December 1, 2023. https://exhibits.lib.ku.edu/items/show/7168.

Palley, Elizabeth, and Corey S. Shdaimah. 2014. *In Our Hands: The Struggle for U.S. Child Care Policy*. New York University Press.

Palo Alto Partners in Education. 2025. "About PiE." Accessed April 8, 2025. https://papie.org/about/.

ParentCo. 2017. "In Defense of the PTA Mom." *ParentCo.*, June 12. https://www.parent.com/blogs/conversations/2017-defense-pta-mom.

Parker, Kim, Juliana Horowitz, Anna Brown, Richard Fry, D'Vera Cohn, and Ruth Igielnik. 2018. "What Unites and Divides Urban, Suburban and Rural Communities." Pew Research Center, May 22. https://www.pewresearch.org/social-trends/2018/05/22/what-unites-and-divides-urban-suburban-and-rural-communities/.

Parker, Kim, Kiliana Menasce Horowitz, and Molly Rohal. 2015. "Parenting in America: Outlook, Worries, Aspirations Are Strongly Linked to Financial Situation." Pew Research Center, December 17. https://www.pewresearch.org/wp-content/uploads/sites/3/2015/12/2015-12-17_parenting-in-america_FINAL.pdf

Parker, Kim, and Eileen Patten. 2013. "The Sandwich Generation: Rising Financial Burdens for Middle-Aged Americans. Pew Research Center, January 30. https://www.pewresearch.org/social-trends/2013/01/30/the-sandwich-generation/.

Pelly, Julia. 2019. "How La Leche League Saved Me." *Today's Parent*, March 28. https://www.todaysparent.com/baby/how-la-leche-league-saved-me.

Peng, Yinni, and Odalia M. H. Wong. 2013. "Diversified Transnational Mothering via Telecommunication: Intensive, Collaborative, and Passive." *Gender & Society* 27 (4): 491–513.

Penguin Random House. n.d. "Love Lives Here." Accessed May 22, 2025. https://www.penguinrandomhouse.com/books/566534/love-lives-here-by-amanda-jette-knox/.

Pitman, Teresa. 2018. "60 Years Later: Celebrating LLLI." La Leche League International, November 22. https://llli.org/news/60-years-later-celebrating-llli/.

Poo, Ai-Jen, and Sade Moonsammy. 2021. "The Care Infrastructure: Building Across Movements." *Generations* 45 (3): 1–7.

Posey-Maddox, Linn. 2013. "Professionalizing the PTO: Race, Class, and Shifting Norms of Parent Engagement in a City Public School." *American Journal of Education* 119 (2): 235–260.

———. 2014. *When Middle-Class Parents Choose Urban Schools: Class, Race, and the Challenge of Equity in Public Education.* University of Chicago Press.

Price-Glynn, Kim. 2010. *Strip Club: Gender, Power, and Sex Work.* New York University Press.

———. 2024. "An Ideology of Collective-Intensive Mothering: The Gendered Organization of Care in a Babysitting Cooperative." *Gender, Work & Organization* 31 (4): 1250–1267.

"Private Facebook Group Offers Haven for Single Parents." 2018. *ABC News,* February 5. https://abcnews.go.com/GMA/Family/private-facebook-group-offers-haven-single-parents/story?id=52834189.

Pryor, Karen. 1963. "They Teach the Joys of Breastfeeding." *Reader's Digest,* May, 103–106.

PTA Equity Project. 2020. "PTA Equity Project: One Fund. One Community." Accessed April 8, 2025. https://ptaequityproject.com.

Pugh, Allison. 2015. *The Tumbleweed Society: Working and Caring in an Age of Insecurity.* Oxford University Press.

Putnam, Robert D. 2000. *Bowling Alone: The Collapse and Revival of American Community.* Simon & Schuster.

QSR International. 2018. NVivo 12 Qualitative Data Analysis Software. Macintosh version.

Quinlan, Casey. 2016. "How Marginalized Families Are Pushed Out of PTAs: Parents with Socioeconomic Resources Are More Likely to Exert Influence on School Officials." *The Atlantic,* July 13. https://www.theatlantic.com/education/archive/2016/07/how-marginalized-families-are-pushed-out-of-ptas/491036/.

Rainie, Lee, Scott Keeter, and Andrew Perrin. 2019. "Trust and Distrust in America." Pew Research Center, July 22. https://www.pewresearch.org/politics/2019/07/22/trust-and-distrust-in-america/.

Rajasekar, Neeraj, Matthew Aguilar-Champeau, and Douglas Hartman. 2022. "Diversity Discourse as Racialized and Double-Edged: Findings from a National Survey." *Sociology of Race and Ethnicity* 8 (2): 315–332.

Ramsey, Sonya. 2012. "Caring Is Activism: Black Southern Womanist Teachers Theorizing and the Careers of Kathleen Crosby and Bertha Maxwell-Roddey, 1946–1986." *Educational Studies* 48:244–265.

Raz, Guy. 2009. "PTA Welcomes First Male President." *National Public Radio All Things Considered,* June 28.

Razavi, Shahra. 2007. "The Political and Social Economy of Care: Conceptual Issues, Research Questions, and Policy Options." Gender and Development Programme Paper No. 3, United Nations Research Institute for Social Development.

Reardon, Sean F., and Ann Owens. 2014. "60 Years After *Brown*: Trends and Consequences of School Segregation." *Annual Review of Sociology* 40:199–218.

Reich, Jennifer A. 2016. *Calling the Shots: Why Parents Reject Vaccines*. New York University Press.

Rembert, Cateia. 2020. "Sharing Resources in a Crisis: How District 15 Leaders Created a Mutual Aid Program During the Covid-19 Shutdown." *PTAlink*, June. https://ptalink.org/topic-areas/activities-events/sharing-resources-in-a-crisis-how -district-15-leaders-created-a-mutual-aid-program-during-the-covid-19-shutdown.

Risman, Barbara. 2018. *Where the Millennials Will Take Us: A New Generation Wrestles with the Gender Structure*. Oxford University Press.

Robinson, Collin. 2019. "Ask a PTA Leader." *Our Children* 45 (1): 25.

Rosen, Hannah. 2009. "The Case Against Breastfeeding." *The Atlantic*, April, 64–70.

Rosenfeld, Jordan. 2014. "Not a 'PTA Mom.'" *Motherlode*, October 3. https:// parenting.blogs.nytimes.com/2014/10/03/not-a-pta-mom/.

Samuels, Robbie. 2017. "Huggies, Boston Dads Group Helping Tackle Diaper Need Issue." City Dads Group, November 2. https://citydadsgroup.com/huggies-boston -national-diaper-bank.

Sanchez, Laura, and Elizabeth Thompson. 1997. "Becoming Mothers and Fathers: Parenthood, Gender and the Division of Labor." *Gender & Society* 11 (6): 747–772.

Schiffrin, Holly H., Miriam Liss, Katherine Geary, Haley Miles-McLean, Taryn Tashner, Charlotte Hagerman, and Kathryn Rizzo. 2014. "Mother, Father, or Parent? College Students' Intensive Parenting Attitudes Differ by Referent." *Journal of Child and Family Studies* 23:1073–1080.

Schilt, Kristen. 2010. *Just One of the Guys*. University of Chicago Press.

Schnell, Alyssa. 2020. "The Role of the Partner in Breastfeeding: How the Support of Dads, Co-Moms and Other People Makes a Difference." *Breastfeeding Today*, August 3. https://llli.org/the-role-of-the-partner-in-breastfeeding-how-the-support -of-dads-co-moms-and-other-people-makes-a-difference.

Schoff, Mrs. Frederic. 1916. "The National Congress of Mothers and Parent-Teacher Associations." *Annals of the American Academy of Political and Social Science* 67:139–147.

School District of Philadelphia. 2021. "Parent Shares Her Experience with the PTA at Charles W. Henry School." April 28. https://www.philasd.org/face/2021/04/28 /19496/.

Scott, Richard K. 2000. "Models of Disability and the Americans with Disabilities Act." *Berkeley Journal of Employment and Labor Law* 21 (1): 213–222.

Sears, William, and Martha Sears. 2018. *The Breastfeeding Book: Everything You Need to Know About Nursing Your Child from Birth Through Weaning*. Little, Brown.

Seligson, Hannah. 2013. "Don't Call Him Mom, or an Imbecile." *New York Times*, February 12. http://www.nytimes.com/2013/02/24/business/fathers-seek -advertising-that-doesnot-ridicule.html.

Shanahan, Charlene. 2018. "As a PTA Leader." *Our Children* 44 (2): 35.

Shefsky, Jay. 2013. "Jay's Chicago: Stories of Life in Chicago: La Leche League." WTTW Chicago PBS. Accessed July 29, 2020. https://interactive.wttw.com /jayschicago/la-leche-league.

Simone, AbdouMaliq. 2004. "People as Infrastructure: Intersecting Fragments in Johannesburg." *Public Culture* 16 (3): 407–429.

"Single Parents: Surviving Single Parenthood." n.d. Facebook. Accessed April 8, 2025. https://www.facebook.com/groups/SingleParents01/.

Skocpol, Theda. 2003. *Diminished Democracy: From Membership to Management in American Civic Life*. Norman: University of Oklahoma Press.

———. 2004. "The Narrowing of Civic Life." *American Prospect* 15 (6): A5–A7.

Smith, Dorothy. 2004. *Institutional Ethnography: A Sociology for People*. AltaMira Press.

Solomon, Catherine Richards. 2017. *The Lives of Stay-at-Home Fathers: Masculinity, Carework, and Fatherhood in the United States*. Emerald.

Sörensen, Silvia, Martin Pinquart, and Paul Duberstein. 2002. "How Effective Are Interventions with Caregivers? An Updated Meta-Analysis." *Gerontologist* 42 (3): 356–372.

Spade, Dean. 2020. *Mutual Aid: Building Solidarity During This Crisis (and the Next)*. Verso.

Stadlen, Naomi. 2020. "Softening into Motherhood." *Breastfeeding Today*, December 7. https://llli.org/softening-into-motherhood.

State of Connecticut, Office of the Attorney General. n.d. "Sandy Hook Promise Foundation and Sandy Hook Promise Action Fund." Accessed May 22, 2025. https://portal.ct.gov/-/media/ag/charities/sandyhook/sandyhookpromise actionfundorginial72313pdf.

Steinmetz, Katy. 2015. "The Dad 2.0 Summit: Making the Care for a New Kind of Manhood." *Time*, February 21. Accessed April 30, 2025. https://time.com/3717511 /dad-summit-manhood/.

Stevens, Emily E., Thelma E. Patrick, and Rita Pickler. 2009. "A History of Infant Feeding." *Journal of Perinatal Education* 18 (2): 32–39.

Stockstill, Casey. 2023. *False Starts: The Segregated Lives of Preschoolers*. New York University Press.

Strauss, Anselm, and Juliet Corbin. 1994. "Grounded Theory Methodology: An Overview." In *Handbook of Qualitative Research*, edited by Norman K. Denzin and Yvonna S. Lincoln. Sage.

Stupi, Amanda. 2014. "A Tale of 2 San Francisco Public Schools: Do PTAs Widen Inequality?" KQED, February 17. https://www.kqed.org/news/126504/a-tale-of-2 -san-francisco-public-schools-do-ptas-widen-inquality.

Sucharov, Mira. 2017. "Upper East Side Moms Facebook Group in Turmoil—Over Israel and the Palestinians." *Forward*, November 20. https://forward.com/life/387997 /upper-east-side-mothers-facebook-group-in-turmoil-over-israeli-palestinian/.

Sweeney, Joan, and Richard J. Sweeney. 1977. "Monetary Theory and the Great Capitol Hill Babysitting Co-op Crisis." *Journal of Money, Credit and Banking* 9 (1): 86–89.

Taylor, Tiffany. 2011. "Re-examining Cultural Contradictions: Mothering Ideology and the Intersections of Class, Gender, and Race." *Sociology Compass* 5 (10): 898–907.

Thelen, Tatjana. 2015. "Care as Social Organization: Creating, Maintaining and Dissolving Significant Relations." *Anthropological Theory* 15 (4): 497–515.

Tocqueville, Alexis de. 1899. *Democracy in America*. Appleton.

Toney, LaWanda. 2016. "National PTA's Commitment to Positive, Safe Environments for All Students." National PTA, November 16. https://www.pta.org/home/About -National-Parent-Teacher-Association/PTA-Newsroom/news-list/news-detail -page/2016/11/15/National-PTAs-Commitment-to-Positive-Safe-Environments-for -All-Students.

Tronto, Joan C. 1993. *Moral Boundaries: A Political Argument for an Ethic of Care*. London: Routledge.

———. 2013. *Caring Democracy: Markets, Equality, and Justice.* New York University Press.

———. 2015. *Who Cares? How to Reshape a Democratic Politics.* Cornell University Press.

———. 2017. "There Is an Alternative: Homines Curans and the Limits of Neoliberalism." *International Journal of Care and Caring* 1 (1): 27–43.

Tyko, Kelly. 2019. "Huggies Puts Dads on Diaper Boxes for First Time." *USA Today*, July 15. https://www.usatoday.com/story/money/2019/07/15/huggies-puts-dads -diaper-boxes-for-first-time/1736077001/.

"UES Mommas." n.d. Facebook. Accessed April 8, 2025. https://www.facebook.com /groups/129399600506031/.

U.S. Census Bureau. 1950. "1950 Census of Population." September 11. https://www2 .census.gov/library/publications/decennial/1950/pc-02/pc-2-40.pdf.

———. 2020. "Census Bureau Releases New Estimates on America's Families and Living Arrangements." December 2. https://www.census.gov/newsroom/press -releases/2020/estimates-families-living-arrangements.html.

Villalobos, Anna. 2014. *Motherload: Making It All Better in Insecure Times.* University of California Press.

Waerness, Kari. 1984. "The Rationality of Caring." *Economic and Industrial Democracy* 5 (2): 185–211.

Walks, Michelle. 2017. "Chestfeeding as Gender Fluid Practice." In *Breastfeeding: New Anthropological Approaches*, edited by Cecília Tomori, Aunchalee E. L. Palmquist, and E. A. Quinn. Routledge.

Walls, Jill K., Heather M. Helms, and Joseph G. Grzywacz. 2016. "Intensive Mothering Beliefs Among Full-Time Employed Mothers of Infants." *Journal of Family Issues* 37 (2): 245–269.

Walzer, Susan. 1998. *Thinking About the Baby: Gender and Transitions into Parenthood.* Temple University Press.

Wang, Jackson. 2012. "Selkirk PTA aids Sandy Hook." *Times Union*, December 22. https://www.timesunion.com/local/article/Selkirk-PTA-aids-Sandy-Hook -4141212.php

Ward, Jule DeJager. 2000. *La Leche League: At the Crossroads of Medicine, Feminism, and Religion.* University of North Carolina Press.

Washington, Kate. 2021. *Already Toast: Caregiving and Burnout in America.* Beacon.

Weiner, Lynn Y. 1994. "Reconstructing Motherhood: The La Leche League in Postwar America." *Journal of American History* 80 (4): 1357–1381.

West, Diane. 2001. *Defining Your Own Success: Breastfeeding After Breast Reduction Surgery.* La Leche League International.

What to Expect. 2024. "About Heidi Murkoff." July 9. https://www.whattoexpect .com/about-heidi-murkoff/.

White House. 2021. "Fact Sheet: The American Jobs Plan." National Archives and Records Administration, March 31. https://bidenwhitehouse.archives.gov/briefing -room/statements-releases/2021/03/31/fact-sheet-the-american-jobs-plan/.

———. n.d. "The Build Back Better Framework." Accessed May 22, 2025. https:// bidenwhitehouse.archives.gov/build-back-better/.

Wiessinger, Diane. 2018. "Breastfeeding in Public Spaces." La Leche League International, November 12. https://www.llli.org/breastfeeding-in-public-spaces/.

Wiessinger, Diane, Diana West, and Teresa Pitman. 2010. *The Womanly Art of Breastfeeding.* 8th ed. Ballantine Books.

William James College. n.d. "Top Ten Tips for New Parents." Accessed April 8, 2025. https://www.williamjames.edu/centers-and-services/forensic-and-clinical-services/yfps/tips-for-parents/top-ten-tips-new-parents.html.

Williams, G. G., and Lydia de Raad. 2022. "New Edition of Our Core Book Coming in 2024!" La Leche League International, August 25. https://llli.org/news/art-of-breastfeeding-news/.

Woyshner, Christine. 2009. *The National PTA, Race, and Civic Engagement, 1897–1970.* Ohio State University Press.

———. 2011. "School Desegregation and Civil Society: The Unification of Alabama's Black and White Parent-Teacher Associations, 1954–1971." *History of Education Quarterly* 51 (1): 49–76.

———. 2021. "Can the PTA Help Americans Be More Civic-Minded?" *Washington Post*, August 20. https://www.washingtonpost.com/outlook/2021/08/20/can-pta-help-americans-be-more-civic-minded/.

Zelenka, Kevin. 2017. "Vegas Dads Rally to Assist National Diaper Bank Network Mission." City Dads Group, December 13. https://citydadsgroup.com/vegas-dads-national-diaper-bank-network.

Zero to Three. 2016. "Tuning In: Parents of Young Children Tell Us What They Think, Know and Need Is a Comprehensive Research Undertaking." National Center for Infants, Toddlers and Families.

Index

About the Author

KIM PRICE-GLYNN is associate professor of sociology at the University of Connecticut. She received the inaugural University of Connecticut's College of Liberal Arts and Sciences Faculty Achievement Award for Excellence in Teaching. Price-Glynn is the author of *Strip Club: Gender, Power, and Sex Work*, and she has published on gender, labor, and carework in several journals, including *Gender & Society*, *Sociology of Health & Illness*, *Research in the Sociology of Health Care*, and *Work, Employment & Society*. With Rutgers University Press, she is coeditor of the book series Carework in a Changing World and the edited volume *From Crisis to Catastrophe: Care, COVID-19, and Pathways to Change*, with Mignon Duffy and Amy Armenia. She is an active member and past cochair of the Carework Network, an international organization of researchers, policymakers, and advocates involved in various domains of carework.